Introduction to

Christianity

Introduction to

Christianity

PAUL   HESSERT
Illinois Wesleyan University

PRENTICE-HALL,   INC.,   *Englewood Cliffs, N.J.*

Christianity ' Essence, genius, nature

To

MY MOTHER AND FATHER
who, by living,
taught the meaning
of being Christian

preface

The revival of interest in biblical theology has brought an awareness that Christianity is a *life*. An inextricable part of this life is a group of ideas about God, but the predominating, pervasive aspect of Christianity is that it is a life shared in an historical, continuing community. This book attempts to interpret Christianity in terms of a people created by God's activity in history, and its pattern is therefore drawn from the implications of the proclamation of the Gospel rather than from the more traditional outline of God, man, sin, and salvation.

The historical development of Christian theology has not been neglected in the book, but the primary intent is to stress the relevance of Christian doctrine to any serious reflection on the meaning of life and to stress this relevance in terms that are understandable to most people. Although I have tried to indicate several positions on any theological issue, the book is not a catalog of theologies. As a reader or a teacher, I have never found this stimulating. Suggested additional readings for each chapter are included to provide a variety of views for comparison and discussion. For reference purposes, the texts of the Apostles' and Nicene creeds and the Christological formula of the Council of Chalcedon are included in the Appendix, followed by sources from which the historic Protestant confessions may be obtained. In this way, one may relate his study to his own tradition, or various traditional formulations of doctrine may be compared.

I have attempted to standardize capitalization throughout the book, including the directly quoted sources. God and the personal pronouns referring directly to Him are capitalized. *Church* spelled with a capital *C* refers to the community called forth by God in Christ, the Church catholic. With a lower-case *c* it refers to earthly embodiments of that fellowship, whether these be local groups or denominations.

Finally, I should like to express my appreciation to my classes at Adrian College and Illinois Wesleyan University, with whom most of this material was worked out, and to my colleagues who made it possible. I should also like to acknowledge the kind help of Dr. Leland Jamison of Princeton University, who first read the manuscript and made helpful suggestions; Mrs. Maurine Lewis of the Prentice-Hall editorial staff, whose careful work has improved the grammar and style of the book; and three students, Miss Donna Benson, Jerry Stewardson, and David Strang, who helped immeasurably in checking the typescript when Judith Ann's arrival in the family upset all established routines and schedules.

The scripture quotations in this publication are from the *Revised Standard Version of the Bible,* copyrighted 1946 and 1952 by the Division of Christian Education, National Council of the Churches of Christ, and are used by permission.

PAUL HESSERT

contents

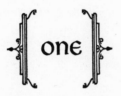

{ one }

preliminary

considerations

introduction

e live in a time when the attitude toward Christianity, and more generally toward all religion, is decidedly ambiguous. The advancement of scientific thought has left many people with a feeling—often indefinite—that old certainties have been shattered, particularly the comfortable belief that some superhuman power watches over human affairs, guiding them for the ultimate welfare of every man. The sheer immensity of the universe, the possibility of the existence of other inhabited worlds, the stark impersonality of the mathematical formulas to which most natural processes have been reduced—all this makes us ask the question "What is man?" not with the awe and wonder of the psalmist assured of God's concern (Ps. 8:4), but in desperation and doubt.

Yet at the same time, perhaps because of this uncertainty about man's place in the universe, there is also a renewed interest in religion. American citizens are voluntarily related to religious groups in a higher percentage than ever before. The words "under God" have been inserted into the national pledge of allegiance. Religious books enjoy an unprecedented volume of sales. Religion, we are sure, is a very good thing, especially when it enables people to adjust wholesomely to their social environment.

Now it may well be that the study of religion in the university is no more than another example of this latter trend. It may be simply a response to a specific interest of students, like courses in photography, or group recreation, or typing, for that matter. Were it no more than this, we might expect the interest to wane in another generation. Yet, we know that religion is a perennial human concern. There has been no civilization investigated by sociologists, historians, or archaeologists that has not shown evidence of religious practices. But now we have raised the question of what we mean by religion.

1. What is religion?

Probably the most ready answer to this question is that religion is one's beliefs about God. God, most people would probably continue, is whatever one may think of as superhuman or supernatural. It is the "power" above us. But what have we actually said in these words? Obviously, they indicate that there is something beyond us upon which we are in some way dependent and which lays some sort of obligation upon us. We do not live our lives completely to our own liking. They are set in a context which we do not create. And there is an order of things over and against us and our world to which all must conform. Religion would therefore involve the way we happen to conceive this "something" above us. Some think of it in personal terms as akin to ourselves. Others think of it as an arbitrary power not primarily concerned with human happiness. Still others are apt to think of it as nature's totality, not something *super*natural but nevertheless superior to any single part of nature. Religion is simply our idea about the superior order on which we are dependent, many people would say.

But if we pursue the question further by asking whether entertaining certain ideas can be religion, we must make an immediate qualification. Such ideas are strictly religious only when they lead to action related to them. Mere opinions, even about the supernatural, are not religion. Opinions become religious when they shape what a person is and does. Hence, if a man feels he is dependent on a power greater than himself and acknowledges his dependency in some way—say in prayer— then he is religious. The person who prays is religious, but the person who merely discusses prayer is not, at least in this one instance.

Yet we still have not finished our investigation. For if we speak of religion as a belief in some more ultimate order, a belief expressed in appropriate action, then we may find religion in areas where we previously had not recognized it at all. Reduce it to its essentials, and what have we been saying if not that religion involves a person's entire response to whatever he feels is of supreme importance in life? If a person regards social adaptability as life's most important concern and consistently makes his choices accordingly, then he is religious, for social conformity is that thing beyond himself which, for him, is ultimate. We can say that it is his god. Or we can put the same idea in other words and say that a man's religion is all that is involved when he formulates or attempts to formulate a meaning for his life. Meaning is the pattern in which all his experiences are organized, and that organization can be made only as all facets of life are seen in relation to one thing supremely important—again, his god. It is in this sense, then, that Dr. Harris Franklin Rall defines religion as "man's life as conceived and lived in relation to a world of higher order, upon which he feels himself dependent, to which he knows himself under obligation, and in relation with which he finds life's meaning and seeks its completion." [1]

In this sense every man is religious, for to be human is to assign values to things. But religion so understood need not have articulated beliefs. That is, the central conviction may never be worked out in a logical system of doctrines. A religious belief is not so much an intellectual opinion as a conviction by which one actually lives, whether it is expressed in language or not. Religion must, therefore, be personal because it involves the whole response of a person. To isolate the articulation of fundamental beliefs is not to isolate religion, but merely to abstract one aspect of it. And to study religious practices is not to study religion, but only certain phenomena of it. In fact, to understand religion, we must come at it from the inside, because only when we are personally involved are we dealing with living religion.

So far we have been speaking of religion in general, though by now we can recognize that it does not exist in general but only in concrete expression in persons. But we also speak of religions referring to Buddhism, or Islam, or Christianity. This is possible because, on the one hand, Buddhism, Islam, and Christianity do fall into a common category. They are attempts

---

[1] Harris Franklin Rall, *Christianity* (New York: Charles Scribner's Sons, 1940), p. 15. Reprinted by permission.

to bind life together in some coherent meaning. And on the other hand, they are religions because people can and do share the same ultimate concerns and ways of expressing them.

The concern and its expression may be simple indeed. Hedonism, for example, means to hold pleasure as life's ultimate concern. There is no particular pattern of expressing this conviction integrally associated with it, hence most people would say that hedonism is a philosophy of life but not a religion. The pattern of expression of a core belief may become complex and stabilized in a given culture, however. Hinduism is an excellent example of this. There is a definite belief: the soul of man is identical with the world soul and individuality is an illusion. Associated with this are characteristic practices ranging from the caste system to the ascetic life of the traditional holy man. Or the core belief and pattern of expression may have their origin with an individual and his followers, tempered, of course, by their culture. Christianity and Islam are examples of this.

Religions as we find them are empirical facts; that is, whether we refer to a group or to an individual, we can say that such-and-such is the basic concern, and it is expressed in a certain way. In this sense, there is no question as to whether a religion is true or false: it simply is. But on the other hand, the basis of a religion—what it regards as ultimate—may correspond to reality or it may not; and the expression of that conviction may be adequate and essentially in character with it, or it may not. I may think that social adjustment is all that finally matters and, consequently, sacrifice everything else to be a member of a particular group. But social adjustment may not really be the center around which all of nature and life revolves; and if it were, concern for the whole of society, rather than some fragment of it, might better express that belief. My religion is a fact, but it may not be sound or valid. My god may not be God.

2.   Can we know God?

There appear to be so many ideas and variations of ideas about what is ultimate, and so many different types of expressions of these ideas, that some people virtually resign from any attempt to distinguish a god or gods from God. They see no real way of discovering what actually is the focus of all meaning. They are likely to say that one man's view is as good as another's.

Something else complicates the problem. We can know the separate facets of our experience because they belong to us. And we can even know something of the whole universe, for here again, although it lies beyond us, it is nevertheless within the range of our experience. It is *our* world. But God, the real foundation of all meaning, must include us and our experiencing. It is not *our* meaning: we are found within it. We cannot know God exactly as we know everything else. Our knowledge reaches only to things that are not ultimate. Professor Etienne Gilson states the problem this way: "How then can He who at all points transcends both the human soul that knows and the sensible object that it knows, fall within the natural grasp of our intellect?" And he goes on to note that the answer of St. Thomas Aquinas, one of Christianity's most important thinkers, was that our intellects "cannot naturally have God for object." [2]

The full consideration of these matters must wait for a more thorough and systematic treatment. We can, however, here point out the direction the Christian answer takes. God can be known only in His relation to us and to human affairs. Or in other words, God is known only as He makes Himself known, as He enters into personal relationships with men. Other religions answer this question differently, some insisting that we

[2] Etienne Gilson, *The Spirit of Mediaeval Philosophy* (New York: Charles Scribner's Sons, 1936; London: Sheed & Ward Limited), p. 250. Reprinted by permission.

may experience a union with God that can never be fully de-
cribed or analyzed.

For a man with rational powers, the choice between such
views must rest on something more fundamental than the accident of his birth in a particular culture. Even if we never fully
comprehend God, we can at least discover the inadequacies of
gods. This process may not be purely intellectual, but it is
rational. That is, as we reflect on our total experience, we may
well be able to make adjustments in our response to what is
vital and in our fundamental concern as well.

3. Why study religion academically?

What we have been describing is a personal process, the sort
of thing any intelligent person might and should do on his own.
But many a student has wondered why a course in religion has
been included in his college curriculum. He is quite willing to
admit that religion is a part of the human scene, for in the face
of the fact that the church is an established part of community
life, it would be foolish to declare otherwise. But religion as a
part of education is another matter. Some people would even
say that for religion to "invade" any field other than established
church life would mean an intrusion into an area where it had
no relevance.

Actually, our nation is somewhat unusual in having so many
people with this attitude, because here religion has traditionally been separated from most public affairs. It is not that our
people are necessarily less religious than others, but that practical necessity forbade any attempt to create a national church.
Few of us have lived under conditions where only one religious
view prevailed, so we find it hard to understand the theory of
one nation-one church. Our ancestors, however, came from
lands with just such a philosophy. An Italian or Pole would be
Roman Catholic, a Swede or Norwegian would be Lutheran, a
Scot would most likely be Presbyterian, and so on. But since

in this country each of these national groups with its own religious ideas and customs had to live with all others in peace, no one religious body could be established for the nation as a whole. Under such circumstances it was felt that by keeping the churches independent of the government, the welfare of all groups would be best served. Even so, Christianity was almost universal, and a common element from it was worked into public life. The Congress had its chaplains, schools had Bible reading and religious assemblies, courts used the Scriptures in tendering oaths.

In more recent years, with larger proportions of non-Christians in the population, this common element has constantly diminished. Since the government assumed and was given the major responsibility for educating children, and since sectarian emphases in public schools would lead only to trouble, religion was for the most part eliminated from the American school curricula, so that the average young person grows up with the idea that religion is definitely an extracurricular matter, something good for those who are inclined towards it, but not a serious consideration in a total educational program, and not necessarily worth profound thought.

In that respect, the elimination of religion from the schools is misleading for one's evaluation of its significance to life as a whole. Christianity has been one of the most powerful shaping factors of our Western civilization, and to be ignorant of its contribution and influence is to have one's whole view of our history warped. Full education requires an understanding of the religious factor.

We might mention, briefly, some of the major contributions to our culture. There is, for one thing, the importance attached to the individual. Where individuality is regarded as illusion, little effort is made to protect human life. Again, scientific thought rests on the belief in the reliability and reality of the world of nature, a belief contributed largely by Christianity.

Still another example is the democratic pattern of checks and balances set up within our national government. These provisions grew largely out of the Calvinistic distrust of individuals or groups who sought to rule absolutely, even for good purposes.

Moreover, since very few churches have been able to maintain an educational program within their own ranks at all comparable to the standards of public school education, a young person's knowledge of religious matters is often far inferior to his scientific knowledge. His religious concepts frequently remain on a childish level, while his other ideas develop with his growing experience. Religious groups, unless they develop their own parochial system, have little time for instruction and must work with voluntary pupils. Even then, such training usually comes to a halt by the time the young person finishes high school. Consequently, one who would not be satisfied with a child's understanding of physics, but who remains content with a child's understanding of religion, is likely to find many discrepancies when he tries to relate his advanced secular knowledge to his stunted religious ideas.

Eliminating religion from the course of study has also made it appear irrelevant to the main issues of life. Religion becomes compartmentalized in action as well as in thought. Problems are viewed and judged without taking religious considerations into account. If religion's central thesis is true—that there is a higher order to which we are related and on which we are dependent and which makes ultimate claims on us—we must seek to understand it, to clarify and organize our present thought, and to relate it to all our concerns and interests.

To some it comes almost as a shock to learn that wise, intelligent, and broadly learned men have given their lives to religious studies, not as a relaxing or inspiring avocation, but as their major concern; or that men famous as scientists, philosophers, and sociologists have found religion worthy of their clearest and most searching thought. Since a university program is designed to introduce one to the vast store of human learning and to enable him to respond wholesomely to life, religion has a place in the curriculum along with literature, science, language, and art.

But which religion? Those who demand objectivity might claim that religion in general would be the best approach. The problem is that no such thing as religion in general exists. There are religions, and one can abstract from them qualities to be labeled "religious," but that abstraction is never religion. In the Western World there can be no question that Christianity is dominant. Probably our only direct knowledge of religion is with Christianity. If there is any wisdom in the old adage about beginning where you are, there is good reason to study Christianity apart from any question of the truth to be found in other religions. Nor does this mean that we study Christianity only as a type of a more general phenomenon. One does, however, need a starting point from which he can look at other people's faiths and back again to his own in renewed appreciation and interest.

This book is not written particularly to plead Christianity's superiority over all other religions. It is an attempt to set forth as clearly as possible important Christian insights. If Christianity makes any claim on us, it is as truth, and truth has its own means of verification apart from special pleading. In other words, Christian faith must stand on its own. It is the author's conviction that Christianity can justify itself if one is careful to learn what it is and, insofar as it is possible, to separate it from misconceptions and misleading simplifications.

4.   How can Christianity be defined?

Although most people feel that they are well enough acquainted with Christianity to know what it is, they are often at a loss to define it. The churches are a respected part of the

American scene. Our nation prides itself in having Christian forebears. In fact, Christianity is often publicly identified with the American way of life. But what is Christianity? There are two extreme and almost opposite definitions, and between them various intermediary ones combining features of both, shading gradually from one to the other.

One of the extreme positions is that Christianity is nothing more nor less than doing good to one's fellow men. After all, it is frequently asked, did not Christ go about doing good, and did he not place more emphasis on how a man acted rather than on the way he thought? So, argue people taking this position, the Christian is not one who professes some stereotyped creed, but one who lives decently, obeying the laws and showing kindness to his neighbor. Many holding this position will assert further that the church is no essential part of Christianity, that anyone trying to lead a good and useful life is in reality a Christian, even though, like the late Mahatma Gandhi, he denies it.

Such a view develops as a reaction in any period when the subtlety of creedal statements comes to dominate the religious scene, drawing boundaries between believer and nonbeliever much narrower than those found in human experience. In this country, the profusion of denominations led directly to this view. There was a time, no doubt, when one could seriously believe that none but those in his little group could be classed as Christian. But as people were forced together in communities and could see at firsthand that denominational label had little effect in itself on a person's daily conduct, the concept of what Christianity actually is had to be broadened beyond denominational bounds. And the fact that kindness, generosity, and humility were not confined to church members led finally to the conclusion that identification with a self-designated "Christian" group was not essential at all. So Abraham Lincoln, noting the divisiveness of church life in his day, and refusing to become identified with it, once said that he would join that church which made as its sole requirement for membership a willingness to obey Jesus' summary of the law: "Thou shalt love the Lord thy God with all thy heart, with all thy soul, with all thy mind, and with all thy strength; and thou shalt love thy neighbor as thyself" (Matt. 22: 37–39).

Pitted against that general view are the more traditional ones at the other extreme. One emphasizes the historical institution. The Roman Catholic Church comes readily to mind as an example, but others hold a similar view. Christianity to them belongs solely to those who are linked to a continuing historical organization that can trace its origin directly to Christ and his disciples. The conditions for membership in such a body come to define Christianity. Requirements include behaving in a certain manner (moral qualifications), holding certain beliefs (doctrinal qualifications), and participating in certain rites (ceremonial qualifications). It is misleading to say that such groups formulate their own definition of Christianity by establishing these requirements: most were established in some form in antiquity by the early church. The creedal formulations, for example, were for the most part settled by the end of the fourth century.

Another position deprecates the institution as such and emphasizes some personal experience. People holding this view often stress that not all church members are Christian. The Christian is one who has undergone a certain experience: emotional, psychological, spiritual—all may be involved. One having had such an experience is Christian; one not having had it simply is not.

Still a third position is taken by those who insist the Christian is one who accepts certain doctrinal statements. These may be historical formulations such as the Apostles' or Nicene Creeds, or the Westminister or Augsburg Confessions; or they may be certain doctrines derived from a literal interpretation of the Bible. Some of these are the literal infallibility of the Bible itself, the Virgin birth of Jesus, and the blood of Christ as God's price for man's salvation. These latter positions arise from the attempt to arrive at a definition of Christianity broader than denominational bounds, yet strict enough to preserve some semblance of a definite body, rather than all kind men in general.

Between these extremes, then, of the kindness and generosity definition and the more rigid ones based on a particular institution, experience, or creedal formulation is the middle ground of those who are willing to admit that Christianity transcends denominational lines, that one of the most important factors is the willingness to live by the example of Jesus of Nazareth in common life, according to the ideals of service, humility, and self-sacrifice. They would further insist on a doctrinal minimum, namely, the assent to the proposition that God has made Himself known in human life on earth in Jesus and that through him men find the reality of their spiritual life, or some more subtle refinement or elaboration of this proposition.

Although it would be foolish to try to find some lowest common denominator of these definitions, any attempt to understand Christianity must take account of their common elements. And certainly one cannot escape the figure of Jesus, himself. From an ecclesiastical standpoint, there is no question of his importance, and even those who look askance at institutional Christianity rejoice in the personality and life philosophy of Jesus. It would be hard for anyone to disagree with the statement that the sum and substance of Christianity is Jesus Christ.

This immediately brings us to the documents about him: the books of the New Testament. There is no secular account of Jesus, and although speculation has made him everything from a disciple of the Greek philosophers to an Indian pundit, no such tale-spinning can compare in significance with the accounts given in the four gospels which early Christianity accepted as authoritative. In other words, any attempt to speak of Jesus while ignoring the New Testament records is to make him no more than a figure of one's imagination rather than an historical person. That the New Testament was created by the church to fill its needs in the generation after Jesus' death is an established fact of biblical scholarship. That it is true to the historical facts of the life of the Man of Nazareth, rather than a collection of first century speculation about him, is apparent from its essential purpose and internal agreement. The claim that one can understand Christianity without a knowledge of the scriptures is an egocentrism that has reappeared many times in the history of the church but which has always been repudiated for its self-inconsistencies, not to speak of its usual irrelevance. To understand Christianity which focuses on Jesus, one must understand the scriptures which are virtually the sole source of information about Jesus and interpretation of him.

The scripture record is more than merely the accounts of the life of Jesus as found in the four gospels. Jesus himself claimed to be the fulfillment of Old Testament prophecies (Mark 14:49, Luke 4:21), and early preachers of the faith were insistent that it was scripture which declared that the Christ should suffer and die and be raised again (Acts 18:28, Rom. 1:2, 1 Cor. 15:3, 4). What this means is that Christianity is not a totally novel arrival on the scene of human history, but that it has a tie in the purpose of the nation of Israel, and that certainly in some respects it is a development of the history of that people. In other words, to understand Christianity, one would need to know its Judaistic background which is found in the writings of the Old Testament.

But the scriptures themselves require interpretation, and this, too, has been recognized from early times. An essential feature of early Christian worship was the expounding of the scriptures, explaining their meaning and application to contemporary situations. Not all men had equal skill in doing this, hence certain figures stand out as authorities in those early years: Irenaeus, Origen, Chrysostom, Jerome, Augustine, and later Thomas Aquinas. But the pattern was established with the first disciples when the Apostle Peter declared the meaning of Old Testament passages in his sermon on Pentecost (Acts 2:14–36). And when, today, the Roman Catholic Church insists on its right to interpret scripture to its people, it justifies its position on the grounds that we are most likely mistaken if, from scripture, we derive any meaning totally different from the meaning the great teachers of the Church have found in it through the ages.

This means that any valid understanding of Christianity must include the fellowship of Christians through the centuries, for it is in this fellowship that scripture has been studied and taught. This does not mean that we must slavishly accept everything one of the Church Fathers—say St. Augustine—taught. It does mean that, at the very least, we must consider their views and their reasoning in establishing it—in short, their witness to what Christianity meant to them.

We need to see that Christianity is not merely whatever we choose to make it. It has a particular meaning handed down through the church through generations, going back to the teaching and work of Jesus, himself, and expressed in the writings contained in the Bible. If we are to understand Christianity, we must know something of this background, though, of course, intellectual knowledge of this material does not in itself make one a Christian. To be a Christian—and there is agreement in this—one must have a personal commitment to Jesus Christ. But if that commitment is to be informed, if it is to have a significant and definite content and be more than a catch phrase, it must be grounded in a wider understanding of what Christianity is.

And just that is the major purpose of this book: to give a

wider perspective of the Christian understanding of God and man and their relationship to each other. Some of it may be an old story to many. Some of it will perhaps be startlingly new. Some of it will simply provide a structure for coordinating and organizing one's own religious thought. But it should make one's concept of Christianity more valid than just personal opinion.

QUESTIONS FOR DISCUSSION

1. What are some examples of the confusion which results from trying to relate immature religious concepts with advanced scientific thought?
2. Why do people differ in their definitions of Christianity?

OTHER SOURCES

Brightman, Edgar Sheffield, *A Philosophy of Religion.* Englewood Cliffs, N. J.; Prentice-Hall, Inc., 1940, pp. 13–18.

Caird, G. B., "The Truth of the Gospel," *A Primer of Christianity.* London: Oxford University Press, 1950, Part III, chaps. 1, 3.

Cherbonnier, E. LaB., *Hardness of Heart.* Garden City, N. Y.: Doubleday & Company, Inc., 1955, chap. 4.

Finegan, Jack, *Beginnings in Theology.* New York: Association Press, 1956, chaps. 1, 2.

Houf, Horace T., *What Religion Is and Does,* rev. ed. New York: Harper & Brothers, 1945, chaps. 1, 2.

Hutchison, John A., *Faith, Reason, and Existence.* New York: Oxford University Press, 1956, pp. 23–27.

Lewis, C. S., *Mere Christianity.* London: Geoffrey Bles, 1952, preface.

Pratt, James Bissett, *Can We Keep the Faith?* New Haven: Yale University Press, 1941, chap. 3.

———, *Eternal Values in Religion.* New York: The Macmillan Company, 1950, chap. 5.

Rall, Harris Franklin, *Christianity.* New York: Charles Scribner's Sons, 1940, chaps. 1, 4.

———, *A Faith for Today*. New York: Abingdon Press, 1936, chaps. 2, 3.

Richardson, Alan, *Christian Apologetics*. New York: Harper & Brothers, 1947, chap. 1.

———, *Science, History, and Faith*. London: Oxford University Press, 1950, chap. 1.

Sperry, Willard L., *What We Mean by Religion*. New York: Harper & Brothers, 1940.

Tilden, Elwyn E., Jr., *Toward Understanding Jesus*. Englewood Cliffs, N. J.: Prentice-Hall, Inc., 1956, chaps. 2, 3.

Wickenden, Arthur C., *Youth Looks at Religion*. New York: Harper & Brothers, 1939, chaps. 1, 2.

Wolf, William J., *Man's Knowledge of God*. Garden City, N. Y.: Doubleday & Company, Inc., 1955, chap. 1.

1

belief, faith,
doctrine, and theology

One cannot long discuss religion without using a vocabulary adapted to religious purposes. Although defining terms can be tedious business compared with the intoxication of speculative thought, definition is necessary if what follows is not to be hopelessly confused by vagueness. Typical words are *opinion, belief, faith, doctrine,* and *theology.* Difficulty arises from a failure to define any of these specifically enough to be used without ambiguous references. Understanding becomes almost impossible if we say that one's beliefs are the same as his theology which, in turn, is no more than the doctrines he accepts as opinions.

Belief can first of all be set apart from mere opinion because belief carries with it the element of personal conviction by which one is willing to act. One entertains opinions, but he guides his life by his beliefs. Actually, the verb *believe* has two meanings that should be distinguished. On the one hand, it may refer to an intellectual acceptance of the truth of certain propositions, without any emotional coloring being involved. Thus, one believes that the boiling point of water at sea level pressure is 212° Fahrenheit. But *believe* can also refer to a commitment that involves one personally. This meaning is usually phrased as *believing in,* whereas the first can be expressed as *believing that* something is so. One could conceivably believe that God exists without believing in God to the extent of venturing one's life on the conviction. In the New Testament, this element of commitment is expressed by the word *faith;* but since English lacks a verb for *faith,* recourse must be made to the double-meaning word *believe.* The significance of the difference and the essentially religious meaning of *faith* can be seen in the initial words of the Apostles' and Nicene creeds: "I believe *in. . . .*" In this sense, the creeds are primarily a statement of personal commitment.

One's beliefs, then, are really the undergirding of life. As such, they may remain only implicit. Many religious people would be hard put to give precise expression in language of their beliefs. When they are formulated in language in order to be communicated to other people, they become doctrines—especially if they are not purely personal, but represent convictions held by whole groups. But the expression of a belief as a doctrine depends on more than the belief alone. It also involves the current thought forms of the culture of the believer. One would not express the same belief in the same way in medieval Europe and twentieth century America. The New Testament itself reflects different expressions of the same basic belief at the same period, but in Jewish terms on the one hand, and in more characteristically Hellenistic (Greek) terms on the other. A comparison of the Gospel of St. Matthew with that of St. John will illustrate this.

Doctrine can be formulated and recorded in writing to be handed from one generation to another. It will remain alive so long as its particular modes of expression are understood and so long as it is grounded on a living faith or belief. Belief itself, however, cannot be given from one person to another or from one generation to another. We believe only that which has a believable quality about it that commends itself to us. We do not believe what we regard as inherently unbelievable. We may believe something that on the surface seems impossible but which, on further consideration, we have discovered to be sound. We do not believe what finally remains impossible to us unless we are dishonest with ourselves.

It is important in this connection to realize that in the last resort there is only one reason for believing anything to be true, and that is that we cannot *help* believing it to be true. At some point or other truth must shine in its own light, must lay hold of the mind with direct, compelling power, so that a man feels that he has no option but to say, "Yes, that is true, and I cannot honestly deny that it is true." [1]

One can learn the words of doctrine—say, that Jesus Christ is God's only Son—but this is not the same as believing it to the extent of making it a pillar of one's life. One may even accept the truth of the proposition granting that the Church through the ages is likely to be more correct than one human mind. But one *believes* it only as the reality itself has entered one's own

[1] Herbert H. Farmer, *God & Men* (New York: Abingdon-Cokesbury Press, 1947), p. 21. Reprinted by permission of Nisbet & Co., Ltd., London.

experience. There is little point in admonishing a person to believe something apart from the inner conviction which constitutes belief. Doctrine, however, can clarify one's basic belief
and reveal its implications. In many respects, the appeal of
Christianity is not as some novel truth but as the true implication of the relation between the individual and God that
already exists. The belief is to some extent present, but its
significance is only potentially present.

In many Christian believers, doctrine remains only implicit.
The reality of belief is there with its significant influence on all
of life, but the person may lack the ability or the time or the
technical capacity to formulate doctrine. At this point he may
simply accept the teaching of his church, trusting that if he did
work out the implications of his belief he would come out with
an answer comparable to that which the great teachers of the
Church have formulated on the basis of an equivalent belief.
But while the doctrinal expression of belief may give it clarity
and open new depths of understanding to the believer, in itself it is not equivalent to faith.

Theology is the organizing and systematizing of the doctrines of a religion to make them consistent with each other and
relevant to the rest of life. This is undertaken not only for the
sake of consistency, but for the sake of clear communication to
other people as well. But theology is more than simply assort-
ing, arranging, and clarifying. It means evaluation and correc-
tion of doctrine. One doctrine is not just as good as another
unless it gives equal expression to the same belief, equal in the
sense of being as true to experience and as easy to understand
in the terms of its expression. A detached study of doctrines in
relation to knowledge as a whole is undertaken in philosophy
of religion.

Some doctrines do not change with changing life but remain
constant because the aspect of experience to which they refer

remains constant. An example, to be discussed more fully later, is the doctrine of the two natures of Christ. Working with the facts of Jesus' humanity and the conviction of his Deity as well, the Church after rejecting doctrinal formulations expressed in terms of dual personalities, or dual wills, or Divine spirit inhabiting a human body, settled on the doctrine of the two natures; namely, that Christ was fully man and fully God, yet one person. The doctrine is held to this day because a better formulation of the central conviction has not been found. And, of course, insofar as there is similarity of belief and culture, there will be similarity of doctrine—hence, the degree of consistency within a particular religion that sets it apart from other religions.

Doctrine can also become dead. This happens when the faith that generated it has disappeared and all that remains are formal statements of expression. But doctrine can also become dead through a change in prevailing thought forms. Then, in order that a doctrine received from the past may be understood, it must be translated into the thought forms of a new age. This, itself, is theological activity. Oftentimes, instead of discarding a doctrine and producing a new one, the historical formulation is retained, but its terms are redefined. For example, in the doctrine of the Trinity—that God is one in three persons—*person* means something quite different from our contemporary idea of person. Failure to appreciate this often makes people think that Christianity affirms the existence of three Gods. Or again, Protestants affirm their faith in the "holy Catholic Church," even though for many of them the first association of the word *catholic* is with the Roman Catholic Church rather than with *the universal body of Christian believers,* as they really define it.

One more word needs to be considered: *dogma,* which has often been abused by being identified with the popular usage of *dogmatic* as a synonym for *unreasonable*. *Dogma* really means "the given aspect of religious teaching." It is something one starts from. For Christians, the doctrine that "God was in Christ reconciling the world to Himself" is a dogma. It is one of the fundamental postulates without which there is no Christianity. It is possible, of course, that one group will regard as dogma what another is willing to question.

A question often asked in Christian groups is why anyone should formulate doctrines or compose creeds instead of simply using the formulations of the New Testament. This question arises from a misunderstanding of both doctrine and the scriptures. Doctrine is not something new to be added to the New Testament. To the extent that it is totally new, it would be regarded as false. It is, rather, the attempt to make explicit what may be only implied in the Bible. The New Testament, especially, was written so close to firsthand experience of the events there recorded that it has little systematic theological reflection. It certainly is not a textbook in theology. What is there needs to be drawn out from narrative to propositional form for study, reflection, and summary. The Apostles' Creed is not found in the New Testament, yet it summarizes in an easily remembered form much of the content of the New Testament message. Doctrine and creeds certainly cannot replace the Bible. Most churches have some statement in their constitutions to the effect that any doctrine which cannot be established from scripture cannot be binding on their members. That at times biblical thought is pulled out into unnecessarily fine distinctions cannot be denied, but so long as the purpose of doctrine is to express belief, and so long as the germ of Christian belief is found in the New Testament insights into the relation of God and man, doctrine will not contradict the Bible. These two references, scripture and experience, serve as criteria for the truth and usefulness of doctrine.

QUESTIONS FOR DISCUSSION

1. Evaluate this statement: Christianity needs no doctrines because doctrines only breed disagreements and arguments.
2. Can one avoid theology in any significant attempt to understand Christianity? Why?

OTHER SOURCES

DeWolf, L. Harold, A Theology of the Living Church. New York: Harper & Brothers, 1953, chap. 1.

Richardson, Alan, Christian Apologetics. New York: Harper & Brothers, 1947, chap. 2.

Spurrier, William A., Guide to the Christian Faith. New York: Charles Scribner's Sons, 1952, chap. 1.

2

knowledge, reason, and faith

Because so many people apparently separate their religion from their other concerns and, in fact, sentimentalize it into a vague feeling, it is easy to charge that religion has no affinity with reason or knowledge. Most people have heard Christian sermons in which the minister counseled the religious person to throw reason to the winds and "just believe." There is some element of truth in the advice, or it would not be heard so often, but such truth as might be found in it is obscured by the apparent contradiction between faith and reason. The result of this contradiction is to make religion a matter of belief while the rest of life and its practical issues are ruled by intelligent thought.

To speak of the relation of these concepts presupposes some knowledge of their meaning. *Belief,* we have already defined as one's basic conviction about the meaning and purpose of life that undergirds all one's thought and action. *Faith* is the living of this central conviction. *Reason* refers to clear, logical thought based on human experience. *Experience* here requires a broad interpretation including all that is involved in one's contact with the world and with God. Limiting experience to sense data only would narrow the province of reason and deny its relevance to all other aspects of life. *Knowledge* refers to facts of experience established, collected, and organized with some reflection on their relationships to each other.

Most difficulty in relating these concepts comes from pairing them off as opposites within a single category rather than recognizing them as belonging to different categories. For example, faith and knowledge are often set against each other as two different ways of presenting us with a body of factual information. Knowledge is then regarded as the direct experience of verifying certain factual data, while faith means accepting the word of an authority that such verification has been made. What we cannot possess as knowledge, in other words, we accept on faith. Of course, the certainty of knowing for oneself is preferable to taking the word of another person. Hence, as knowledge increases, faith is supplanted. When knowledge is meager, the importance of faith is enhanced.

A question that arises with this approach to the problem is how one can evaluate the authority in which he places his trust.

To accept whatever an authority declares without any critical appraisal is simply gullibility. When authorities make conflicting statements, one must somehow evaluate their claims in order to decide which one he will accept. This appraisal can be valid only as one's knowledge of the authorities and their particular subject matter is increased. But as one's knowledge increases, his need for faith and authorities is overcome. New knowledge either shows an authority to be false or misleading, or simply bears it out—actually making it unnecessary.

It may be objected that if the pronouncements of an authority have been found to be reliable up to a certain point, this justifies any faith in the balance of the declarations of that authority. But the point at issue is not what one has been able to check in the past, but how he will settle the question at hand. Always a new situation arises in which the authority must be accepted or rejected, but accepted only provisionally until one's own knowledge is adequate to the problem involved.

But the principal objection to pitting faith against knowledge is that such a contest comes only from a gross misunderstanding of faith. Certainly the New Testament does not refer to faith as something finally to be supplanted by knowledge (1 Cor. 13:8, 13). Faith involves one's understanding of the meaning and purpose of life, his attitude toward God. As one's knowledge—his grasp of truth—grows, his faith should grow, if his faith has been placed in the true God. Knowledge exposes a false faith: it strengthens rather than displaces a true one. That there is place in religion for accepting the word of an authority is not to be denied, just as its place in science is not to be denied; but this is not the primary meaning of faith. Faith does not supply what is missing in knowledge. It helps us obtain knowledge, not as a method, but as an attitude in which learning is made possible. The significant content of our religion is defined not by what we do not know, but by what we know.

Similar to pitting faith against knowledge is pitting it against reason. In this it is implied that if faith does not give knowledge directly, it is a short cut in obtaining knowledge. Faith then becomes equated with intuition, in contrast to the process of logical thinking. *Reason* means thinking things through clearly, while faith appears to be a leap to the conclusion. Contrasted to each other in this way, they cannot be made relevant to each other. Reason has no jurisdiction over faith in terms of criticism or evaluation. Faith is either held to be beyond all criticism or else is regarded as foolishness. The pronouncements of faith can be subjected to no appraisal. Faith, if one accepts its claim, is its own guarantee of its truth; and if one does not accept that claim, he ignores it altogether.

Of course, every other claim to truth in life must be evaluated and related to all other claims to truth. Scientific hypotheses are not accepted without some verification through other aspects of experience. Ethical theories are related to facts about people living in society. Philosophy is judged by internal logic and its adequacy to all relevant facts. But religion in its relation to faith is exempted from such a process. Yet, an uncriticized religion is apt to confuse grossest falsehood with truth.

It makes no difference if one is a foe or a friend of religion: the result is the same if one places faith opposite reason. The man who does this because of his utter regard for faith and the one who does it because he feels reason can have no competitors—both separate religion from any attempt to relate it to the rest of life or to distinguish from its true element any admixture of superstition, falsehood, or irrationality.

But again the difficulty arises from a false view of faith. Faith is here thought of as a challenger of reason, of the same category as reason, whereas in the New Testament, faith is not a substitute for reason. St. Paul did say that the wisdom of God seen in the cross of Christ was foolishness with men (1 Cor.

1:18). He did not mean, however, that this was a final and unresolved foolishness, for his life was spent in the attempt to convince men that this was really their deepest wisdom just because it was the wisdom of God. Not less thought or shallower thought, but more and deeper thought would show faith's insights to be true. And so it must be if religion is to claim the whole man rather than one small compartment of his life. Jesus commanded men to love God with all their minds as well as with all their hearts (Matt. 22:37).

Perhaps the Christian attitude toward the relation of faith and knowledge and reason can best be summarized in terms of its practical results. For one thing, the Christian is always the seeker after truth because his God is a God of truth who must be worshiped in truth. Therefore a Christian is never afraid to learn facts, never afraid that true knowledge will destroy his faith or supplant his God. And that attitude has tremendous significance because it has been in Christian lands that modern science has developed. Sometimes that fact has been obscured by the attention given to the opposition of the churches to certain scientific theories. The trouble Galileo encountered when he rejected a geocentric astronomy comes readily to mind. But the basis of science—the firm reliability of the processes of nature and the ability of the human mind to comprehend them— has followed upon the Christian faith in a God of truth who alone is absolute and who is not challenged in His dominion by man's knowledge of the natural order.

At the same time, the Christian will be conservative in his attitude toward new ideas, and that conservatism ought to be respected, neither disparaged nor exaggerated. In other words, as the Christian is interested in truth, he will be sure that mere opinions and unverified theories are not mistaken for established facts. His search for truth demands that he be critical of new ideas as well as receptive to their possible truth. Of course, such conservatism can be perverted by the assumption that all truth has already been discovered for all time, that no further inquiry is necessary or desirable. But neither is it sound to say that the past has given us nothing worth the keeping.

QUESTIONS FOR DISCUSSION

1. Why is scientific knowledge sometimes thought to be destructive of religious faith? What concept of faith does such a fear presuppose?
2. In what way is religious faith dependent upon reason?

OTHER SOURCES

DeWolf, L. Harold, *A Theology of the Living Church*. New York: Harper & Brothers, 1953, chaps. 2, 4.

Farmer, Herbert H., *God & Men*. New York: Abingdon-Cokesbury Press, 1947, chap. 1.

Pratt, James Bissett, *Can We Keep the Faith?* New Haven: Yale University Press, 1941, chap. 6.

Rall, Harris Franklin, *Christianity*. New York: Charles Scribner's Sons, 1940, chap. 11.

Richardson, Alan, *Christian Apologetics*. New York: Harper & Brothers, 1947, chap. 10.

3

religion, science, and philosophy

Religion, we have said, is man's total response to what he regards as of ultimate importance. It can never be isolated from his attempt to understand the natural world or to arrive at a coherent picture of reality. But it must not be confused with these other concerns.

1. Religion and science

The relation of science to religion has been the focal point of the conflict between faith and reason, at least in popular thought. And much confusion has arisen because the methods and principles of science have not been clearly understood. Science deals with measurable quantities and accepts them as reality for its starting point. With that as its foundation, it should be obvious that the conclusion of science is that only measurable quantities are real. A study that excludes certain considerations cannot be expected to shed any light on those considerations. Science is a system which includes only a part of human experience. As a system it is remarkable, and its contributions to human welfare cannot be gainsaid, but it remains an exclusive rather than an inclusive system. If, from the start, it excludes complicated personal reactions like love or the intricacies of religious experience, there should be no surprise that, in turn, it does not verify these experiences and establish them on the same basis as, say, the atomic structure of hydrogen. In other words, if science gives no absolute proof of God, that should not come as any surprise or even as a disappointment to the religious person. Nor does it mean that religion is therefore divorced from reason. Reason is important to all human mental pursuits—literature or philosophy, for example—that are not included in science.

It has been the supposed conflict of science and religion, however, that has drawn most attention, and in America, at least, no phase of the problem has achieved more notoriety than the subject of evolution. Did God create man, it is frequently asked, or did man just evolve from lower forms of life? These alternatives are taken as the epitomes of the religious and scientific outlooks. Now, while it might be interesting to argue the issue on this basis, it will be more constructive to discover the basic presuppositions of both sides, as well as their approach to any specific question.

We have already noted that science is grounded on the faith that the universe is orderly and rational and therefore understandable by man. This rational order is understood by science in terms of cause and effect. It is assumed that any event can be understood only in relation to the events preceding it and related to it, events that brought it about or caused it. This, in essence, is what science means by *cause:* those natural events preceding and related to the one in question. When a pail of water that I left outside overnight freezes, I note that the temperature dropped after sundown and conclude that it was the drop in temperature that caused the water to freeze.

Of course, it is science's task to discover which of the antecedent events are actually related. There can easily be an arbitrary factor in the early stages of this search. Primitive science is usually the fallacious *post hoc ergo propter hoc* type of reasoning run wild—the idea that if one event follows another, the first caused the second. For example, if a tribe in desperation does a particular dance and rain follows, it is concluded that the dance caused the rain. Science continually works to free its concept of cause from irrelevant factors. In other words, scientific cause is a sequence cause, and scientific explanation is made in these terms. In this sense, science would look for the "cause" of man in natural events preceding his appearance on this planet and related in some way to it, hence the whole system of evolutionary thought that accounts for the arrival of man by an unbroken chain extending through decreasingly complex forms of life to the simple living cell, and even beyond that to the development of complex inorganic compounds from even simpler constituents.

It should not be hard to see that any event in this natural order would have a scientific cause given in terms of the preceding events, because any event occurring within the natural order would be preceded by other events related to it. This is why science countenances no miracles and why God does not enter into scientific investigations. God is not a natural event at all, the only sort of thing with which science is equipped to deal. For example, a person might, from a religious standpoint, count the Israelites' crossing of the Red (or Reed) Sea a miracle. The scientific student, by the very nature of scientific investigation, would have to discount such an interpretation *for his purposes* and concentrate instead on the succession of natural events that led to the phenomenon of the parting of the waters. And he would note, perhaps, the strong east wind of the biblical account (Exo. 14:21). The wind, he would likely say, was the cause of the sea's parting; and he would not mention anything about the intervention of God. Even supposing east winds to be exceedingly rare in the area, he would look for something in the natural order that would account for it. The religious explanation, on the other hand, centering on the meaning of the event for the Israelites, would be that God saved His people by parting the water to allow them to pass.

Let us be sure to note at this point that it was only as science thus interpreted the rational order in terms of sequence causation that it was able to discover the things which make our lives today so much more pleasant than human life just a few generations ago. So long as the "will of God" was introduced to cut short investigation of natural cause, progress in this field was held back. So long as epidemics were dropped into God's lap, no one bothered with the problems of sanitation and infection. It was when all considerations other than temporal sequence were ruled as extraneous that science could come into its own.

But while the scientific approach to a problem through the concept of natural cause is a helpful one so far as human need is concerned, it is not adequate to our total experience. While we know the significance of the cause of an event in terms of antecedent events, we know, too, that events must also be understood in terms of some purpose which they fulfill. In other words, we do something today not merely because we have done certain other things yesterday and cannot help ourselves, but because it must be done if we are to have something else tomorrow on which we have set our minds. The future planned event determines our present course. It is this purposive response to external conditions that is characteristic of life. The conduct of a scientific investigation cannot be understood then in purely scientific terms. Not only preceding events must be taken into consideration, but also—and primarily—the purpose of the scientist. One could, for example, explain a person's walking to town in a purely physical manner: the contraction of the muscles in relation to his skeletal structure that enables him to move his legs and feet. But if we ask the person why he walks to town, it is much more likely that we want to know his purpose: what he intends to buy, or whom he intends to see, or even whether he merely wants physical exercise. Purpose is as necessary to our way of thinking as scientific cause.

But natural science has no way of dealing with this consideration. It is not a scientific concept at all. Particularly when that purpose involves life's ultimate meaning, to ask about it is not to raise a scientific question but a religious question, and a religious question can only be answered with a religious answer. We must note carefully, however, that whatever cannot be explained in scientific terms is not necessarily a religious matter. The thinking of the past that ascribed to the will of God whatever could not be explained scientifically, that brought in the concept of purpose to cover the deficiency in knowledge of temporal cause, led to much confusion when human knowledge was expanded by research. It was as though God were confined to a diminishing realm, that the more human knowledge grew, the less reason there was to be concerned about God. Some people, in the name of religion, tried to limit the expansion of human knowledge, for fear that the need for God would be completely outgrown. And many others, although they found it possible to relate their religion to such science as they already knew, recognized that their faith might easily be challenged by new developments, as more and more formerly unaccountable things were tied in with the whole chain of cause and effect.

Religion does not necessarily deal with a set of events completely different from those which are the province of science, but it approaches them from an entirely different standpoint. Using again our example of the Israelites' crossing of the Red Sea, the issue is not which of the accounts of it, the scientific or the biblical, is true—implying that only one can be. The question is, rather, whether the scientific account—as complete in its own way as we might wish to conceive it—does not leave out some important consideration of the event, namely, its significance to the people involved in terms of their understanding of life's meaning. Science is a colorless approach to reality—at least, it strives to be. But human life is not colorless, and to consider it apart from its color is to consider it only in part, not as a whole.

Some simplify the distinction between science and religion by saying that science tries to answer the *how* question of life, while religion concerns itself with the *why* question. This is certainly a truer distinction than saying that science is interested only in facts, while religion is concerned only with values. But the point to be made here is that the answers which science supplies do not eliminate the need for religion, not because science leads us back to where our knowledge fades out, but because many important questions—many would say the most important questions—are not scientific questions at all. They are religious, and only religion can answer them. Expanding knowledge of the natural order cannot usurp God's place because God is not in competition with the natural order.

The scientist and the man of faith may, in fact, be the same person, but the two roles are not the same and are not meant to be. Conflicts come when the roles are confused, when one attempts to give religious answers to scientific questions, or scientific answers to religious questions. Thus, the statement sometimes heard that there is no God because science has not discovered Him in the natural order is not only misleading, it is nonsense. So, also, the view that religion can supply the factual data of natural phenomena before the time of human history is nonsense. The relation of these two approaches should become clearer as we work through the main points of Christian thought.

2. Religion and philosophy

Another human concern sometimes confused with religion is philosophy. Philosophy is the attempt to obtain a comprehensive, coherent picture of life in which all aspects of human experience are fitted together in one over-all view. The analysis we have made of religion and science and their relation to each other is a phase of philosophy. Philosophy uses the data of the sciences along with aesthetic, moral, and religious experience, appraising them through reason and logic to trace their mutual relations. It seeks to answer such questions as how we know what we do, what life's true values are, and what the nature of reality is.

This attempt to see life as a whole is decidedly close to religion, but the two are not the same. Philosophy attempts to be a study in which objective truth can be sought as completely divorced as possible from personal idiosyncrasies. Philosophy can be discussed in the abstract, as though one were not himself directly involved. The attempt to speak abstractly about religion falsifies it, making it something other than religion. Religion is one's complete response to what he regards of such supreme value in life that it demands everything of him, a response seen not only in an internal concern but in the expression of that concern emotionally, intellectually, and volitionally. Religion involves the whole person.

To that extent, no religion—certainly not Christianity—can be conveyed in a book. One cannot understand a religion thoroughly merely by reading books about it. Doctrine can be expounded. Patterns of response can be described. But religion goes beyond this, because the whole person is religious, whatever his beliefs may be. As Immanuel Kant pointed out nearly two centuries ago, while one can dispute with his mind the reality of the higher order called God, he cannot act as though it were not real and still act rationally. To be rational means to live in terms of purpose and meaning, and even when the mind cannot define the meaning, its influence continues to be felt in life. This aspect of religion must always be kept in mind. We do not deal solely with the realm of ideas but with the response of the whole person to what he regards as of supreme importance.

QUESTIONS FOR DISCUSSION

1. What is the nature of the questions which science seeks to answer? What type of question does religion seek to answer?
2. Evaluate the statement: Science can take us back so far in its search for cause, and beyond that point is God.

OTHER SOURCES

Baillie, John, *Natural Science and the Spiritual Life*. New York: Charles Scribner's Sons, 1952.

Caird, G. B., "The Truth of the Gospel," *A Primer of Christianity*. London: Oxford University Press, 1950, Part III, chap. 2.

Farmer, Herbert H., *Towards Belief in God*. New York: The Macmillan Company, 1943, chap. 12.

Houf, Horace T., *What Religion Is and Does*, rev. ed. New York: Harper & Brothers, 1945, chaps. 5–7.

Marney, Carlyle, *Faith in Conflict*. New York: Abingdon Press, 1957, chap. 1.

Raven, Charles E., *Christianity and Science*, World Christian Books. New York: Association Press, 1955, chaps. 1–5.

———, *Science, Religion, and the Future*. New York: The Macmillan Company, 1943.

Richardson, Alan, *Christian Apologetics*. New York: Harper & Brothers, 1947, chap. 7.

———, *Science, History, and Faith*. London: Oxford University Press, 1950, chap. 2.

Wickenden, Arthur C., *Youth Looks at Religion*. New York: Harper & Brothers, 1939, chap. 3.

{ two }

revelation, the bible, and faith

4

REVELATION

Religion, we have noted, differs from philosophy in that it is the response of the whole person, not merely his rational faculties, to what he finds of ultimate value in life. Intellectual problems invite our curiosity and thought, though we may feel no obligation to tackle them ourselves instead of leaving them for others to solve. Physical restraint may force us to act in a certain way, but it cannot compel us to change our world view. Aesthetic experience may bring our emotions into play, but it does not necessarily lead us to action. But the concerns of religion are not met merely by a consistent theology, or a program of charitable acts, or a satisfying emotional glow. Our religion involves our whole personalities.

But what are the implications of this fact that we are thus completely involved? There must be something outside ourselves that makes its claim known upon us; yet, because we often think of ourselves as seeking for life's meaning, this may not be so obvious. The concept of seeking seems to imply activity on our part and often passivity on the part of the object sought. It "waits" to be discovered by us. A deeper consideration of the matter, however, would indicate that we seek only in response to a prompting that suggests to us there is something to be found, something that, in a sense, beckons us. Our search is a response to something that claims our attention.

But *things* do not make a claim on us. Things in themselves are indifferent. They do not suggest what we shall do about them. They are simply there to be used or avoided as we see fit. Whatever it is, then, that calls forth this whole response on our part cannot be of the nature of a thing. It is, rather, of the nature of a person, for only persons can lay claim on us by making themselves known. This claim is not an explicit "Do this" or "Don't do that." It is a claim on us as persons.

This search for life's meaning has a peculiar nature all its own. It is different from that involved in scientific investigation, for its object is not so much how things actually are but how they ought to be. Its nature is normative rather than descriptive. If we fail to note this difference, we may think of God as some remote object, albeit the most important object, waiting to be discovered by us. And we shall likely think in terms of projecting our experience of this world to what is beyond this world—from the natural, in other words, to the supernatural. For example, when we find a piece of complicated mechanism on this earth, we note that a human intelligence has been active in its fabrication. Therefore, when we observe the delicate balance of so many factors in nature which makes our lives and the entire universe possible, we conclude that only a Supreme Intelligence—God—could have fashioned it all. God, thus seen, is a rational inference from our knowledge of the world.

The search for natural law is a far different thing from the search for ultimate meaning. We often speak of natural law, not realizing that unlike human or statutory law, natural law is a description of how things actually behave under definite conditions. This can be the proper object of research and study. But obligation refers not to how things actually behave, but how they ought to behave even though they may not, in fact, do so. The attempt to learn the law governing the fall of an apple from a tree is quite a different undertaking from the attempt to learn what life is about and why we should not live aimlessly. Natural law waits to be discovered and formulated. Philosophical principles wait to be deduced. There is something optional about such studies. But God lays a claim upon us which is not optional because it involves our very being as men.

1.   The meaning of revelation

This movement from God to man through which all of a man is involved is called *revelation*. It is God making Himself known to us, disclosing Himself so that we, in turn, must do something in response. Our problem, therefore, is not to project our thought to Him: it is more simply to recognize and understand His approach to us. Revelation in some form is basic to all religion. It accounts for the experience of complete involvement apparent in the sense of obligation. But the crucial question, the answer to which distinguishes Christianity from other religions, is how God reveals Himself and what is actually given in this revelation.

Often when people think of revelation, they think in terms of specific information given to men in a manner outside the usual ways of obtaining it. Revelation, it is thought, gives us knowledge of specific events to take place in the future. We usually think of the prophet in this role of learning the secrets of the future from God and announcing them to the people concerned. In ages past, men thought that answers to specific questions would be given them by revelation, that the gods would declare their will in such matters as launching a war or planting crops. And methods for discerning the gods' answers varied from watching for certain patterns in the flight of a released flock of birds, or looking for a particular coloration of the internal organs of an animal purposely sacrificed, to throwing dice or drawing straws. In more sophisticated cultures, the revelation of God was sought from seers especially gifted, and later from religious texts which were usually the writings of religious men of an earlier day. The date of the end of the world has been sought for centuries in the cryptic words found in the books of Daniel and the Revelation. Others have tried to make predictions about the future from the mysterious writings of Nostradamus. In fact, the very mention of revelation is apt to call up a host of thoughts about bizarre and unsupported ideas, esoteric teachings, and voices out of the darkness.

Or revelation is thought to supply information about the past that is otherwise unobtainable. Some feel, for example, that our knowledge of man's origin would be forever closed to us because no one was witness to the event, but that God has given us this interesting information by revelation in the Bible. Others feel that historical facts such as the length and extent of the reign of King David of Israel are given by revelation. But while this information, if it were so given, might be interesting, it cannot be regarded as of scientific or historical accuracy. This does not mean that it is untrue; but if it is accepted as fact, it must be verified on grounds other than revelation. Whatever claims to be scientific data must be scientifically verifiable, and whatever claims to be historical fact must be verifiable as history. No scientist can introduce into his line of reasoning data which he obtains not by scientific methods but rather from his dreams or from consulting prescientific books. In other words, revelation cannot guarantee the truth of what is rightfully a matter of scientific or historical investigation and confirmation.

This recognition has led people to confine revelation to purely religious matters. Many would therefore say that what God reveals are the great eternal truths of the Christian faith, such as that God is one in three persons, or that Christ and God are of the same substance; or the truths of other religions such as the Hindu axiom that Brahma is Atman. But doctrines vary not only from one religion to another, they vary from one group to another within any one religion. The problem may focus in man's faulty apprehension, but revelation cannot be successful if it results in obscurity or contradiction. In either case, it is hard to see how revelation could really be relevant to life.

A more promising approach begins with the question as to why revelation should be given at all. The answer is not to expand our scientific or historical knowledge. Revelation is given primarily to answer or to help us answer the question of the meaning of life as a whole. It does not give us something that lies within our powers to supply. It gives us, rather, that which we can receive in no other way. Since life as we know it neither guarantees its fulfillment nor defines its own meaning, we can see that knowledge of the scientific or historical sort can furnish no answer to the questions for which revelation must supply the answers; hence, scientific or historical data cannot be the content of revelation at all. And while perhaps it is easier to regard doctrine as the content of revelation, even here we have

a human response that in itself cannot answer the human problem. What we may expect to find as the content of revelation,
then, is not impersonal information but that quality of knowledge that elicits our entire personal response. But since that
sort of response is generated only by trust and commitment
which are personal qualities, the content of revelation must,
itself, be personal. This distinction should save us from ignoring revelation in religious matters because we know its irrelevance to scientific matters and because we see it does not save
us from inconsistencies in philosophical thought.

The real meaning of revelation can best be seen in the relationship of persons to each other. We may know about a person
in the sense of knowing certain facts about his life, facts which
we have learned either for ourselves or from a third party. This
type of information can be obtained from an encyclopedia
article or a biography and may be very general or quite de-
tailed. To know a person, however, one must have knowledge
of a different sort altogether. It cannot be had at secondhand,
but only in personal encounter. It does not add to our factual
knowledge at all; for when we know a person, we find it exceedingly difficult to say what it is we know and how we have
come to know it. And we cannot know a person unless he is
willing that we should know him, unless he "reveals" himself to
us. Our response to such self-giving is our giving ourselves in
return. To know a person is, by its very nature, a mutual relationship. We can know only as we are known. And, finally, this
self-giving is complete. A symbol of it is the sharing of secrets
which has little to do with an increase of factual knowledge
but has much to do in putting each person in the other's power.

Revelation is akin to the self-giving of a friend who is willing
to be known. In the same way, it involves the response of faith
in wholehearted personal involvement or commitment. It does
not necessarily increase our factual knowledge, although—just
as in friendship—we may make statements on the basis of this

mutual relationship, but statements that at best are always incomplete because they refer to living persons rather than to things. Revelation, in short, is God's disclosing of Himself that elicits our response of faith, the whole-person response which is of the essence of religion.

With this understanding of revelation in mind, we should be able to see why men should have thought of it as supplying data of a scientific or historical sort. These data were not just information for its own sake but, rather, information essential to one's understanding of the purpose and meaning of life. Not every person has identical observational or rational powers. Some may be able to reason their way to religious certainty, but not every man can follow the intricate arguments, nor can every man hope to verify the historical facts related to the experiences of Israel and the Church. Although these differences of ability would be relatively inconsequential on insignificant matters, they would be crucial on matters involving life's purpose and meaning as a whole. Hence, it was thought, God in His mercy would reveal to men whatever they were not able to discover for themselves in regard to their soul's salvation. Since this limit was not the same for all men, there naturally would be considerable overlapping of revealed knowledge with discoverable knowledge. This duplication would instill confidence in the source of revelation because if one could verify part of the content of revelation, he might well assume that the balance of it would be equally trustworthy.

In revelation, God seeks to give us Himself. This is what is really pertinent to our religious questioning, and this alone will satisfy us. An excellent example of what we are talking about is found in the biblical story of Job. Job, plagued with the question of why he, a righteous man, should suffer—when suffering was regarded as the result only of personal sin—is totally unsatisfied by the religious counsel of his friends as they try to speak to him in behalf of God. Job says the only thing that can possibly satisfy him is to have an answer directly from God to his question "Why?" But when God does answer him, Job receives no direct reply to his question, yet he is satisfied because the question has resolved itself on a higher level in which Job freely declares his faith. What satisfies Job is not a philosophical answer to his question, but the direct revelation of God to him, which never finds adequate intellectual expression because it involves levels of his personality that cannot be expressed in words.

This is what is involved when the Christian speaks of revelation, and it can be readily seen that this is something quite different from the idea that revelation supplies scientific or historical data or even doctrinal statements. If we can keep our analogies personal, we shall find it easier to understand revelation, which is integral to an understanding of Christianity.

2. How revelation takes place

In reply to the question as to how revelation takes place, three principal answers are given: in nature, in mystical experience, and through events in history. This first answer, looking for God's manifestation in nature, is not to be confused with finding in nature's orderliness and system evidence of the purpose and workmanship of God, Who is beyond nature. Rather, it is to find the only final meaning of life within the processes of nature itself. The cycle of the seasons, the death of vegetation and its renewal again, the succession of one generation after another in the pattern of birth, growth, death, and decay —in relation to these everything takes on meaning. In short, this is God.

Such was the understanding of life embodied in the old myths of Pluto and Persephone, or of Isis and Osiris, or of Dionysus. In the Bible, this concept of religion is called "Baalism." The imagery used was largely sexual because of the intimate relation between reproduction and the natural cycle.

But though these ancient myths are no longer taken seriously, this approach to revelation (though it may not be called this) is characteristic of all who attempt to find the meaning of human existence and man's final destiny within the system of nature, who see man as nothing more than natural processes completely explainable in naturalistic ways.

The second answer is that God makes Himself known in mystical experience in which the individual, totally oblivious of his physical situation, is caught up into direct communion or even actual union with God. This type of thinking can be found to some extent within nearly all religions, but it is definitely characteristic of Eastern religions which usually regard the world as illusion. What is real is thought to be changeless, and, consequently, whatever changes is but a deceptive appearance of reality. God, therefore, must be sought apart from the material order in an experience not dependent upon it. Unconscious of his surroundings, even of his own existence, the mystic contemplates changeless, eternal truth; and this he takes to be the true source of all meaning.

But the biblical answer to the question of how God makes Himself known is neither of these. It is, rather, that God reveals Himself in action in the course of human events (which we shall call "history," noting that it applies not only to what has happened in the past but to the present as well, and even to the possibilities of the future). Since revelation is essentially personal, it must come in personal ways, through action in human affairs. This initial concept must be made clear, for the Judeo-Christian approach is not through the religious seer contemplating eternal truth unmoved by the world's events, nor through the processes of nature which are never self-explanatory. It is, rather, through the man in action who must make decisions in his daily life. These decisions are made on the basis of his present understanding of life's purpose. In other words, God reveals Himself to the whole man as he is involved in life, not merely to his mind or to his soul. This emphasis on action may help us to counteract the unhealthy idea that revelation means we ought to listen for voices speaking in some mysterious or miraculous way.

Moreover, God's revelation in history is found in definite, unrepeatable acts that call forth the response of faithful trust on man's part. This subject will be discussed in greater detail in the next section of this book. Here, in order that we can grasp the main line of thought, we might look briefly at the crucial event of Israel's history: the deliverance from Egypt in the miraculous crossing of the Red (Reed) Sea. We have discussed this event in connection with the relation of scientific to religious thought. So far as the meaning (not the natural cause) of the event is concerned, we, as well as the Israelites, have two possibilities before us. On the one hand, it might be considered as only a most fortunate coincidence, or in our day of natural science, as simply a natural occurrence governed by definite, definable natural laws. Such an interpretation would have given the people absolutely no counsel for the future except, perhaps, to kindle an ungrounded hope that similar coincidences might happen again.

On the other hand, it can be regarded as one event in a much wider pattern of purpose. And this view does give guidance for the future: it encourages the search for purpose, and in the meantime leads to responsible choices rather than the surrender to chance. These choices may, in turn, bring other succeeding events into the scope of the original purpose. In terms of our example, the Israelites saw in the Red Sea crossing the totally unmerited deliverance of God, and succeeding decisions were made in the light of this awareness that God had saved the people to be the agent for His work within history. The nature of His purpose was not fully evident at this time, but it could be revealed only in future events brought about by decisions called for by trust in the earlier revelation.

When, in the wilderness, the Israelites ran short of food and began to murmur about returning to the relative security of Egyptian slavery, it was the prior interpretation of the Red Sea crossing as God's deliverance that made them push on rather than go back to the old conditions. And this decision to go on, itself became a further evidence to them of God's continuing redemption. This interpretation, incidentally, in no way voids the modern scientific attempt to account, in entirely natural terms, for such unusual happenings as the parting of the waters. God does not necessarily substitute for natural processes or for human agents. The relationship of God to the natural world will be discussed in detail later.

Yet, the question of how one can be sure that God really was behind the escape of the Israelites has not been answered. Is there any way of being certain that these people interpreted the event correctly? We must note here that the event apart from any interpretation does not constitute revelation. To the Egyptians, the escape of the Israelites may have been only one more incident in the conflict between their established civilization and tribes of nomadic invaders, or it may have meant no more than a bit of bad luck, if not a lamentable turn of fate in the loss of useful laborers. None of these equally likely interpretations would indicate that here God was revealing Himself to men.

We do wrong in trying to find some one interpretation demanded by the facts of history as simply a logical development of those facts. We do not even find an inherent relationship in science between observed fact and scientific theory based on that fact. There is no inevitable progression from noting the fall of an apple to the conclusion that the force of attraction between two bodies is directly proportional to their masses and inversely proportional to the square of the distance between them. Between these two things lies the brilliant mind of an Isaac Newton. And between the historical event and its interpretation as the revelation of God lies the mind—and faith—of a prophet.

And here, too, in the interpretation of history conceived by the prophets, Israel saw the activity of God, for the one who can interpret history correctly does so, not from mere human ability, but by the inspiration of God. It is the man of faith whose eyes are opened to the significance of the present moment. Not everyone has the eyes to see, nor the ears to hear. This is why, even in the matter of interpretation, God's action is deemed prior, and why revelation is found in the union of event and interpretation.

But what makes one interpretation preferable to another? The Israelites would answer that it is the subsequent course of history. In terms of our example, the succeeding events leading to the establishment of the nation, and through the nation the formation of a religious faith that survived even national ruin, showed that this interpretation had more to commend it than our hypothetical Egyptian ones. It provided the foundation for understanding all history. The important point is that through this conjunction of event and its interpretation, Israel learned to know God—His faithfulness and steadfastness enduring far beyond human fickleness. It was in relation to this God, manifest within history, that she learned in action the meaning and purpose of life.

Much more information about Hebrew history ought to be included in clarifying this basic idea. Enough has been said, however, to indicate the biblical concept of revelation in which two points stand out. First, God's revelation is to the whole person in the midst of his life, even though it relates to a meaning beyond that life. Second, the meaning disclosed is never complete in itself. It is always a call to the venture of faith. Like all personal relationships, it involves the risk of self-commitment.

QUESTIONS FOR DISCUSSION

1. What are some examples of the appeal made to revelation to settle arguments about the natural world? To what extent are such appeals valid?
2. Is it merely anthropomorphism to think of revelation in personal terms? Why?

OTHER SOURCES

Baillie, John, *The Idea of Revelation in Recent Thought.* New York: Columbia University Press, 1956, chaps. 4–6.

DeWolf, L. Harold, *A Theology of the Living Church.* New York: Harper & Brothers, 1953, chaps. 3, 7.

Finegan, Jack, *Beginnings in Theology.* New York: Association Press, 1956, chaps. 3–5.

Rall, Harris Franklin, *Christianity.* New York: Charles Scribner's Sons, 1940, chaps. 8–10.

Richardson, Alan, *Christian Apologetics.* New York: Harper & Brothers, 1947, chaps. 3–6.

———, *A Preface to Bible Study.* Philadelphia: The Westminster Press, 1944, chap. 4.

Spurrier, William A., *Guide to the Christian Faith.* New York: Charles Scribner's Sons, 1952, chap. 3.

Wolf, William J., *Man's Knowledge of God.* Garden City, N. Y.: Doubleday & Company, Inc., 1955, chaps. 2, 5.

Wright, G. Ernest and Reginald H. Fuller, *The Book of the Acts of God.* Garden City, N. Y.: Doubleday & Company, Inc., 1957, prologue, chap. 2.

5

the bible

Stated simply, the Bible is the written witness to the revelation of God to Israel and later to the Christians. It is a recording of the interpretation of the events in which the action of God was seen. It bears witness to the reality and nature of God. It exists as a response to God's prior movement and, consequently, in no place seeks to prove God's existence. Such a thought would not occur to those who saw themselves confronted directly by God and saw their whole lives as a response to that confrontation, any more than we feel the urge to prove the existence of a friend who is asking us to do something with him. This outlook of the Bible has often been neglected by those who sought to interpret it.

Two views which sound like polar opposites, but which are derived from the same misunderstanding of the Bible as basically the presentation of timeless truth, are those found in fundamentalism and modernism. Both words, like most labels, are highly ambiguous and therefore dangerously misleading when applied generally to the opinions of whole groups of people.

Fundamentalism tends to regard the Bible as literally the "words of God," the final revelation of God to man, inerrantly objectified for present-day use. This view is sometimes explained by saying that since God is no longer with us as He was with the patriarchs, prophets, and apostles, He has compensated for His departure by giving us a book in which all we need to know about life and salvation can be found in clear form. This carries with it the idea that God's revelation is given in actual sentences which an earthly writer merely transcribes. Sometimes the relation between God and the human writer is expressed as that of an official to his secretary. We might receive a letter from such a man, but actually his secretary would have written it. Yet, we would not think of saying that we had a letter from his secretary, but from him. In an exactly parallel manner, according to this view, the Bible is God's direct word to us. All the human authors contributed were writing materials and mechanical skill.

The truth, then, of the biblical message in no way depends on who wrote it, or when, or under what conditions, because none of these factors influenced the message. Whether we understand it or not is not the issue, since even the original writers did not need to understand it. Some of the prophets, for example, wrote of events that would not take place for centuries. They merely wrote what God told them to write; hence, their writings form a continuing but constant and definite revelation lasting through the centuries. We need to adjust our ideas to correspond with the Bible. True experience can merely verify what the scriptures say not only about God and man but about the natural world as well. The Bible, in other words, *is* the revelation, and as such it is equally true in all its parts. In fact, were there a single demonstrable error in it, the whole would be useless. But actually, according to this view, there are no errors to be found in it.

This view of the Bible is difficult if not impossible to maintain in the light of the discovery of the historical process through which it grew. The Bible reflects, for example, the picture of the universe that ancient minds conceived: a four-cornered flat earth surmounted by the dome of heaven on which the stars were fixed and through the windows of which rain poured down on the earth. Underneath was water and the abode of the dead. The world of the Bible is inhabited by spirits and demons. To make it *the* revelation of God is to absolutize these ancient concepts. Although our world view of atoms and electrons and microbes and viruses may need to be corrected in time—that is, none of these can be regarded as final and ultimate truth—the search for truth surely is not aided by accepting first-century views as final, merely because the men who wrote the Bible happened to hold them.

The second position, which we shall call "modernism," holds that since outdated concepts of the universe characterize the Bible, what we must do is extract its timeless element, rejecting everything else, and put this in the new framework of thought developed by modern science. Those holding this view emphasize the evolutionary character of the biblical concepts.

The understanding of God, they point out, shows definite development chronologically from crude anthropomorphism to refined spirituality, and this development did not cease when the last of the biblical books was written. While they regard the Bible as an interesting example of religious thought, they classify it along with the Vedas of the Hindus, or the Koran of the Moslems, or the Avestas of the Zoroastrians, or even with contemporary religious writings. Insofar as the Bible is compatible with modern scientific thought, it is regarded as true; but present-day ideas are held to be the critique by which it is to be judged.

Here, again, the Bible is thought of as claiming to be eternal truth; but whereas in the first view it is regarded in the whole as ultimate truth, in the second, much of it is rejected because it is so characteristic of the period in which it was written. For example, those holding the first view would say that since the Bible regards disease as produced by evil spirits, this is the correct explanation and science should discard its theories of microbe infection for the spirit idea; or conversely, some might attempt to show that the biblical writers really meant "microbes" when they said "demons." They might rejoice in developments in psychosomatic medicine as demonstrations of the "truth" of the biblical outlook. And they would hold that sooner or later, as we approach the truth, our ideas will more and more fall into line with those found in scripture. Those holding the second view, on the other hand, would consider the belief in spirits and demons as primitive superstition long since discredited and would seek in the Bible only such truths as are independent of time, perhaps found to be more clearly stated in our own day. Instead of regarding the Bible as *the* revelation of God, they would regard it as a compound of some true ideas with much useless, outdated materials that are best forgotten.

Both of these views, though they are contradictory, start from the same premise that the Bible's claim to truth is on the basis of the ideas it presents, the first accepting it because it takes those ideas as true, the second rejecting it because they are regarded as false. In either case, the principal content of the Bible—God's personal confrontation of men—is neglected. On the one hand is the idea that we have a book held to be true, word for word, and on the other hand only primitive concepts that need to be brought up to date. But if what we have said is correct, what God reveals is not a body of information, nor even timeless truths, but Himself. Revelation is not something we can tabulate and memorize but an event in which God confronts us. And to make scripture itself the revelation is to short-circuit the process which should lead us to God Himself.

Anyone who seeks to define the truth of the Bible ought first to look at our ways of expressing truth in language form. There are simple factual or empirical statements that are verifiable in some way by our senses. Examples of this type would be "The chair has four legs," or "The barn is red." Anyone with the necessary observational equipment can disprove or verify these statements. Other statements involve the very structure of language: "Quantities equal to the same quantity are equal to each other." This is axiomatic because it is fundamental to all meaning. Other statements involve judgments: "Killing is wrong," or "Kindness is good." These statements are not verifiable merely by sense experience. Their truth is of a different order.

But in each of these cases a truth is conveyed that, in good measure at least, is external to the person declaring it. If, however, a person were to try to tell something of the truth he has discovered in his own life—a truth that involves him as a person —he would find these types of statements inadequate. He would discover that they deal in abstractions rather than in living reality; and in order to get his point across, he would probably resort to the story form, either as a true incident from life, or as a parable meant to illumine some life situation. Truth involving us as persons cannot be conveyed wholly by statements objectively true. It must be conveyed in some form in which the subjective aspect is also made real. And this is what the Bible does.

Anyone reading the Bible, noting the nature of what he reads, should be able to see that it is not presented as timelessly true propositions. With the exception of the wisdom books like Proverbs, the bulk of the Bible is what we would call "narrative," relating one incident after another in which real people caught in specific historical situations had to make real choices, either in obedience to their understanding of life or in defiance of it. We are introduced to men and women who found God in their actual living. The truth of the Bible, therefore, is to be found not so much in definite statements that can be lifted out of context, conditioned as it was by ancient views, but in its whole approach toward life, related so that we, living through similar situations, recognize that we are confronted by God and must decide the nature of our response to Him.

The seeds of a much better understanding of the Bible were sown by the Reformers in their concept of the "Word of God." *Word* here is understood in its biblical sense: more than a sign —a living means of communication between persons through which one is called to respond to the self-disclosure of another. A word is a bridge between two responsible persons, conveying something of the reality of one to the other. What the Reformers meant by this term when they used it in connection with the Bible is that through its words, God conveys Himself to those who read with understanding. The Bible is not an objective statement of God which can be absolutized for all time; it is a means of communication between God and men of any time. As we read the Bible, noting the words of prophets and faithful men as they interpreted the events of their age in the light of their faith, we hear God speaking to us in a way that is relevant to our own situation. What Isaiah, for example, heard God say is not necessarily a timeless truth pertinent to any period of history in any place in the world, for God's revelation to Isaiah was in terms peculiarly appropriate to the specific situation in eighth-century Judah, caught in the maelstrom of Assyrian and Egyptian power. In what Isaiah heard, pertinent to his time, we find God telling us something pertinent to our time, though the ancient confederations of power have long since disappeared, the world of science has banished many older concepts of the natural world, and we, unlike the officials to whom Isaiah directed many of his words, do not have direct control of our nation's foreign policy.

This view places us under no obligation to reconcile science and biblical thought. Some people show great delight if a passage of scripture can be harmonized with recent scientific discoveries. "Again," they declare, "the truth of the Bible has been vindicated. This is one more piece of evidence showing that we can trust it entirely." While such correspondence may be interesting, while it may demonstrate that the ancients were not so stupid in their observation of natural phenomena as is often thought, it is not really relevant to the main point of scripture. The Bible could be completely true from the scientific point of view and still fail to confront us with God. And on the other hand, certain views found in scripture can be false according to the standards of today's science, and the main thought of scripture can be true; for when God confronts us, He does so in terms we can understand, whether we live in the tenth century, B.C., or in the twentieth century, A.D., just because the confrontation is personal rather than ideological.

It was for this reason that the Reformers gave up any final attempt to "prove" the inspiration of scripture. What is the point of claiming an objective status for the Bible as inspired truth if the person reading it does not accept that claim? How can we, for example, distinguish between the claims of a Christian for his Bible and a Moslem for his Koran if each insists his book is God's final utterance? We have already noted that one believes not at a command or request, but only in response to what presents itself as believable. The Reformers thought this was the point where God had to vindicate His own word. And here they spoke of the inner testimony of the Holy Spirit. What they meant by this is that God gives us an inner awareness. As we read the Bible, we sense that there is more here than human ideas, that in and through it God is making Himself known to us, putting His claim upon us and offering us His help. Or, to put it in the religious terms we have been discussing, the Bible calls up in us the response of faith.

In short, revelation is a present reality. It is God's making Himself known to us now. Regardless of what has happened in the past, if this communication does not take place with us, there can be no revelation for us. And if in reading scripture we find only ancient world views, or details of history in the Middle East, or interesting examples of Semitic folk literature, we cannot say in the religious sense that we have received revelation of God. It is only as His living reality confronts us personally that we can say we know God Himself. And in the sense that through the Bible we grasp the outlook on life of the Hebrew people and are enabled to see our own lives in the same way they saw theirs, recognizing the response of faith as pertinent not to life only in general, but to specific events within life—to life in the concrete—then God speaks to us personally. In this sense the Bible is the Word of God.

The Word of God, then, comes to us not simply through the sense of hearing, nor can it be reduced completely to writing and so come to us through the sense of sight. The Word of God means God's living communication of Himself to us, an experience that transcends both sound and sight and involves everything that we are. To "hear the Word of the Lord" in the biblical sense is not merely to listen to spoken sentences: it is to respond in faith with one's whole being. One who can testify to no unusual experiences of hearing superhuman voices can nevertheless truly say he has heard God speak if his life is one of obedience to God's purpose. And to anticipate a later portion of this book, we might note that for Christians the full expression of the Word of God could be given only in a person—Jesus Christ.

It is for this reason that citing isolated verses of scripture to give authenticity to an argument is usually beside the point. The method depends on a prior belief that biblical references are in every detail final truth. Biblical references throughout this book are not given with the intent of cutting short discussion of a problem. They are illustrations of the type of thought that is found in the Bible. Personal or denominational interpretations vary. The purpose of the Bible is not to bolster or refute human arguments, but to serve as a channel of revelation.

But is God's revelation not wider in scope than the Hebrew nation? Yes and no. Yes, certainly, in the sense that granted the biblical insight that God makes Himself known in action, men can learn to recognize His presence in all of life. In this sense, the response of faith is a continuation of prophetic insight. And yes, also, to the extent that any religion has as its basis this personal relation between God and men, even though that relation may not be understood or may even be covered over by doctrines essentially contrary to it. The answer is no, however, to any attempt to make God's revelation general and impersonal rather than particular and personal. God may reveal Himself to another, but this does not constitute revelation for us unless, in this relation to another, God is directly related to us. More will be said in this regard when we consider the relation of Christianity to other religions.

QUESTIONS FOR DISCUSSION

1. On what basis have claims for the truth of the Bible been made? Evaluate them.

2. What advantages for biblical interpretation are there in regarding the scriptures as timeless truth in ancient garb? What difficulties are involved?

3. What can the historical and literary study of the scriptures contribute to our understanding of their central purpose?

OTHER SOURCES

Anderson, Bernhard W., *Rediscovering the Bible*. New York: Association Press, 1951, chaps. 1, 2.

———, *The Unfolding Drama of the Bible*. New York: Association Press, 1953, Introduction.

Bowie, Walter Russell, *The Bible*. New York: Association Press, 1940, especially chap. 3.

deDietrich, Suzanne, *Discovering the Bible*. Nashville: Source Publishers, 1953, chaps. 1–5.

DeWolf, L. Harold, *A Theology of the Living Church*. New York: Harper & Brothers, 1953, chaps. 8–10.

Fosdick, Harry Emerson, *The Modern Use of the Bible*. New York: The Macmillan Company, 1924, chaps. 1–6.

Jenkins, Daniel, *Believing in God*. Philadelphia: The Westminster Press, 1956, chap. 3.

Neil, William, *The Rediscovery of the Bible*. New York: Harper & Brothers, 1954, chaps. 1–7.

Richardson, Alan, *Christian Apologetics*. New York: Harper & Brothers, 1947, chap. 9.

———, *A Preface to Bible Study*. Philadelphia: The Westminster Press, 1944, chaps. 1–3, 8.

Wickenden, Arthur C., *Youth Looks at Religion*. New York: Harper & Brothers, 1939, chap. 5.

Wright, G. Ernest and Reginald H. Fuller, *The Book of the Acts of God*. Garden City, N. Y.: Doubleday & Company, Inc., 1957, prologue, chaps. 1 and 3.

6

the response of faith

Earlier in this section we noted that whereas the movement of God toward man is called "revelation," the response on man's part is called "faith." Our discussion of revelation, emphasizing that it is the self-disclosure of God to individual men—rather than the giving of factual information or even creedal statements—should indicate the direction that an interpretation of faith will take.

It can be readily seen that with such a concept of revelation, faith cannot be thought of primarily as accepting the truth of certain propositions. Propositions, in and of themselves, are not directly given in revelation. Faith is response to a person, and the response to a person is never contained in an acceptance of objective statements. Response to a person must be reciprocal self-giving that is at heart a trust and a commitment. When a friend makes himself known to us, our response is not to regard this as an interesting bit of data to be added to our expanding knowledge, but to make ourselves known to him. We may say that we "give ourselves" to each other. We do things together as a physical and psychical expression of our friendship. In fact, no facet of our human make-up is extraneous to such a relationship. Every part of us comes into play.

Such a response is what is called for in God's giving of Himself to us in revelation. But a friend confronts us within the context of this life; God confronts us in what may be called the context of eternity—in terms that involve the meaning and purpose of life itself. And the response on our part is not one that can be put on and off as we choose, but our whole life is that response, our action as well as our thought, our basic philosophy of life as well as our emotions. Faith is life lived in obedience to God's revelation to us. When we accept the fact that life has meaning in God, when, in that very acceptance, we put ourselves in a position to learn and fulfill that meaning, then we are responding in faith.

It can be seen, then, why faith should be differentiated from knowledge in the sense of a collection of data and from reason. Life does not provide its own answers to the questions it raises. One's basic attitude toward life cannot rest, therefore, on reason or on knowledge in its usual sense, although that attitude ought not to be inconsistent with either. Faith involves a response of life for which nothing else can substitute, just as nothing can substitute for knowledge or for reason. Faith sets the context in which all of life is lived, in which reason is exercised and knowledge obtained. Some sort of faith, then, there must be. There is no real choice between faith and no faith. The only choice is between faiths, unless one's life is to be the complete irrationality of insanity. So the Bible presents man's basic decision as between idols and the true God, not between God and no god. But when faith rests in the true God, life has consistency and purpose and an expanding meaning; when faith rests in a false god, life is characterized by increasing fragmentation and frustration.

But there are other aspects of faith, because one's trust is never in a vacuum nor is one's commitment to the totally unknown. Even the personal relationship disclosed in revelation requires some expression in language if it is to be communicated to others. And the way this relationship is expressed is no matter of indifference. We have examined the relation of belief to doctrine and both to theology. Doctrine, we said, is true or false according to whether or not it gives adequate expression to the experience which stimulated it and on which it is grounded, an expression intelligible within the context of prevailing language and thought patterns. If there is to be any community of faith, this expression cannot be divorced from the faith itself. Hence, the formulation of doctrine is important.

This is the reason for creeds, though the principal emphasis of the creed is not the statement of propositions but the declaration of faith. Even so, to believe in God is to trust in One of definite character and nature, and this character must be defined. It is crucial whether one thinks of God as a drinking bout on Mount Olympus or as the high and holy Lord of history. This is never merely a matter of choice. It is rather a matter of giving honest and competent expression to God's revelation. No scientific theory, for that matter, is purely a creation of the personal choice of the scientist. It must be adequate to the facts discovered in scientific investigation. And as God is God, not some indefinite summation of our personal prejudices, so we are under obligation to bring our concepts into line with His truth.

When we said that faith is not a substitute for knowledge, it was necessary for us to define knowledge as the assembling of facts. If we think of knowledge, however, as the understanding of what life is really all about, then the close relationship between the two can be seen. For such knowledge is never derived apart from the personal commitment of faith. No one learns the answers to life by retiring to a study where they might be worked out. He discovers them in living. But the results in his faithful living he does know. The knowledge contained in faith, then, is of this practical sort. It is not speculative, seeking to explain how this world might be if there were no one on it to see it, or how the end of it all might come. The knowledge is knowledge of life. It does not exist for its own sake, but in order that we may find our way.

Expressed differently, such knowledge is faith understanding itself, and in this process reason finds its most significant use and its most demanding challenge. Christian faith makes claims as truth, a deeper truth than objective scientific fact, just because it is truth that involves the whole person. But it is truth, not the effervescence of emotion alone. Faith means something definite for one's whole outlook on life, and this something must be made specific to be understood and to be communicated. Books can deal with Christianity on this level. No book can ever be Christianity or the essence of Christianity. But reading a book which seeks to clarify the witness of the Bible and the testimony of the Church in contemporary terms can help us to comprehend and deepen that faith which God alone can call forth.

Finally, then, in this sense faith has an additional meaning of confession (perhaps *profession* would be a better word for our contemporary vocabularies), the proclaiming of its insights to others, the witnessing to the ground of one's own life. It is this confessing which, on the one hand, brings together those others who have made the commitment of faith into the community of faith and, on the other hand, becomes an instrument of revelation. Just as we find God addressing us in the testimony written in the Bible, so others may find Him addressing them through our witness.

But just as faith is the whole life response to God, not merely a warm feeling or an intellectual declaration, so faith, as confession, involves the whole person, not just his spoken or written words. To make a "good confession" in New Testament times meant not a well-organized speech, but a testimony in action and speech, grounded in personal conviction, and given to others for their personal decision.

Summary

In short, then, we have seen that whereas revelation has in some cases been regarded as general, or as conveying particular information of a factual nature, its basic meaning is a personal disclosure of God—His making Himself known to us. This concept is basic to Christianity. If the Bible is to be regarded as revelation, it must be seen in this light, so that in the record of God's dealings with His people in the past, we discover God speaking to us or confronting us with His demands and promises. Faith is our response to this prior movement of God and its essential element is the trust that produces obedience. But such faith has other implications: first, by way of clarification of the nature of the One in whom faith is placed, and second, in the declaration of faith that at the same time generates a community of the faithful and becomes a channel for revelation to others.

QUESTIONS FOR DISCUSSION

1. What understanding of faith goes logically with the concept of revelation as giving factual information? Creedal statements? God Himself?
2. What relation does reason have to faith conceived as trust or commitment?

OTHER SOURCES

Baillie, John, *Our Knowledge of God*. London: Oxford University Press, 1939, chap. 2.

Richardson, Alan, *A Preface to Bible Study*. Philadelphia: The Westminster Press, 1944, chap. 10.

Wickenden, Arthur C., *Youth Looks at Religion*. New York: Harper & Brothers, 1939, chap. 4.

Williams, Daniel Day, *God's Grace and Man's Hope*. New York: Harper & Brothers, 1949, chap. 6.

Wolf, William J., *Man's Knowledge of God*. Garden City, N. Y.: Doubleday & Company, Inc., 1955, chap. 6.

{ three }

the biblical proclamation

jesus of nazareth

Most books on Christianity begin with a consideration of the Christian concept of God and the philosophical reasons for believing in God's existence. Following this usually comes a discussion of the human situation with its problem of sin, and then the solution of that problem through the redemption found in Jesus Christ. Often the approach assumes that people have an understanding of God, man, and the world which Christianity merely augments. While this approach is systematic, it overlooks the fact that people generally do not become Christians as the result of an intellectual inquiry into Christian theology.

People become Christian by their whole response to the Christian message—a response much broader than syllogistic reasoning or intellectual accepting. They do not come to believe in God as the logical conclusion to an argument. Their belief stems from the active decision called for by the proclamation of the Gospel. Therefore, instead of beginning with a philosophical examination of the "theistic hypothesis" we shall attempt to understand Christianity religiously, beginning where it begins with the Gospel of Jesus Christ.

1. The life of Jesus

The Christian message is based on the life and teachings of Jesus of Nazareth. Any attempt, then, either to propagate the faith or to understand it begins by recounting the "simple gospel story." This is usually taken to mean the major events of his life. Although there is no complete biography of him on anything like the modern scale, the general pattern of his career can be traced through the first four books of the New Testament, which are known as the four gospels: Matthew, Mark, Luke, and John. Of these, the first three are decidedly similar, in contrast to the fourth. The three are called the "synoptic gospels" because they present a comprehensive view of his activities. They are remarkably alike, with many almost identical passages, although there are also significant differences in content. Particularly is there lack of consensus on accounts of Jesus' birth and his resurrection appearances.

Mark, the earliest and shortest of the three, begins the account with Jesus' baptism in the Jordan River by John the

Baptist. John was an ascetic figure, reminiscent of Elijah of old Israel, living a rugged life in the wilderness. His message was akin to his way of life, for he called people away from their urban pursuits to repentance for their sins. Baptism had been a rite by which proselytes were initiated into the Jewish community, but John added a new note in insisting that even those who were Jews by birth repent and undergo baptism as a symbol of their cleansing. Even they, belonging to the religiously privileged nation, could not stand unpurified in the presence of God who was already beginning the destruction of all evil.

Jesus came to be baptized by John, apparently identifying himself with the most humbly devout part of the population who earnestly sought God's will for themselves and for their nation. Jesus' own preaching career began when John was arrested by Herod, king of the region. Possibly there was fear that the fiery prophet would incite rebellion, though the New Testament says the sore point was the extension of John's attacks to the notorious immorality of the ruling family. Like John, Jesus called the people to repentance, but instead of appealing only to the threat of impending disaster, he had a positive message of the nearness of God's rule of righteousness —the Kingdom of God—into which people were invited as citizens through repentance and faith. His preaching won huge crowds of people. From his many followers he selected twelve men to be his constant companions, the disciples.

The proclamation of the Kingdom had other overtones. His ministry included teaching the quality of life characteristic of those who belonged to the Kingdom. But attracting more attention were the healings of the sick who came to him for help. These healings or "mighty works" he regarded as special manifestations of God's power and goodness breaking into the present world order. The gospels contain story after story of such healings. Even the disciples, as fellow-proclaimers of the good news, were empowered to heal.

But Jesus' very success stirred up opposition to him. His seeking out the lowly and those rejected by respectable society brought him into conflict with the religious professionals and the Pharisees who saw the possibility of national salvation only in an even stricter adherence to the law of Moses. Moreover, Herod, the king who had silenced the Baptist, threatened action because of his superstitious fears that John had returned to life. Avoiding Herod's jurisdiction, Jesus left Galilee and began the journey to Jerusalem.

It was on this trip that he first began to predict the coming crisis at Jerusalem which would lead him to death, a death he interpreted in some sense as an "offering for many." Appalled by this news, the disciples protested, trying to dissuade him from going on. With utmost firmness he dismissed their advice and stood by his original purpose. But important to these predictions was his admission that he was the Messiah, God's promised deliverer for His people. Yet the role of the Messiah, he insisted, would not be that of the glorious conqueror, but rather that of a suffering servant. Such a reinterpretation of the traditional hope the disciples could not then understand.

Not long after his arrival in Jerusalem, trouble came to a head between him and the religious authorities. Always his apparent carelessness with the age-honored legal code had disturbed them. Consequently, they looked on him as one who would destroy everything for which they stood. Particularly, a remark of his about the destruction of their sacred temple alarmed them. But the act that apparently united the opposition against him was his driving out of the temple area the merchants and money changers attracted there by the profitable trade in sacrificial animals during the high religious festivals when pilgrims thronged Jerusalem. Smoldering resentment against him now flamed into a definite determination to have him put out of the way, though not in such a manner as would arouse his followers and sympathizers.

One of his own disciples, Judas Iscariot, betrayed him to the authorities, either by telling them where he could be arrested quietly or by disclosing the nature of his views of himself and his role. (The later charge against him was blasphemy—that he made himself equal with God.) The authorities moved quickly, seizing Jesus in a night arrest on Judas' identification, rushing him through the mockery of a rigged trial that ended in his condemnation, having Pontius Pilate the Roman governor confirm the death sentence, and finally having him executed by crucifixion—all within less than twenty-four hours. The speed of the action caught his followers off-guard, and none was with him through the trial to raise the slightest protest.

The subsequent events were most amazing. Utterly discouraged and defeated by the death of their leader, the disciples were astounded by the news brought them a few days later that Jesus had been raised from the dead and had been seen alive. Their inspection of his empty tomb was confirmed by their seeing him and talking with him themselves, though there is variance in these accounts. But there is no disputing the fact that instead of disheartened and defeated followers, they became the enthusiastic proclaimers of the Gospel—that the events to which they were witnesses were no mere incidents in the life of their people, but events determining the meaning of world history for all men. With this experience and proclamation began the history and missionary enterprise of the Christian Church.

2. The teachings of Jesus

When the question of the meaning of all this is raised, the usual answer given to it is that these events were simply the life context in which Jesus' teachings were set, the biography—sketchy, it is admitted—of a teacher whose message is relevant not just to his own day, but to all time. It is the teachings of Jesus which are the most important consideration in this view. And the teachings are usually organized in some summary such as the Fatherhood of God, the brotherhood of men, and the realization of the Kingdom of God in human society.

This more systematic order is usually altered by human interest to begin with the brotherhood of man. The foundation for this principle is seen in Jesus' teaching of the importance of the individual. Jesus had the unique ability of singling people out from crowds for special consideration, and especially for giving identity to those who were lost in broad impersonal categories. One example of this is his consideration for a repentant woman of the streets whom all others simply dismissed from their concern as a sinner (Luke 7:36–50).

Even laws of justice, he taught, could be subordinated to the welfare of individuals. Perhaps the favorite example is his story of the prodigal son (Luke 15:11–32). In this parable, a young man asks for his inheritance early in order to seek his fortune in the world. The father acquiesces, but soon improvident spending and bad luck reduce the boy to abject poverty. Yet, even with such a wastrel, the father does not lose interest, nor is he eager to teach the boy a lesson. When the son returns, beaten and humble, the father gives him an elaborate homecoming, much to the disgust of the steadier elder brother. The parables of the lost coin and the lost sheep for which a shepherd risks the safety of his whole flock amplify the same point.

This teaching of the importance of the individual has been looked on as a foundation of democratic government and is one of the things people often have in mind when they talk about the religious foundation of democracy. "Each man counts" is another way of saying the same thing. And since this emphasis on the individual was not often found in ancient civilizations, it is held that this constituted the good news which Jesus brought to men.

The more discerning recognize, however, that the belief in the importance of each individual man cannot be established with authority merely as an opinion of those who are inherently kind-hearted. There must be a more solid foundation beneath it. Hence, there is the acknowledgment of the significance of another teaching of Jesus held to be unique with him—the Fatherhood of God. One's ultimate importance, regardless of earthly judgments, must rest in eternal things. If, as Jesus taught, each man is dear to God for his own sake, then among men he must have value in his own right simply as a man. If, with God, a man matters not because of his social status, his productive capacity, his mental ability, the influence of his friends, even the correctness of his religion, but solely because he is God's creation, then he must be treated so in human society. This teaching is set in opposition to the earlier view that a man mattered only as a member of a larger group—a tribe, nation, race, or religion—with which his own fortunes rose or fell.

This very relationship of love in which God gives status to individuals is held to be something new, something that Jesus first taught. Earlier concepts of deity stressed justice, it is said, or wrath, instead of the pure love found in Jesus' teachings. Throughout the Old Testament, God appears vengeful and warlike, often immoral by our standards, a God to be feared, who dwelt in the pitch blackness of the temple's holy of holies. The Gospel, in this view, is the teaching that Jesus first brought to mankind, that instead of such a terrible and fearsome deity, God in reality is love and kindness that would harm no one. Jesus taught us that we can approach God in the love and confidence bred in familiar relationships because He is the Father of each one of us.

Another teaching held to be unique with Jesus is that of the Kingdom of God. It was his proclamation of the positive features of God's righteous rule that differentiated his message from the Baptist's. What this actually means, however, is variously interpreted. The inwardness of the Kingdom as a quality of the heart is stressed. Jesus is said to have lifted up the question of a man's motives in contrast to his outward actions. When, therefore, one is ruled by pure love rather than by the urge to dominate people, or the demand for prestige, or the desire to hurt others, regardless of the outward appearance of his actions, then he is living in the Kingdom of God. As this quality of love among men develops, God's Kingdom becomes an outward reality as well.

The Kingdom is also often interpreted as the good society where justice and consideration prevail, and where there is such wholesome environment that children can grow into their full stature as sons of God. The Kingdom comes as men seek to orient their society by the example of Jesus. Often the idea of a progressive coming of the Kingdom is included here. This means that as the years go by, as more people can enjoy a more leisurely life, as the benefits of education are more widely distributed, as one generation succeeds another, more and more God's rule will be evident in human society. And this, too, is held to be the Gospel: that God's Kingdom is being established through the call to love leading to progressive social measures, though its complete realization may wait for many more generations.

In all this there is the common idea that the Gospel is essentially teaching given by one whose capacities enabled him to have a closer fellowship with God than the rest of men enjoy. This teaching is not foreign to other human experience, however, hence its innate attractiveness. When appropriated by men, it can lead them into a similar close fellowship with God. All we need to do today, according to such a view, is to take these timeless teachings of Jesus from their first century setting and apply them to our own situation.

QUESTIONS FOR DISCUSSION

1. Why should the New Testament contain four "gospels" rather than only one comprehensive and corrected account of Jesus' life?
2. In the gospel accounts, when Jesus speaks of the will of God for man, to what does he refer as his authority?

OTHER SOURCES

Bowie, Walter Russell, "The Parables," *The Interpreter's Bible*. New York: Abingdon-Cokesbury Press, 1951, VII, 165–75.

Branscomb, Harvie, *The Teachings of Jesus*. New York: Abingdon-Cokesbury Press, 1931, chaps. 1, 6, 8.

DeWolf, L. Harold, *A Theology of the Living Church*. New York: Harper & Brothers, 1953, chap. 28.

Dibelius, Martin, *Jesus*. Philadelphia: The Westminster Press, 1949.

Goodspeed, Edgar J., *A Life of Jesus*. New York: Harper & Brothers, 1950.

Houf, Horace T., *What Religion Is and Does*, rev. ed. New York: Harper & Brothers, 1945, chap. 17.

Laymon, Charles M., *The Life and Teachings of Jesus*. New York: Abingdon Press, 1955.

Lyman, Mary Ely, *Jesus*. New York: Association Press, 1937, chaps. 1, 2.

Manson, T. W., "The Beginning of the Gospel," *A Primer of Christianity*. London: Oxford University Press, 1950, Part I.

Taylor, Vincent, "The Life and Ministry of Jesus," *The Interpreter's Bible*. New York: Abingdon-Cokesbury Press, 1951, VII, 114–44.

——, *The Life of Jesus*. New York: Abingdon Press, 1954.

Tilden, Elwyn E., *Toward Understanding Jesus*. Englewood Cliffs, N. J.: Prentice-Hall, Inc., 1956, secs. 2, 3.

Wilder, Amos N., "The Sermon on the Mount," *The Interpreter's Bible*. New York: Abingdon-Cokesbury Press, 1951, VII, 155–64.

Wolf, William J., *Man's Knowledge of God*. Garden City, N. Y.: Doubleday & Company, Inc., 1955, chap. 7.

See especially the Gospel according to St. Mark.

8

the significance of jesus

The approach we have been describing, while it does provide a relation between the first and the twentieth centuries, fails to answer two questions that are crucial to any genuine understanding of the Christian Gospel. First, why should Jesus' teachings be preferable to those of other great teachers of the world? Why should they in any sense be regarded as authoritative? And second, what is the purpose of the narrative type of presentation that characterizes the gospels? Why do they take a story form, conditioned so inescapably by a particular time and location, instead of a form which more suitably expresses timeless truth?

The first question raises some definite problems, because it is rather easily shown that Jesus' teaching is not completely novel. He was not saying things that had never been said before. In seeking parallels to his teaching, we ought not to confine our search to the Old Testament, because much had happened in Jewish religious thought since the canon, for all practical purposes, had been closed. The rabbis had made significant compilations of the most important parts of scripture and had condensed these to easily remembered, pithy sayings. Several hundred years before Jesus' birth, man's religious situation had been summarized in these terms: "He [God] has showed you, O man, what is good; and what does the Lord require of you, but to do justice, and to love kindness, and to walk humbly with your God?" (Micah 6:8). In all likelihood, the summary of the entire law in the two commandments of love of God and love of neighbor had been made before Jesus lived. In the Gospel according to St. Luke, it is a lawyer who thus epitomizes the law (Luke 10:27).

Or again, addressing God as Father was not unique with Jesus, although he gave the word an unforgettable poignancy so that it virtually displaced all other names. The attitude of love toward God can certainly be found in those Psalms that breathe a quiet assurance and trust in God who will hear the cry of the downtrodden and rescue the oppressed and strengthen the faithful. The message of the Kingdom of God, while new perhaps in the tone of its present realization, was in many respects the age-long aspiration of the prophets who yearned and worked for the day when God's righteous rule would be supreme.

All this is in no way an attempt to say that Jesus had nothing but a recapitulation of old themes to offer people. Even Jewish scholars have commented on the fact that his seeking out sinners to help them was a very new emphasis. But it is nevertheless significant that the New Testament writers do not attempt to claim uniqueness for Jesus on the basis of the novelty of his teaching. In fact, they go to considerable lengths to relate what he said to Old Testament foundations. It is rather the *authority* of his teaching to which they appeal (Matt. 7:28, 29), and only what he was in himself lends this quality of authority to what he said. Their regard for Jesus is not so much for one who preached the Gospel as for one who himself is that Gospel, so that for them, to preach the Gospel meant to preach Christ.

The situation as it is represented in the New Testament by those closest to the events is not that the immediate appeal of the teachings made people ready to accept any other claims of the teacher, but that the teacher, being what he was, invested the teachings with an authority they otherwise would not have had. We are not to judge the teachings, but to use them as the criteria for our judgment. (Should this sound arbitrary, it is because we need to consider more fully the relation between God and man which is discussed in the next section.)

The traditional view held that this authority was indicated in Jesus' ability to work miracles. People were willing to accept what he said because of the mighty works he did. Any man who could give sight to the blind, and restore hearing to the deaf, who could even bring the dead to life again surely should be listened to and obeyed implicitly. This view regards the miracles as signs which attested the truth of the teachings. But this is not the prevailing New Testament view of miracles. To those who believed, they were signs. But for Jesus, these mighty acts were not performed as proof of his authority. In fact, he specifically refused to give signs to people who would not accept him on any other basis (Mark 8:12).

In order to go on here, we must state a New Testament conviction, show its relationship with these two questions, and then examine the content of the conviction more fully. Put quite simply, the New Testament theme is that God was in Jesus Christ revealing Himself to men for their salvation. What this means is that, in accordance with the conclusions of our discussion of revelation, where we said that God reveals Himself as active in events rather than as the abstract truth of teachings, the good news of the Gospel is Jesus Christ himself—his life, death, and resurrection. It is this that explains why the teachings should be regarded as authoritative, rather than merely as more material to be added to the vast fund of religious and ethical instruction contributed by the world's long line of devout and sincere men.

Moreover, it explains why the Gospel should take the form of narrative, the reciting of the events in the life of a man, Jesus of Nazareth. The Gospel is news of something that has happened, and this can be recounted only in narrative form. Hence, when St. Mark starts writing: "The beginning of the Gospel of Jesus Christ . . ." he tells of Jesus' coming to the Jordan to be baptized and continues with other events in his life. The main principles of Jesus' teaching are considered later. Early Christian preaching took this same form. It is recognized that St. Luke in the Book of the Acts is not transcribing early sermons *verbatim*, but increasingly it is seen that these reconstructed sermons represent in the main the typical apostolic preaching. The essence of it, with its many allusions to the Old Testament, centers in the facts of Jesus' life in relation to God's on-going purpose. It was these events, or if one wants to consider them as a unit, this Event that constitutes the Gospel.

This very point can also explain Jesus' method of teaching through parables. The parable had been used as a teaching device by the rabbis, and rabbinical literature contemporary with Jesus abounds with examples, though they usually lack the incisiveness and appeal of Jesus' parables. The rabbis, however, used them to bring their teaching to those initiated to this type of presentation and to keep it from the superficial persons who listened only from curiosity. While at one place in the gospels this same reason is attributed to Jesus (Matt. 13:13), it is incongruous with Jesus' announced purpose of his mission. The reason for the parabolic teaching with Jesus is not that he wanted to cloak his message with ambiguity, but rather that the truth in it can be seen only in life situations where people are called on to make responsible decisions. The truth is found in life with all its fullness, not in abstract principles (Matt. 13:35). The key to the meaning of the parables is not some code of allegorical interpretation. It is Jesus, himself.

QUESTIONS FOR DISCUSSION

1. What reasons can be given why Jesus' teachings should be followed rather than those of any other teacher?
2. What reasons did Jesus himself give for heeding his words?

OTHER SOURCES

Anderson, Bernhard W., *Rediscovering the Bible*. New York: Association Press, 1951, chap. 7.

Branscomb, Harvie, *The Teachings of Jesus*. New York: Abingdon-Cokesbury Press, 1931, chap. 22.

Craig, Clarence Tucker, "The Proclamation of the Kingdom," *The Interpreter's Bible*. New York: Abingdon-Cokesbury Press, 1951, VII, 145–54.

Gilkey, James Gordon, *A Faith to Affirm*. New York: The Macmillan Company, 1940, chap. 1.

Lyman, Mary Ely, *Jesus*. New York: Association Press, 1937, chaps. 3–5.

Neil, William, *The Rediscovery of the Bible*. New York: Harper & Brothers, 1954, chap. 23.

Richardson, Alan, *A Preface to Bible Study*. Philadelphia: The Westminster Press, 1944, chap. 9.

Wright, G. Ernest and Reginald H. Fuller, *The Book of the Acts of God*. Garden City, N. Y.: Doubleday & Company, Inc., 1957, part iv, chap. 2.

9

jesus and the gospel

In order to clarify the questions about the authority of Jesus' teaching and the narrative form of the gospel story, we had to anticipate a fundamental conviction of Christianity, namely, that God was in Christ. Now we need to turn more definitely to this conviction to see it in relation to the whole line of biblical thought. A succinct statement of God's activity is found in Peter's first sermon on Pentecost: "Let all the house of Israel therefore know assuredly that God has made him both Lord and Christ, this Jesus whom you crucified" (Acts 2:36). This is the conviction that guided the whole New Testament interpretation of the events in the life of Jesus. And as we noted earlier that revelation is found in interpreted events, so it is in this understanding of Jesus' life that the revelation of God is found, according to Christianity.

In order to make this clear, however, we must note that there is no such thing as the facts of the life of Jesus apart from any interpretation whatsoever. This is true even of secular history. No historian can record all the facts of a situation, for this would mean a complete reliving of the situation. The historian is interested in giving only the significant facts, so that those who read his writing can gain an over-all view of the period— long or short—of which he writes. But in order to do this, the historian must have some view as to what constitutes significant fact in any particular case. History can be written, then, only on the basis of some prior principle of interpretation. This does not mean that the historian chooses only those facts that prove his point. This would be warped history indeed. His principle of interpretation must be justified by the facts, but the interpretation is not created by the facts.

What is true of secular history is also true of the Bible, and particularly of the life of Jesus. Men recorded the events of his life only because he meant something to them. There is no impersonal record of his existence such as might be obtained from a government bureau of vital statistics. The New Testament shows no foundational stratum of fact not involved in the presentation of its main theme. Moreover, any attempt to reinterpret the "facts" of Jesus' life apart from New Testament thought must be based on some prior assumptions. What we have in the gospel record are those facts the people who knew him best thought it necessary to preserve in order that we might understand who he was and what he meant to them. Before attempting to justify this interpretation, let us see more carefully what it is.

We have noted that the fundamental idea is that God made Jesus both Lord and Christ. To put this in other words, we might say that through—or in—Jesus, God has overcome human sin and has lifted him to the position of Lord of all creation, overcoming in him the fragmentation and divisiveness of life that sin has produced. This bald statement requires considerable expansion. For this purpose we shall break the core thought into two parts: overcoming sin and establishing Christ as Lord. After this biblical line of thought has been presented, we shall then consider its relevance and importance to the understanding of our human situation.

1. Overcoming sin

The simple proclamation of the Gospel is that in Christ God has triumphed over sin. As such, the proclamation is good news. But this simple proclamation must be related to the biblical understanding of human need. Probably the best single treatment of the problem is found in St. Paul's Letter to the Romans (see Rom. 1:16–3:31).

Paul begins with an analysis of the human situation, noting the prevalence of evil in the world. As in our day, so in his, anyone with even a modicum of sensitivity could catalog the evils of society in terms of problems in the home, within the nation, and in the relation of nations to each other. The picture, just as it is often conceived today, is drawn in black. Gross immorality, sexual perversion, corruption—all these are evident. They raise a serious question about the goodness and power of God who is supposed to reign supreme over all creation. How can such things be if God is in control?

Paul's answer, in line with the main stream of biblical

thought, is that these things are not to be seen as challenges to either God's power or His goodness, but are rather manifestations of that power. They represent God's judgment on an evil society. In other words, these evils do not prevail in spite of God: they prevail in a sense because of God. It is because of God's moral ordering of the universe that any attempt of men to live apart from Him leads to such chaos and disintegration of human society.

The significance of this interpretation comes out only as one looks for a remedy for the evil. Seen from the human perspective as denials of God's goodness, these evil phenomena appear as something men should be able to overcome themselves. And men have actually attacked the problem from this point of view. They have tried to root out evil, to destroy it, and to educate themselves to avoid it. The first of these is found in the human drive to secure perfection in society through law and order. Paul later lends his support to the maintenance of social stability through government. But at this point he seriously questions it as a cure-all for the human problem. He points out the fallacy of the idea that all we need to do to improve our situation is to root out evil wherever we find it, and as an end product we shall enjoy the perfect society. Again and again man has given himself to this program in inquisitions, blood purges, reforms, and revolutions, but he has never achieved his goal. The reason is that no man has the moral pre-eminence to judge absolutely what is right and what is wrong. The judge himself is corrupted so that his pronouncements are prejudiced and he has no way of evaluating his judgments. Consequently, his very attempt to establish perfection develops into a new form of evil. A nation, for example, that is over-zealous to eradicate a particular form of evil is apt to develop into a police state, or an individual who overcomes gross immorality is likely to become unlovely through spiritual pride. What this approach to the problem actually does is build more impregnable walls of hatred and mistrust dividing men from each other, and by misrepresenting the truth of the human situation it blocks off through false pride the only possible source of external help—God.

The second, the way of education, is the idea that if people can be directed to live properly, the evils of which we speak will, in due time, take care of themselves. This, however, simply begs the question of what final standard is to be the goal of an educational program. Educators assume that they have such a standard, that were the whole world remade according to their hearts' desire it would be a world of peace and justice. But is this so? Paul questions whether we do have such a standard (Rom. 2:19–21). "You who would teach others not to steal," he writes, "are you free of dishonesty yourselves?" Particularly in our day, when educational techniques are being perfected and propaganda methods are thought to be virtually irresistible, we might reconsider this point. Aims of education have changed radically in only the last twenty-five years, so quickly have educators discovered the weaknesses and inadequcies of their plans. Educational programs are found to have fatal flaws, not just in techniques but in over-all goals. When any program is carried out, we soon learn that it cannot fully answer the basic human need.

Both of the approaches to the problem stem from the same fundamental assumption that trouble in human society has no higher reference than man himself. And both come short of solving the problem for just the reason that it is not solely a human one. It is the problem of the relation of man with God. Social chaos is the evidence of God's judgment on a society that has not acknowledged Him as God (and this can apply as readily to the individual). Hence, the remedy for it cannot come from man directly but instead must be initiated by God. Men have broken a relationship with God, the break resulting in the painful facts of the human situation; and standing in that broken relationship they can do nothing to mend it, just as a car mired in the ditch cannot pull itself out. This, in biblical terms, is the problem of human sin—the wrong relation to God which breeds the host of human evils.

Now the Gospel is the announcement that in the face of this hopeless situation God has done something to set things right. He has sent Jesus Christ to show us first of all the seriousness and pervasiveness of human sin. Men assume that they can recognize goodness when they see it, and yet when God's own Son came to earth, he was misunderstood, maligned, and finally killed. It is easy, of course, to say that unusually wicked men did this, but the New Testament lays the blame on ordinary people doing for the most part what they thought was right. The religious leaders were holding the integrity of their tradition against an innovator; the Roman government was maintaining the peace of the nation against one who seemed to be inciting rebellion; and the people were obeying their officials instead of taking the law into their own hands. Paul elsewhere says that had the rulers of this world understood the situation they would not have crucified the Lord of glory, implying that they did not grasp the reality of the situation (1 Cor. 2:8). Lack of adequate punishment of sin in past times had led men to discount its seriousness, but the death of Jesus under the circumstances involved shows for all time the tragedy wrought by sin. Far from recognizing goodness when they saw it and giving themselves in obedience to it, good, respectable men treated it as their worst enemy. In Christ, then, we are finally driven to acknowledge the truth of our human situation. Our supposed attempt to achieve goodness actually is found to work against it.

But more than this, through Christ God opens the possibility of righteousness to men through faith. Here is a totally new way of dealing with sin. Men could not be made righteous by punishing them, for this left them where they were, though it prevented complete chaos in the world. They could be made righteous only by treating them as if they were righteous, by breaking the chain of evil that held them in bondage. This God did in the free forgiveness offered through Christ, a forgiveness which men can accept only as they are willing to admit the use-lessness of their own attempts to set things right. Only in this restored relationship can the human problem be worked out. God has done something to alter the situation in Jesus Christ. This is the Gospel.

2.   Establishing Christ as Lord

The second aspect of what God has done is the lifting of Christ to the position of Lord, which means the highest object of men's allegiance and obedience. Christ, in other words, is supreme over all things. This is necessary to confirm what has been said about Christ in relation to sin. Had Jesus been left at the mercy of evil men, he would have been no more than a martyr to a cause. In the resurrection, God vindicated his faith-fulness and established him as Lord to whom men can give themselves completely. This aspect of the Gospel can best be seen in the Letters to the Ephesians (see Eph. 1:3–2:22). The point made here is that life under the influence of sin has be-come fragmented. Men have divided allegiances. There are in-dividual as well as social interests. There are the demands of the family conflicting with the nation. There are national interests against human interests in general. Life is pulled in many direc-tions because there is no center by which it can be unified. No one thing has absolute claim upon us.

But this is precisely what God gives us in Jesus Christ. Every-thing subordinated to him can now be ordered in the right relation within itself. Instead of chaos and conflict, there is peace and unity. As an example of this new unity based on a new center of loyalty, Ephesians introduces the breakdown of the old dichotomy between Gentile and Jew that marked a fundamental division of the human race—so fundamental that no Jew was supposed to eat with a Gentile. And yet even that radical cleavage was overcome as men gave their allegiance not to Gentile nor to Jew, but to Christ who surpassed the distinction. The Church, then, was the first area of a growing unity. "So then you are no longer strangers and sojourners, but you are fellow citizens with the saints and members of the household of God" (Eph. 2:19).

Christ alone has this claim over us. All other claims on us are in some sense relative. His is absolute. Hence, he alone is Lord. This, in fact, was the earliest Christian confession of faith: "Jesus Christ is Lord." Everything written about Jesus in the New Testament is based on this fundamental conviction. The facts that we have about him were recorded to establish this meaning and purpose. God had acted in history to unify all life under one head.

Before we attempt to justify such an interpretation, however, we need to see its roots in the religious faith of Jesus and his followers. Especially is this true since the Christians were convinced they were preaching no novel doctrine, but actually the culmination of all Israel's previous experience with God. Again and again when specific events in Jesus' life are considered, they are related as happening "according to the scriptures," meaning, of course, our Old Testament, since the New did not exist at that time. In other words, the meaning of Christ must be seen in relation to all that we have said about revelation as event and interpretation, an interpretation directed by past revelation and bearing it out in its ability to relate the significance and meaning of the events in question.

QUESTIONS FOR DISCUSSION

1. How does St. Paul alter the interpretation normally given the problem of man-caused evil?
2. How is God's judgment of evil made evident in human society?

OTHER SOURCES

Anderson, Bernhard W., *Rediscovering the Bible*. New York: Association Press, 1951, chap. 8.

DeWolf, L. Harold, *A Theology of the Living Church*. New York: Harper & Brothers, 1953, chap. 29.

Farmer, Herbert H., *God & Men*. New York: Abingdon-Cokesbury Press, 1947, chap. 4.

Filson, Floyd B., *Jesus Christ the Risen Lord*. New York: Abingdon Press, 1956, chap. 2.

Finegan, Jack, *Beginnings in Theology*. New York: Association Press, 1956, chaps. 9, 10, 15.

Fosdick, Harry Emerson, *The Modern Use of the Bible*. New York: The Macmillan Company, 1924, chap. 7.

Gilkey, James Gordon, *A Faith to Affirm*. New York: The Macmillan Company, 1940, chap. 2.

Houf, Horace T., *What Religion Is and Does*, rev. ed. New York: Harper & Brothers, 1945, chap. 18.

Hunter, Archibald M., *Introducing New Testament Theology*. Philadelphia: The Westminster Press, 1958, chap. 2.

Kee, Howard Clark and Franklin W. Young, *Understanding the New Testament*. Englewood Cliffs, N. J.: Prentice-Hall, Inc., 1957, chap. 2.

Lyman, Mary Ely, *Jesus*. New York: Association Press, 1937, chap. 6.

Neil, William, *The Rediscovery of the Bible*. New York: Harper & Brothers, 1954, chaps. 24, 25.

Richardson, Alan, *Science, History, and Faith*. London: Oxford University Press, 1950, chaps. 4, 5.

Wolf, William J., *Man's Knowledge of God*. Garden City, N. Y.: Doubleday & Company, Inc., 1955, chap. 4.

10

GOD'S WORK IN ISRAEL

Probably the most rewarding line to follow in seeking the source of this interpretation of the role of Jesus is to consider what meaning Israel found in her own history, since Christians were convinced it was this that reached its culmination in Christ. We have mentioned the fact that the key experience in developing such an understanding of her history was the deliverance at the Red Sea. This was the key experience not because it was the first, but because it is referred to throughout the Old Testament as the fundamental example of God's call and redemption. As the key, it was used to interpret all other events of Israel's life. She was convinced that the deliverance was not sheer chance, but that God had some significant purpose, and therefore the life of the nation had to be guided by a search for, and obedience to, that purpose rather than to the directionless impulses of opportunism.

But the clear definition of the purpose was not easily derived. Israel's religious history might be conceived as the attempt to define it. The feeling of wonder that God had chosen her often degenerated into the belief that somehow she would be lifted above the nations for her own glorification. Repeatedly the prophets had to challenge this misconception. Yet in spite of it, the nation was able to nurture those who did question such a view and who consequently sought a more profound meaning of "chosen people." They had the conviction that God was making known to them in the events of history what that meaning was.

As a matter of fact, three series of events stand out as of crucial importance. The first of these is the calling of Abraham and the promise made to him and renewed with the other patriarchs. The Bible regards the patriarchs as distinct individuals, although modern scholarship has indicated that they are also ideal figures on which the faith of Israel can focus. Archaeology has demonstrated the general reliability of the social and political background of these stories. Our point here, however, is not to argue whether or not these accounts are strictly historical but to show that Israel saw life in relation to the purpose of God rather than in relation to merely natural pressures.

We now know, for example, that the context of the story of Abraham is accurate. There was a vast migration of peoples from the fertile and cultured Mesopotamian region at that time, a migration brought on by social and political upheavals. But the significance of his participation in the migration is seen as more than chance. It is regarded as his obedient response to the call of God. There was a deeper meaning here than political or economic pressure, and this meaning was important not only for Abraham's subsequent life, but in its influence on later generations as well. Joseph, for example, did not succumb to aimlessness as the result of his brothers' treachery in selling him into slavery. Because he was convinced of some final meaning to this experience in the purposes of God, he disciplined himself, rising to a position of power in Egypt, not—note this carefully—for his own aggrandizement, but in order to be an effective agent of God's on-going purpose for his people.

It was this relation of past revelation to present event that bothered Moses as he noted the condition of his people. God's purpose could hardly be thought to culminate in a slave status. Hence God, Himself, true to His promises to the patriarchs, commissioned Moses for his role as emancipator. We have perhaps said enough about the events of the exodus that were convincing evidence to the Hebrews that God was active in history on their behalf. The point is that in these events—the exodus from Egypt, the settling of Canaan, and the establishing of the nation—God was seen making clear and fulfilling His purpose.

The establishment of the nation as something more than a collection of tribes depended on the work of David. Here again the same pattern repeats itself. David could have been regarded as a fortuitous leader, happening on the scene in the crucial hour. He is, instead, regarded as God's anointed, specifically raised up for a unique task—the consolidation of Israel against her enemies. The Philistine invasion could have destroyed Israel not only by political domination, but in the corruption of her religious faith by the nature-fertility cults of Baalism. In other words, David the king was granted his large powers in order that he might fulfill his role defined by God's purpose. It was in this sense that the glorification of the king and his domain went along with the idea of the fulfillment of God's purpose, but led also to the mistaken notion that the direction of history pointed to Israel's pre-eminence as a nation.

Along with this understanding of the kingdom was another contrary to it. There were those who saw that the development of such absolute power was carried on through a gross misunderstanding of God's purpose; in fact, it was a perversion of that purpose. This was the theme of those prophets of the northern kingdom who encouraged one revolution after another with all the attendant atrocities of civil strife and blood purges. The idea is frequently repeated in the nostalgic glances at the older, freer days of tribal life in the wilderness when God was king. Yet as time went on, the very concept of monarchy was taken over to express the religious hope of fulfilled meaning. Attention was directed to a future ruler whom God would bring forth and who in purity and righteousness would institute God's new order, fulfilling the promises of the old.

In addition to these developments, incidents within Israel's history led to a reappraisal of the meaning of God's purpose. The nation was nearly always at the mercy of her powerful neighbors, the Assyrian and Egyptian empires. Although the tragic fortunes of the kingdom were at first interpreted solely as the result of Israel's sin of disobeying God, this could not be the final explanation. The agents of Israel's punishment were acknowledged to be oftentimes more vicious than she. Finally, in the writings of the unknown prophet of the exile found in the latter part of our book of Isaiah, came the recognition that God's purpose was wider than the glorification of Israel, that it included all nations in its scope, that Israel's role was really that of a servant or agent of God in history. And this new insight led to the setting of Israel's history within the context of all world history in the opening eleven chapters of our book of Genesis.

Two other developments need to be mentioned, chiefly because they do not form the connecting link with the main line of Christian thought. One of these is legalism, the idea that God has given his final revelation in a law that needs only codification and enforcement to bring about the realization of the meaning of history. Here revelation could only be conceived as a past event, and creativity could be exercised only in casuistical efforts to relate it to the changing scene of contemporary situations. Christianity rejected legalism even though there was a tendency to develop some form of it within the Church. The rejection was based on the recognition that God's relation to men is dynamic and living.

The other development was apocalypticism that tended to deny any significant meaning to the present in the idea that earthly conditions would become steadily worse until God was prompted to intervene in some final cataclysm in which evil would be completely destroyed and good permanently established. Certainly elements of this view are found within Christianity. But Christianity sees more to the present than signs of the end of all things. This world, though it is affected by sin, is nevertheless God's world over which Christ is Lord.

Excluding, for the most part then, the developments of legalism and apocalypticism as the truest expressions of the meaning of history, what the Christians saw in Christ was a fulfillment of this whole attempt to learn the purpose of history. In Christ the meaning of God's purpose had now become evident. And as we have noticed, that purpose was two-fold. For the individual it meant release from sin and growth into a man of the stature of Christ. For society it meant one center of organization and loyalty, the true Kingdom of God, the reuniting of all things under one Lord.

Yet we must carry our thought further to note that it was this conception of purpose which alone gave continuity and significance to Israel's varied fortune in the world. Moreover, it is this conception of purpose that makes sense of the life and death and resurrection of Jesus. The concern of the disciples was not with a national martyr-hero, for there had been many of those in the endless conflict of the Jews with their various captors—the Persians, Greeks, and finally Romans. Their concern was with the good news that in Christ God had made His purpose clear and had granted to them the earnest of its fulfillment.

QUESTIONS FOR DISCUSSION

1. How did New Testament people see Jesus fitting into their understanding of God's purpose in Israel?
2. Why should Abraham be taken as the precursor of the Christian? (Note references in the epistles to the Galatians, Romans, and Hebrews.)

OTHER SOURCES

Anderson, Bernhard W., *Rediscovering the Bible*. New York: Association Press, 1951, chaps. 2–6.

———, *Understanding the Old Testament*. Englewood Cliffs, N. J.: Prentice-Hall, Inc., 1957, Introduction.

———, *The Unfolding Drama of the Bible*. New York: Association Press, 1953, studies 1–8.

Bright, John, *The Kingdom of God*. New York: Abingdon-Cokesbury Press, 1953, chaps. 6, 7.

Filson, Floyd V., *Jesus Christ the Risen Lord*. New York: Abingdon Press, 1956, chaps. 3, 4.

Hunter, Archibald M., *Introducing New Testament Theology*. Philadelphia: The Westminster Press, 1958, chap. 4.

Neil, William, *The Rediscovery of the Bible*. New York: Harper & Brothers, 1954, chaps. 14–22.

Richardson, Alan, *A Preface to Bible Study*. Philadelphia: The Westminster Press, 1944, chaps. 5–7.

Wolf, William J., *Man's Knowledge of God*. Garden City, N. Y.: Doubleday & Company, Inc., 1955, chap. 3.

11

OUR RESPONSE TO THE GOSPEL

The apostolic preaching to which we have referred raised a particular question in the minds of those who first heard it. Strange as it may seem to us, that question was not "Is this true?" or "What are your credentials for delivering such a message?" but rather "What must we do?" And in asking this question those early hearers indicated a much better understanding of the Gospel than we often have today. They understood it as news to which they had to respond in action of one sort or another, and this was precisely what the Christian preachers intended. Because God had done something, men were called to do something. It is important that we are clear about this point, about the nature of the Gospel and the area of life to which it applies. The Gospel is a call to action, a call to organize life about the right center. This new center is not an abstraction, nor is it a mere possibility. It is a fact. This is what the disciples meant when they said, "Jesus Christ is Lord." But men can accept this fact grudgingly or joyfully, and their attitude will be borne out in action.

The attempt to verify the Christian proclamation can therefore never be a purely intellectual matter, although the intellect has an important part to play in the process. We need to study the record of the past with as little distortion as possible, particularly since Christians look for God's revelation within the events of history. Knowledge of the relation of first-century terminology to our own can help us understand what the New Testament people had in mind when they wrote and spoke as they did. We can clarify philosophically what we mean in asking religious questions in comparison to scientific questions. But none of these things in themselves can verify the Christian proclamation which involves the whole person.

If the Gospel is true, it will be found to be so not by an abstract discussion or study of its principles, but by its becoming the basis of actual living. Truth is always more than an impersonal collection of facts. Particularly in the Bible, truth means the right ordering of life. Whatever unifies life, giving it a direction and significance that do not at the same time lead to its eventual destruction—this is true. Whatever breaks life into fragments which are irrelevant to each other is false.

The truth, therefore, of the Christian revelation is found only as we participate in its meaning. All meaning is meaning for the present. The meaning of history is the meaning of it for us today, even though that meaning may point beyond us. The meaning the Israelites found in their history had significance not for academic research but for decisions the nation was constantly called to make. The meaning of the Gospel is the meaning of it for our lives today. The truth of it cannot be verified with the labors of New Testament scholars or students of antiquity. It cannot be verified by contemporary psychologists, as psychologists, either. It can be verified only as it becomes the basis for decisions that must be made in the present. And the principal decision to be made is not about one's opinion of the past—even an opinion about the career of Jesus—but whether or not one's life shall have some direction and what that direction shall be.

This means two important things. First, it means that the verification of the truth of the Gospel is not confined to the intelligentsia of any culture, but can be the experience of the most common man. In no sense must this be taken as a depreciation of learning. All men, whether wise or simple, must make decisions in life. If these decisions are to be rational— that is, if they are to conform to some pattern—they must have some directing purpose. Christ is that true purpose by which, alone, life can be organized as a whole with all of reality. And the demonstration of this can be found in any life so lived. This is why, when we talk of real knowledge of living, we often must turn in respect to some very humble person whose life "makes sense" or as it may be said "counts in the long run."

Second, it means that there is a place for honest doubt even in the expression of our faith. One may believe all the New Testament statements about Jesus. Or one may have doubts about either their accuracy or their relevance. But one's faith in Christ is seen more fundamentally in the whole way one lives and thinks. If one is convinced that life is not hit-or-miss but has direction and purpose, and if, on that understanding, one decides the questions with which life confronts him—even the issue of searching for the truth—then basically he is a man of faith. And if one's decisions are based on that understanding of life declared in the affirmation "Jesus Christ is Lord," then one is a person of Christian faith, though he may doubt biblical miracles and seriously question statements of Christian doctrine. If one looks forward to full maturity as a son of God so far as his own life is concerned, and to rightness in the sight of God in all one's interpersonal relationships, and his decisions are made on this basis, then he is responding in faith to the Christian proclamation.

Such a faith may not be so profound as it might be, but it is faith. Faith is found in this sort of fundamental attitude toward life. And it was such faith that Jesus and his disciples sought to stimulate. In the gospels—even in St. Paul's letters—there is very little said about the exact content of creedal statements. Affirmation of faith meant the confession of where one stood in his basic commitment of life. In later years as fallacious interpretations of Christian commitment arose, creedal details were necessarily formulated. Sometimes we find it hard to understand these details because we are not participants in the controversies that made them necessary.

Yet this quality of faith does not originate with any man. It is a response to what he has found of most significance in life. But he cannot discover this apart from the venture of life. Christian faith involves life as a whole—not as the sum of its many parts so that one would speak of faith found in worship, in work, in study, and in play, adding one to the other—but in the sense of the foundation of it all, its inner consistency, its over-all direction. It is this fundamental decision that the preaching of the Gospel calls from men, and it is in responding to this call in the action of life that people become Christian.

The news is, "God has made Jesus Christ Lord," and the question is, "Where do you take your stand as a result?"

QUESTIONS FOR DISCUSSION

1. What concept of truth underlies the biblical emphasis on action rather than contemplation?
2. Why does faith, though grounded in fact, always entail risk?

OTHER SOURCES

Anderson, Bernhard W., *The Unfolding Drama of the Bible.* New York: Association Press, 1953, Introduction.

Baillie, John, *Invitation to Pilgrimage.* New York: Charles Scribner's Sons, 1942.

Baly, Dennis, *Chosen Peoples.* Philadelphia: The Christian Education Press, 1956, chap. 5.

Farmer, Herbert H., *God & Men.* New York: Abingdon-Cokesbury Press, 1947, chap. 7.

Finegan, Jack, *Beginnings in Theology.* New York: Association Press, 1956, chap. 13.

Lyman, Mary Ely, *Jesus.* New York: Association Press, 1937, chap. 7.

Rall, Harris Franklin, *Christianity.* New York: Charles Scribner's Sons, 1940, chap. 13.

{ four }

god and man

12

implications of a
call for decision

The Christian proclamation calls men to make a decision concerning their lives, the decision of faith. This decision holds the key to the meaning of all of life, and is one of the determining factors in all subsequent events. But the very fact that men are called to decide discloses a definite understanding of men and of their relationship to God, to each other, and to the natural world. It is to the consideration of this relationship that we now turn our attention.

Any discussion of human nature can easily resort to the use of the impersonal "man" as representative and typical of each individual man. Of course, there is no such thing as "man," but only "men." Generalizations must be made, but they are valid only to the extent that they relate and interpret data of genuine human experience. The Christian view of man is based on experience interpreted by faith.

Many attempts to understand man begin with an appraisal of his "nature." Based on an observation of other people, these studies de-emphasize the more personal elements, but the Christian approach is immediate and personal, depending more, though not solely, on the analysis of one's own experience not only with other men, but with God and with oneself.

Many would say that such an approach is subjective, as indeed it is. But too often *subjective* is taken to mean that there is no reference involved to anything outside of the subject, and consequently subjective data are thought to be so shaded by personal idiosyncrasies that they are not worth much in discovering truth. The elimination of the subjective factor is taken as necessary to discovering truth which demands a reference wider than one individual. Objectivity is equated with reality (although this identification is often only inferred), while subjectivity is equated with illusion or falsity.

Although the demand for objectivity has borne important results in the sciences, it is not strictly applicable to the study of man himself. In the observation of physical phenomena, for example, the personal factor can mean only falsification. If my peculiarities should enter into my determination of the boiling point of a compound, I would not have an accurate representation of that compound. In our scientific observation, then, we seek to eliminate the personal factor as much as possible, using objective measurements of quantity in place of human qualitative judgments. At one time the pressure of steam in a boiler was determined by noting the sound it produced escaping from a petcock, but a pressure gauge which does not depend on acuteness of the human ear gives a more reliable indication of pressure.

In seeking an understanding of man, we now want to consider precisely those things which we want to eliminate in a scientific inquiry. It is man as a self-conscious, thinking, planning being that we would study. We want to know him not only as an object, but as a subject. In other words, we want to know from within what it means to be a man. The Christian understanding of man is based on this inner experience of living rather than on some abstract concept that is dead from the start because it never takes into consideration the uniquely human experiences.

Furthermore, the Christian understanding of man is practical. It is not sought as a mere expansion of the body of human knowledge. It is sought as a guide to living. Hence it is interesting not only to the connoisseurs of intellectual fabrications, but to all who are involved in the business of living.

Some who have been influenced by a current philosophy would call this whole approach *existential*. Existentialism as a philosophy, the attempt to understand man from within, raises a host of questions which we cannot examine, much less answer here. But without going into details, we can admit that our approach is existential in its attempt to understand the human situation through the full interior experience of what it means to be a man. To be a man who is conscious is different from the existence of a stone, and methods which give us data pertinent to a stone's existence do not give us the significant aspects of human existence.

The most important thing we note in examining our own lives for that element which is distinctively human is that we are constantly called on to make decisions for which we feel some sense of responsibility. Unlike other physical objects we do not merely react to stimuli from outside ourselves. A stone, when it is struck, will move a definite amount calculable by physical science. A rat in a research project of some psychologist will behave in a predictable way. To some extent we will also. When we are struck, however, while we will behave physically like any other physical body, we must decide our further response. This response will depend on the circumstances under which we were struck. We will behave differently if we were struck by a falling limb than if another person deliberately hit us. And if it was a person, we will decide whether to strike back or refrain, whether we will bow in submission or secretly plot vengeance.

What this implies is that to some extent, at least, we determine our own lives in a way that other animals cannot. Nature rigidly regulates the career of a horse or frog. Such animals behave according to patterns established by their natures. While they may adapt themselves to some degree to a change of environment, such adaptation is strictly limited. Horses may thrive on a wild meadow or on baled hay, but horses themselves can make no provision for an adequate food supply. Frogs cannot reproduce unless their natural environment is right.

But we are not thus completely determined by nature. We do have a psycho-physical organism with certain capacities and potentialities and, consequently, limitations. We cannot, for example, obtain our required oxygen from water, as fish do; we must take it from the atmosphere. But we can adapt our living to desert or jungle, to polar icecap or midwestern prairie, to seacoast or mountain top. We can even alter prevailing conditions if this becomes necessary for our survival. The fact that we are to an important degree self-determinative constitutes our basic problem. Nature does not regulate our lives as it does with the animals. So Jeremiah could complain about his nation:

"Even the stork in the heavens knows her times; and the turtledove, swallow, and crane keep the time of their coming; but my people know not the ordinance of the Lord" (Jer. 8:7).

This is borne out by our behavior toward each other. While we would not think of admonishing a table for structural failure, or even a dog for undoglike conduct—if such were even possible—we do not hesitate to speak to another man who is living as though he were less than a man, because we assume he can respond in some way to what we have to say and that he can more wisely respond to the circumstances of his life.

We may, of course, deny the significance or possibility of personal decision in such matters; but this denial destroys the whole question of distinguishing between truth and falsehood. This book, for example, is written to enlighten, instruct, and perhaps even convince those who read it. If the readers could not decide for themselves, if they merely reacted to it in a pattern determined completely by factors beyond their control, there would be little point in writing or publishing it, unless this, too, was beyond all human decision. It is written because readers can weigh its statements against their own experience and hence either modify or reject its premises or re-evaluate their own experience. And it is only because people have some capacity to evaluate and appraise what they read that they read such books at all. Decision and responsibility are found at the very core of our lives as men.

QUESTIONS FOR DISCUSSION

1. Read Deut. 30:15–20, Hosea 14:1–3, and Matt. 7:24–27. What do these three biblical passages imply about man?
2. What would you say, on this basis, is man's unique capacity that sets him apart from the other creatures?

OTHER SOURCES

Barry, F. R., *Recovery of Man*. New York: Charles Scribner's Sons, 1949, chap. 3.

Calhoun, Robert L., *What Is Man?* New York: Association Press, 1939, chaps. 1–3.

Cherbonnier, E. LaB., *Hardness of Heart*. Garden City, N. Y.: Doubleday & Company, Inc., 1955, chap. 2.

DeWolf, L. Harold, *A Theology of the Living Church*. New York: Harper & Brothers, 1953, chaps. 19, 20.

Farmer, Herbert H., *God & Men*. New York: Abingdon-Cokesbury Press, 1947, chap. 2.

Fosdick, Harry Emerson, *A Guide to Understanding the Bible*. New York: Harper & Brothers, 1938, chap. 2.

Harkness, Georgia, *Understanding the Christian Faith*. New York: Abingdon-Cokesbury Press, 1947, chap. 7.

Houf, Horace T., *What Religion Is and Does*, rev. ed. New York: Harper & Brothers, 1945, chap. 8.

Miller, Alexander, *The Renewal of Man*. Garden City, N. Y.: Doubleday & Company, Inc., 1955, chap. 1.

Pike, James A., *Doing the Truth*. Garden City, N. Y.: Doubleday & Company, Inc., 1955, chap. 2.

Pratt, James Bissett, *Can We Keep the Faith?* New Haven: Yale University Press, 1941, chap. 8.

Rall, Harris Franklin, *Religion as Salvation*. New York: Abingdon-Cokesbury Press, 1953, chaps. 1, 2.

Spurrier, William A., *Guide to the Christian Faith*. New York: Charles Scribner's Sons, 1952, chap. 4.

13

the problem of freedom

T his observation of the element of decision in our
lives raises a further question as to what extent such decisions
can really be our own, and to what extent we are actually
capable of shaping our own lives. This, then, is the problem
of freedom.

1. The meaning of freedom

Freedom must be distinguished from determinism on the one hand and indeterminism on the other. The determinist holds that there are no free choices, that our lives are completely structured by factors that are beyond our conscious control. To say that a child's life is entirely the product of his heredity and environment is to take this position. The indeterminist, on the other hand, holds that everything depends on conscious choice, that past conditions have no direct control on events following upon them. According to this view, a child's life is the result of his personal choices regardless of hereditary and environmental factors.

Freedom, however, is neither determinism nor indeterminism. Freedom does not rule out the existence of conditioning factors, for these provide its setting. We can choose within limits, not just as we happen to please. Obviously, our characters, extending far into the background of psychological depths which we do not fully understand or control, affect the way we choose. Our human natures as well as any unique physical or mental ability lead us into a particular type of life. We are creatures of time in the sense that we are located at a definite point in history, with all its possibilities and limitations, as well as in the sense that our lives are characterized by growth and development which leads to eventual death. The decisions of other people—from our parents to the world's statesmen—shape our lives, as do the results of our own past choices that now are unalterable.

These are limitations on us, but they do not strictly determine our response to them. We may be severely handicapped by our ignorance, but there is a wide range of possibilities open to us within our capacity for knowledge. Freedom is thus a denial of determinism because it is antithetical to the idea that we can be no more than what factors beyond our control make us. It also is a denial of indeterminism because it allows for the influence of conditioning factors. Indeed, these provide the context in which our freedom is exercised. Our lives are shaped not only by external factors, then, but by what we are in ourselves and by what we want to become. Our response to these factors beyond our direct control is not simply a reaction (as a rock reacts to physical pressure) but a response of which we are the controllers.

Few people today hold the indeterminist position. There is too much evidence refuting it. Habit and character would be meaningless. But many are likely to regard determinism as true because past events usually show a multitude of conditioning factors which make us seriously wonder whether we could have done anything different. We remember our previous experience, our established patterns of behavior, the prevailing conditions, and we see our action as directly shaped by these. But our experience of the present moment is rather that we are faced with alternatives that demand our decision. When we reflect seriously on life, we cannot avoid the actuality of freedom.

Suppose, for example, a man should insist that he is what he is by no choice on his part, but only because of the parents and training he has had and the sort of neighborhood in which he was raised (or some more refined analysis of such factors); or if he is willing to acknowledge the possibility of personal decision, suppose he should insist that whatever choices are presented to him are made strictly according to his previous conditioning. Freedom still intrudes itself in the question of what he shall do now, granted that this may be so. Is his arguing thus also determined, or can he speak differently? Is our understanding of his predicament determined? Why should he seek to convince us of his plight if our response is not within our conscious control?

But freedom makes itself known not only in our experience

of the present moment that calls for our decision but also in our experience of remorse for something in the past. As we look back, we may not only regret what has happened (because we can regret happenings that were completely beyond our control), but we may be sorry that we made the choices we did, recognizing that we could have made them differently. We may also feel guilty if we think we have decided contrary to our own understanding of what was best or right. While feelings may not be the most accurate approach to reality, they are an unavoidable aspect of our personal experience; and as with physical sensation, it is logical to assume that they do reflect reality.

It is often asserted that were we to know enough of the past life of an individual we could predict reliably his next move and that, therefore, freedom is a delusion. Such a statement has a basic fallacy in it—the argument from ignorance. Were we to know enough of the past, we might discover that predicting the future was even more hopeless. Our understanding of ourselves dare not be grounded in ignorance, but in the knowledge we have at the present moment. In the future we may have to adjust our understanding of ourselves, as new data are available. But our concept of truth must rest on our present experience. We are conscious of making choices for which we are responsible because they are ours.

2. Possibilities and limitations of freedom

If we are able, then, to shape our own ends, why is it that life does not correspond with our dreams? Why is it, considering human society at large, that we find it virtually impossible to live at peace among ourselves, that in spite of the achievements of civilization and the spread of culture we can, on provocation, drop back into a state worse than barbarism? Why is it that universal justice is so long in coming? Or considering the more personal level, why do we find our own personal inte-

gration so difficult? Why is our life characterized by a continuing struggle between competing drives and forces? Why is
unity of purpose so elusive?

There are two types of answers to these questions and
numerous variations within each type. We have said that our
lives are shaped by our natural endowment and by our own
choices. The first set of answers attributes all the difficulty to
our natural endowment: we are at the mercy of drives and
forces beyond our control, and these are the source of our
frustration.

Regardless of human ideals, for example, we are creatures
that require food. Consequently in the long run, according to
this general approach, economic pressures are more certain to
shape our destiny than beautiful dreams of the ideal society.
Marxism comes readily to mind as a philosophy which regards
economic factors as completely determining human destiny.
Ideologies are regarded as only surface indications of deep-
running, irresistible forces. Whereas there may be some
freedom of choice, it does not hold the possibility of the
achievement of our dreams.

Another variation of this line of thought looks to an uncom-
pleted evolutionary process as the explanation of our present
difficulties. Human existence at one time depended on a relent-
less self-assertion that put no interest in life higher than self-
preservation. While society now permits and even encourages
the development of other social and personal qualities, an over-
emphasis on self-preservation carries over in our personalities
through sheer inertia from an earlier age, tempering, even corrupting, all our activity. This drive can be expressed econom-
ically, psychologically, or even ideologically.

Such a view is more hopeful than the first one we have mentioned, because it looks to the passage of time for our deliverance from these things of the past that we have not yet outgrown. There seems to be the possibility that our "higher

selves" will eventually triumph over the "beast" that is in us. But the question which continually arises in spite of such optimism is whether such a view is true to our experience. That we have within ourselves deep and mysterious drives that baffle us in our attempts to realize our dreams can hardly be denied, but whether our failure is due solely to these or rather to our misuse of the control that we are able to exert is the crucial question. Our experience seems to point to the latter.

An animal's nature with all its limitations prevents its running amuck: it may kill, but nearly always for food and not for sheer wantonness. It may assert its leadership over a herd, but it does not plunge nature into chaos by trying to dominate the whole earth. Our chief difficulty, in other words, stems not so much from the carryover of our evolutionary history, but from the possibilities of our highest capacities. Therefore, while we may progress in moral achievement in some ways, that very progress introduces new problems not found in an earlier stage of development.

The second type of explanation for our failure to achieve our ideals consequently looks not to some phase of our natural endowment as the source of our difficulty but to the possibilities of our freedom. What betrays our hopes is our use of the basic equipment with which we must work. Our problem is continually with us regardless of our achievements. We will not outgrow it in time. While the context in which man exercises his freedom changes from one age to another—the details of social organization, for example—the human problem remains pretty much the same. It is always what we shall do with what we have, which in turn is ultimately determined by our final loyalty in life. The problem facing us in the twentieth century A.D. is basically the same as that which faced men in the tenth century B.C., although there are great differences in the external conditions of two such widely separated ages.

This can easily be overlooked when we consider the technological progress of our own day. Comfortable homes and daily work that does not utterly exhaust us, or stable government and consequent peace within a geographical area as large as our nation, or the division of labor which permits us to do those things at which we excel, leaving to others those things which they can best do—all this comes as reassurance that we have improved our lot. But the obverse of such accomplishments—the technology that threatens destruction along with the promise of cheap and abundant power, that brings economic exploitation which in some areas has created slums far more dangerous to health and morals than were the huts of savages, that binds us together so intimately that riots in India reverberate in midwestern barbershops—all this was unknown to an earlier generation.

Time is not automatically solving our basic problem. It is changing the context of this problem. It does permit recognizable technological advance, but the basic problem only alters and shifts. It does not disappear. The reason is simple: we carry our problem with us not as a hangover from the past, but as something with which we infect every present moment. We are more than just nature. We exert a measure of control over nature. But it is this "more than nature" that is our downfall. It is our highest capacity, our self-determination that leads us astray.

And our highest capacity, the final significance of the self-determination that we possess is the choice of the God we shall serve, by what conviction and final purpose we shall live. Granted any one orientation of our lives, our choices will follow on it. Our understanding of the purpose of life inevitably guides our decisions. But no one decides for us what we shall live for. This must be our decision. "In other words, within limits, we are free to choose our gods. Apparently we are free as to nothing else. Thus ultimately the *only true freedom is religious freedom.*" [1]

QUESTIONS FOR DISCUSSION

1. What is the difference between the Christian understanding of man's freedom and "doing what you want to do"?
2. In what sense has man "evolved" within recorded history? Is there any evidence that his basic nature is changing?

OTHER SOURCES

Calhoun, Robert L., *What Is Man?* New York: Association Press, 1939, chap. 4.

Cherbonnier, E. LaB., *Hardness of Heart.* Garden City, N. Y.: Doubleday & Company, Inc., 1955, chaps. 3, 10–13.

DeWolf, L. Harold, *A Theology of the Living Church.* New York: Harper & Brothers, 1953, chaps. 21, 22.

Marney, Carlyle, *Faith in Conflict.* New York: Abingdon Press, 1957, chap. 2.

Pike, James A., *Doing the Truth.* Garden City, N. Y.: Doubleday & Company, Inc., 1955, chap. 1.

Rall, Harris Franklin, *A Faith for Today.* New York: Abingdon Press, 1936, pp. 142–48.

———, *Religion as Salvation.* New York: Abingdon-Cokesbury Press, 1953, chap. 4.

[1] From: *Doing the Truth* by James A. Pike, p. 22. Copyright 1955 by James A. Pike, reprinted by permission of Doubleday & Company, Inc. and Victor Gollancz, Ltd., British publishers. Italics are Dr. Pike's.

14

IMAGE OF GOD
AND ORIGINAL SIN

We contain within ourselves the strange dualism of what we know we ought to be and what we recognize ourselves as actually being. But what is the source of this dualism? What does it really mean? It should be obvious that the meaning of life is not to be found solely within a human reference.

In relation to ourselves, we see confusion. We are not able to create a meaning for life consistent with our entire experience, nor are we willing or even able to surrender to complete meaninglessness. This can be interpreted, according to Christianity, by seeing ourselves as creatures dependent upon God in whom alone can be found the meaning of our existence, and yet creatures of a unique sort that possess something of the nature of their Creator.

Two concepts must now be introduced to clarify our understanding of ourselves, and both of them must be seen in relation to our dependence upon God. Much confusion can be avoided if we realize from the outset that these are not two component "parts" of man, but rather concepts which shed light on the complex situation in which we find ourselves.

The first of these is the *image of God*. In the history of Christian theology it is not easy to find a single accepted definition of the phrase suggested by the words of Genesis 1:26: "Then God said, 'Let us make man in Our image, after Our likeness. . . .'" It has always meant that to some extent we have a basic kinship with God. Sometimes a distinction was made between the image of God, which was interpreted as a capacity of man, and the likeness of God, which was thought to be moral similarity. The parallel construction of Hebrew poetry does not justify this distinction. The theologians, in making it, were attempting to clarify the meaning of the image of God in relation to the other major one, *original sin*. The image of God has been corrupted by original sin.

The biblical story which links these two concepts is that of the "Fall" of Adam and Eve (Gen. 2:4–3:24). In this account, God creates man and woman and places them in the garden to live obediently to Him. The serpent, however, entices Eve to disobey God's command not to eat the fruit of the tree of the knowledge of good and evil, suggesting that equality with God —independence from Him, in other words—will be the result.

The man and woman eat the fruit and suddenly recognize their sin which now is evident in their guilty attempt to hide from God, in their refusal to accept the blame for their own disobedience, and in their perverted consciousness of sex.

Much difficulty has come as people tried to interpret this story in a strictly historical sense. Thus the attempt to relate it to archaeological and anthropological data about Neanderthal or Cro-Magnon man has given rise to questions such as: were these creatures truly men in the sense of possessing the image of God, and if so did they live before or after the Fall? In trying to answer these questions, some have suggested that the story is true of every individual, that each of us experiences the Fall in his own life.

Although analysis of the complex human situation is not to be oversimplified, we may find help in understanding these terms by keeping in mind that they center in human experience —our experience. In taking this approach we will recognize how impossible it is to speak of any capacity for action entirely apart from its use. Strength, for example, cannot be determined—certainly not measured—if it is never put into play. We may say that an individual has mental capacity which he is not using; but such a statement, if it is at all valid, is based on some observation of the use of that capacity—the filling out of a test form, perhaps.

So in our consideration of man, the image of God is not some abstract quality which we can think of as man's possession before he was active in history. Its reality becomes evident only as man participates in history, but his activity indicates a misuse of that capacity, just as a man's strength may be seen in his smashing a valuable machine as well as in saving a child from a burning house; or just as mental capacity in school children may be indicated by the ingenuity of their mischief as well as by their proficiency in their class work. Man's first use of his God-given potentialities is their misuse, whether we are speaking of man in ancient days or in the present day. Yet apart from such use, or misuse, there could be no knowledge of the potentiality.

This consideration saves us from trying to date the Fall in personal, rather than racial, history. People often speak of an "age of accountability" before which wrongdoing cannot be considered sinful because the individual involved cannot yet recognize its significance. This leads to hopeless speculation about such an age of accountability. The point, however, is not that we try to date the end of the period of innocence, but rather that we recognize that when the gift of self-determination is evident by its use, the use will be found in some measure to be a misuse.

But what really is the image of God? We have already noted that it means some sort of kinship between man and God. Obviously this is not a physical likeness. Childhood concepts of God may involve a huge, dignified old man somewhere in the sky, but very little of the scientific attitude toward the world is enough to dispel such ideas as strictly childish. At times the image of God has been identified with man's rational powers. It is held to be man's ability to formulate purposes and carry them out in action that is a reflection of his basic kinship with God, Who gives life meaning.

A wider, though similar view regards the image of God as man's strange, almost mystifying ability to transcend himself, the ability to see not only the circumstances of life, but to see himself in the setting of those circumstances and to a degree independent of them. We all have that power to look at ourselves. This power, moreover, is always one step beyond our comprehension of it. When we contemplate ourselves, we know that the subject who is contemplating is never identical with the object contemplated. This is perhaps our unique capacity as men: we are always something more than the situation in which we find ourselves. And it is this capacity that gives us our freedom.

It is this power of self-transcendence that enables us to attach meaning to life because we can see more than a mere succession of events. Life's meaning is not derived from life itself. It is something by which we can organize the experiences of life in some pattern. We can thus interpret life only because, to some extent, we stand outside of it. Yet as human beings we are also inescapably involved in it. Our lives have the natural dimensions of time and space from which we never completely escape. We are born and we die. Though we are self-transcendent, we are unable to set the major dimensions of life, nor can we determine its larger setting. Hence, while we can attribute meaning to aspects of life, we cannot do it for life as a whole. This is what it means to be creatures. We are not equal with God. It is the resulting tension between human transcendence and limitation that Professor Reinhold Niebuhr sees as the occasion for human sin—the attempt to assert that we are beings complete within ourselves rather than creatures.[1] In terms of the biblical story of Adam and Eve it is the temptation to "be like God" (Gen. 3:5). In other words, we are sinners because we misuse our superiority over nature to rebel against our dependence upon God.

But since our pretensions do not alter the facts of our existence, since we must have something by which we can interpret life, we put something else in God's place. This is what the Bible means by idolatry—not necessarily making an idol of wood or metal, but trying to derive life's meaning from something other than God. To see that meaning solely in terms of material success, or fame, or power—this is idolatry. Idolatry leads inevitably to our own betrayal because only the true God

---

[1] Reinhold Niebuhr, *The Nature and Destiny of Man* (New York: Charles Scribner's Sons, 1941, London: Nisbet & Co. Ltd.), I, 181. Used by permission.

can give life a consistent, coherent meaning. False gods are unable to make sense of all of reality.

Sin, then, is our denial of our true relationship to God and the attempt to organize life on some other basis. Consequently, any Christian definition of sin must involve both man and God in the wrong relation to each other. This fundamental consideration underlies other definitions of sin.

For example, sin is sometimes defined as lawlessness (1 John 3:4). Man, no longer willing to live in obedience to God, becomes, or tries to become a law to himself. But since those who reject God have no more of a mind to be obedient to each other, utter chaos or lawlessness results. Again, sin is sometimes defined as selfishness: man's putting himself at the center of his concern. Yet selfishness is often seen as involving man only in his relation with other men rather than with God. Sometimes sin is equated with pride, since it is man's inordinate pride in himself which leads him to deny his dependence upon God. All these interpretations of sin are to an extent true, but they are true because the foundation of them all is the alienation of man from God. Man in his freedom tries to find the meaning of his life within himself or within nature, thereby denying its only real meaning—that which God, who created it, gives it.

We should now be able to see that original sin refers not so much to the sin of the first man as to the first sin of man.[2] Many times it is thought that original sin pertains only to the sin of Adam and Eve who tainted the whole race, transmitting the guilt of their act to every human being following them. Such transmission has been seen in the process of natural generation, or in a more complicated concept of the whole race being represented in Adam as its head. Such an explanation has been made by theologians and is not without meaning, though it may

[2] H. Richard Niebuhr, *Christ and Culture* (New York: Harper & Brothers, 1951; Harper Torchlight edition, 1956; London: Faber & Faber Limited), p. 211. Used by permission.

be easier for us to understand original sin if we remember that it refers to the basic sin of rejecting God and rebelling against Him, which in turn leads to all other forms of human sinfulness.

The world into which we are born has already been affected by the sinful attitudes of the generations preceding us. It is not the pure world of God's creation. It is a world that leads us to distort our view of ourselves, so that acting on that distorted view we add to the world's wrongness. In this other sense, too, sin is original. It is part of the human picture before we were born, and as soon as we enter the world we are inescapably affected by it.

In conclusion, we must note that the same man is both created in the image of God and a sinner, and this is true on every level of his being. If there is one insight of the biblical view which stands out, it is that man is a unity, perhaps driven by cross-purposes, but cross-purposes which make themselves evident in every aspect of his personality. There is thus no one level which is pure, as against another which is sinful. We do not deliver ourselves from our human predicament by forcing one phase of our personalities to dominate the others. Image of God and original sin are not two parts of us, not even two sides of our nature, but two concepts that help us study and understand the complexity of our experience.

Perhaps this is more easily seen if we compare the Christian analysis of man with others. Some, for example, have identified reason with the "good" part of man, and his material body with the relatively "bad" part. In this view man can deliver himself from his problem by allowing his reason to dominate his physical body and appetites. Others have simply reversed this judgment and have looked for man to overcome his difficulties by identifying himself with nature instead of seeking to "upset" the order of things by his arbitrary control. Others have spoken of a "spark of God" in every man which somehow remains free from contamination and thereby gives man a base from which he can rebuild life in a perfect pattern. Some Eastern religions have identified man's religious consciousness with Ultimate Reality itself.

The analysis we have made, however, is based on the recognition that in our experience there is no taint-free base from which to launch an all-out attack on evil. We are not schizophrenics, although we may be driven by cross-purposes. We do not have a good nature as opposed to an evil one, but rather, as men, we have potentialities which in actual use are put to selfish ends; and despite our ability to recognize this situation, the recognition does not deliver us from our problems.

Let us now review what we have said. We have noted from our own experience the complexity of the human situation. The constant demand of life for our personal decisions indicates that we are creatures of freedom, but a freedom which is exercised only in the context of natural and human limitations. Then we observed that in spite of our freedom we are not able to make of life what we will, to realize our dreams and achieve our goals. This failure, we said, is sometimes attributed to the deficiencies of the world in which our lives are set, but a more careful examination shows that the difficulty lies not only here, but also, even primarily, in the use of our freedom. Something we *are* leads to our predicament.

Christian theology interprets this experience in terms of the image of God and original sin. Created by God to a degree transcendent over nature, able to see life in its larger setting and thereby able to appreciate and give ourselves to its meaning, we have actually sought life's meaning not in God, but in principles of our own choosing. We alienate ourselves from God by our own idolatry.

QUESTIONS FOR DISCUSSION

1. To what realities of our own experience do the terms "image of God" and "original sin" refer?

2. What other ways are there of accounting for the human experience of decision and responsibility?

3. What is the human need to which Christianity addresses itself?

OTHER SOURCES

Cherbonnier, E. LaB., *Hardness of Heart*. Garden City, N. Y.: Doubleday & Company, Inc., 1955, chaps. 4, 5, 13.

DeWolf, L. Harold, *A Theology of the Living Church*. New York: Harper & Brothers, 1953, chaps. 24, 25.

Farmer, Herbert H., *God & Men*. New York: Abingdon-Cokesbury Press, 1947, chap. 3.

Finegan, Jack, *Beginnings in Theology*. New York: Association Press, 1956, chap. 6.

Gilkey, James Gordon, *A Faith to Affirm*. New York: The Macmillan Company, 1940, chap. 5.

Lewis, C. S., *Mere Christianity*. London: Geoffrey Bles, 1952, Book I.

Miller, Alexander, *The Renewal of Man*. Garden City, N. Y.: Doubleday & Company, Inc., 1955, chap. 2.

Pike, James A., *Doing the Truth*. Garden City, N. Y.: Doubleday & Company, Inc., 1955, chaps. 4, 6.

Rall, Harris Franklin, *A Faith for Today*. New York: Abingdon Press, 1936, pp. 148–54.

——, *Religion as Salvation*. New York: Abingdon-Cokesbury Press, 1953, chaps. 3, 5, 6.

Spurrier, William A., *Guide to the Christian Faith*. New York: Charles Scribner's Sons, 1952, chap. 5.

Whale, J. S., *Christian Doctrine*. New York: The Macmillan Company, 1941, chap. 2.

15

the need for redemption

So far, we have attempted to examine the human situation as we find it, the interpretation of which is clarified by the Christian concepts of image of God and original sin. Now we must turn to a discussion of the significance of this approach for our actual living.

138

Sin, we have said, is fundamentally the breaking of the relationship of trustful dependence upon God by our refusal to live in obedience to Him and by putting something else in His place. Unsatisfied to remain in the unstable position of being great enough to recognize our limitations, we seek to overcome them. But since our fundamental limitation is of the very nature of our existence as creatures, in attempting to overcome it we falsify our situation, denying God's dominion over us. We create a god after our image, not in the sense of making a physical idol, but in the sense of attempting to derive life's meaning from something within the created order of things, which is not ultimate. This falsification breeds a host of problems in our relation to God, to our fellow men, and to ourselves, problems which we may think of as the effects of sin.

1. The effects of sin

a. Alienation from God. Religiously speaking, the first effect is our alienation from God. So perverted is our real relationship that we look on God's goodness and see it as evil. Our choices, significant as they are, cannot alter the basic structure of reality. God remains God, in supreme control over all creation. Sin does not deliver us from God's jurisdiction. But this jurisdiction is now seen as being at radically cross-purposes with our own interests. The universe cannot function as a universe with multiple centers of control and organization, hence the result of our attempt to establish life apart from God is continual frustration within ourselves, in our social relations, and in nature as well. Such frustration we tend to view as the problem of a natural order inherently at odds with human efforts to achieve meaning in life.

Primarily is this so when we try to learn from the experiences of life. Any attempt to learn involves the assumption that there is some order outside ourselves to which we must conform. We take this for granted in our scientific investigations. Similarly, we can learn from the experiences of life only to the degree that we can admit a meaning to life which we do not make for ourselves and into which we must somehow find our way. This is borne in upon us by the frustration we experience in trying to be a law to ourselves, the experience of seeing life refuse to bend to the pattern that we would impose upon it. Were we truly open-minded, these frustrations would demonstrate to us that there is a truth of life which is either escaping us or which we are deliberately avoiding. Being open-minded, we would welcome the opportunity to learn. And if we were living in the relationship to God of faith, we would see these experiences as God's leading us into fuller truth and consequently more satisfying living.

But it is just this relationship to God which permits such receptivity—a receptivity resting squarely on the foundation of the trust of faith—that sin destroys. Seen from the perspective of our broken relationship, God is not the One who would lead us into truth, but rather One who would destroy such meaning as we have been able to create for ourselves. His every approach we see as a threat, something outside of us which limits us and frustrates our efforts.

b. Guilt. Moreover, this broken relationship with God has repercussions within our own personalities. It destroys our own integration and inner peace. Responsibility of decision is not something from which we can escape; but when our lives are wrongly oriented, that sense of responsibility expresses itself negatively as guilt. Guilt may be magnified to the point of mental distraction, and it may manifest itself in physical illness. Because we are *person*alities, there is no isolating one aspect of our lives to prevent its influence on any other.

If our sense of responsibility is at all related to God, we may view God's approach to us as punishment for our wrongdoing. It is this aspect of the relationship between God and man to which the Bible refers as God's wrath. True enough, there may be biblical usages of the term that lack this deep significance, as when God is said to blaze forth in anger to destroy a whole people (Exo. 32:9–10, for example). But even in such instances there is often the underlying reason of their refusal to "learn" God's will. It is this inability to read the lessons of history in faith and at the same time to escape a sense of the dominion of God that makes men feel that God's wrath is "kindled against them."

Yet, as we noticed earlier in our examination of the opening portion of St. Paul's Letter to the Romans, this interpretation may not be at all evident to us if we stand apart from God through sin. From our point of view there may be no personal antagonism of a Deity whose wrath is kindled against us. Rather, the problem may be seen merely as the forces of nature, which do not include our welfare in their action, going their own way, and this may give way to a more religious but still unchristian acknowledgment of a fate which ultimately holds us as pawns in its control. The ability to see the problem in the context of God's concern for men is a break-through from outside ourselves. It is part of our redemption.

c. *Disharmony in society and in nature.* Sin also has an objective result in the broken sense of community among men and the shattering of the harmony both with and within nature. It is this aspect of sin's effects that the biblical writer points out in the story of the expulsion of Adam and Eve from the garden into the hard world of toil, pain, and treachery. It reaches its poignant climax in the story of Cain's murdering Abel (Gen. 4:1–16). The same theme is put in the larger context of human society in the story of the tower of Babel, where, in the attempt to lift themselves to God, men discover that they can no longer communicate with each other (Gen. 11:1–9).

Sin leads us to exploit other people for our own purpose and makes us view our neighbors' prosperity as coming in some way at our own expense. Wrongly related to God, we have no basis for genuine community in society apart from self-interest. The relative order and stability which self-interest can generate when it is enlightened easily give way to sheer bestiality when it is threatened. Our efforts to establish peace always rest on a realistic appraisal of balance of power, for we have lost the condition which would enable us to achieve it on some idealistic basis.

The Bible also speaks of the disharmony in nature as a result of human sinfulness (see Rom. 8:19–22). Some concrete examples of this point come readily to mind. Human greed that exploits natural resources upsets nature's delicate balance. Hills denuded of their forests release normal rainfall in torrents that flood inhabited valleys. Grasslands unwisely plowed and sown to wheat become deserts of drifting dust. Short-sighted attempts to control pests or to profit from the propagation of certain species often wreak more havoc than they accomplish good. Sometimes the unique fear wild creatures display toward men seems to indicate that there is a basic distrust that reaches back into something like a memory of the species.

Whether everything in nature that does not contribute to human welfare can be understood in this light is another matter. In the next section we shall discuss the problem of natural evil. To argue beyond our knowledge is not wise. Our point here, however, is only to indicate that the problem of sin which we find within ourselves has repercussions outside ourselves, that apart from the right relation to God we find ourselves tragically at odds with our fellow men and with nature.

d. *Spiritual blindness.* But sin, in addition to its effect on our relationship with God, ourselves, our fellow men, and nature, compounds its own seriousness by producing spiritual blindness. Not only does it alienate us from God and our fellows, it disguises such alienation. While personal uneasiness and experienced frustration will remain, their source is hidden, and so is their cure (see 1 John 2:11). Unable to see things as they really are, we seek solutions to our problems vainly and in such foolish efforts preclude any true help. The last place we would look for the source of our difficulties is where they originate.

Sometimes sin is defined as a known violation of the law or will of God. The definition, true so far as it goes, implies that only when one is conscious of what he is doing can he violate his relation to God. The Bible insists that sin befogs the real issue, producing an ignorance which we did not intend and of which we are not aware. If there were some dramatic warning when we were about to take a false step, some unmistakable notice that here lay the parting of the way, our situation would be simpler. But the basic sin of unbelief, of distrust of God arising in the heart, in itself has the power to blind us. Such blindness allows us to move from the lesser evil to the greater, a phenomenon recognized in many religious traditions. The connection between blindness and conduct is always close: "This is the judgment, that the light has come into the world, and men loved darkness rather than light, because their deeds were evil" (John 3:19). Or from another New Testament author: "They are darkened in their understanding, alienated from the life of God because of the ignorance that is in them, due to their hardness of heart" (Eph. 4:18).

2. Attempts to deal with sin

It has been defining sin in terms of its results that has often led to seeing it falsely only in a human dimension and attacking it on this basis. Since the basic sin of unbelief or distrust of God gives rise to the host of human social evils or personal problems, sin comes to be defined in these terms only. It is true that if we do not see our lives under God's dominion we tend to orient everything to our own pleasure. Our concept of sex, for example, is warped so that it becomes instrumental

only to the end of personal enjoyment. Apart from any higher
reference, sex may lead us to exploit other people for purely
selfish reasons and may give rise to vicious forms of perversion.
Hence, sexual misbehavior is regarded as sin. Or because a person bent on his own pleasure is apt to disregard the value of
time and give himself to dissipation, sin is identified with those
acts most often associated with dissipation. And because the
person who deserts God often worships at the shrine of chance,
gambling is taken to be sin. Some people, unable to distinguish between that which is sinfully used and the sinful use
itself, frequently regard sex generally or all card-playing or
dancing as sin.

Because of this identification of sin with the acts resulting
from it, dealing with sin has often been equated with dealing
with these specific acts, and the attitude toward them has
varied from uncritical permissiveness to the most severe repression. For our study we shall consider three attitudes: naturalistic surrender, retreat into spirituality, and legalism.

a. Naturalistic surrender. There are those who insist that
such acts are no more than the inevitable product of our
psycho-physical make-up. Since these things are inevitable,
they are not to be taken too seriously, certainly not to the point
of disturbing our inner serenity. This approach to the problem
is taken by all those who attempt to define the standard of
human conduct by nothing more than a statistical average of
observed human behavior. Should they discover through investigation that a majority of those in a specific age group in-
dulge in illicit sexual relationships, they would conclude that
this is "natural" and that since little can be done to change
nature, we ought not to be overly concerned about it.

We may call this *naturalistic surrender* because the assumption lying behind it is that man is nothing more than nature,
that his life is the product of forces over which he has no real
control, and that nothing more than present circumstances need

be taken into account. Christianity has always insisted that man must be understood not only as he is, but as he may become, that sensuality is fundamentally unnatural because man was made for something better, apart from which he cannot find life's fulfillment. As we observed at the beginning of this section that the Christian understanding of man is evident only from the standpoint of faith, so here we may see that the naturalness or unnaturalness of sinful acts must be judged from the standpoint of what man was meant to be and what he is through faith.

b. Retreat into spirituality. Attacking specific acts as the attack on sin is easily criticized when one understands the primary meaning of sin as a violated relationship with God that brings these evils in its train. Particularly in sophisticated circles is this apt to be emphasized as against identifying sin with certain acts, an identification often termed "repressive morality." Such criticism may also indicate one of the ways that sin is dealt with on the human level. That is, a radical distinction is made between physical acts and spiritual realities. Our relation to God, some say, is purely a matter of the spirit: these other things are physical. Life's significant meaning is sought in a realm completely divorced from our daily life in this world.

This process of reasoning serves as a warning that religion *per se* is not necessarily a good thing. A man's religion may be the very means he uses to excuse himself or to obtain a cheap peace. The end result is a type of antinomianism—a refusal to accept responsibility for the results of sin. The Church has often had to do battle with those who would so spiritualize Christianity that they make it irrelevant to life.

The New Testament is much more realistic in reflecting the interaction of spiritual and physical matters. Rejection of God results in moral degradation, but moral indifference produces spiritual blindness. It is hard to see how, in this context of interrelation, sin could be significantly separated from specific acts which it produces and which can harden the individual against God. The claim of God on men, according to Christianity, is not a partial but a total one; and our religion is our total response to it.

c. Legalism. The attempts to regard sin's results as thoroughly natural, or the easy separation of spiritual concerns from the rest of life have nothing helpful to offer the human predicament. Neither does the identification of sin with such acts. When this identification is made, it would appear that we could avoid sin by avoiding just those acts. This is the negative side of legalism which is the attempt to define the will of God in such specific terms that we can chart the quality of our obedience by a check list.

On the surface it seems logical. What could be simpler than to improve one's relationship to God by avoiding those things that can destroy it! But legalism has two basic flaws. In the first place, it leads to self-righteousness. One is apt to define sin as those specific things which he does not do but of which other people are guilty, and he may refuse to consider his own shortcomings. Self-righteousness may be the overt, nasty attitude of "I am better than you are." But it can also be a more subtle thing that manages to avoid criticizing others, yet still reflects the very essence of sin in trying to maintain an independent goodness before God.

The more sincere the legalist, the more evident is the second flaw. The more he tries to eliminate sin in striving for perfection, the more he is driven to desperation by the impossible size of the project he has marked out for himself. Life not only refuses to respond in obedience to our best desires, but it has its own way of mocking them. Modern psychology has illumined the problem by showing that an attempt to achieve perfection may arise from dubious motives, among them the repression of quite contrary desires. This is recognized in the Bible: "The heart is deceitful above all things, and desperately corrupt; who can understand it?" (Jer. 17:9). And even the genuine desire for goodness is tragically frustrated by the inability to implement it with action. The result for those who try to be honest with themselves is despair, either in their impotence to do what they know is right or in the impossibility of ever having done enough to stand uncondemned in the eyes of God or to compensate for past wrong.

As an example of the first we have St. Paul's lament expressing a universal experience, "I can will what is right, but I cannot do it. For I do not do the good I want, but the evil I do not want is what I do" (Rom. 7:18, 19). An example of the second is the almost pathological worry of Martin Luther that somehow —even only in ignorance—he was failing to obey God's complete will, "For whoever keeps the whole law but fails in one point has become guilty of all of it" (James 2:10). Nor is it possible to compensate with obedience today for disobedience yesterday: "So you also, when you have done all that is commanded you, say, 'We are unworthy servants; we have only done what was our duty'" (Luke 17:10).

Legalism is doomed if it cannot bring assurance that in its prescriptions the full will of God is declared, that these prescriptions are within the range of human ability, and that somehow one can make up for past sin by an obedience over and above what is required today. Experience indicates it can do none of these. In the first place, even though it is necessary to make our knowledge of God's will specific, our codifications must be continually revised according to newer insights. This role of criticism was played by the prophets of Israel, and in our day their line is continued by those who remind us of the total claim of God. In the second place, experience indicates that the attempt to follow legalism's codes results only in despair or an uncritical self-righteousness. And in the third place, God's claim on us in every moment is a total one, so our hope to exceed our duty is based on some truncated idea of what God asks of us.

What we have considered, then, is the nature and complexity of the problem with which sin confronts us. Most obvious are the evils in human society that set man against man and group against group. Yet more fundamental is the problem of spiritual blindness that prevents our seeing life in a true perspective which would reveal the source of, and remedy for, our difficulty or, seeing this, that understands God's approach to us as condemnation and wrath.

We have looked at the possibilities of human attempts to deal with the problem, either in some fashion ignoring it, or light-heartedly or legalistically cutting down God's claim to fit our performance. Somehow the situation must be set right. Somehow there must be a break-in of a new light and a new power. And yet this is impossible from the human standpoint. Human potentialities do not hold the promise of the resolution of the tension which they create and sustain. We do not achieve the full life by developing ourselves as we are.

This is the truth embodied in asceticism encouraged by many of the world's religions. Certainly some aspects of our lives must be negated. But the Christian view goes deeper than most of these prohibitions that asceticism formulates. "These have indeed an appearance of wisdom in promoting rigor of devotion and self-abasement and severity to the body, but they are of no value in checking the indulgence of the flesh" (Col. 2:23). Rather, we need remaking at the very core of ourselves.

QUESTIONS FOR DISCUSSION

1. What possibilities and resources within himself does man have for dealing with his fundamental problem?
2. How do guilt and remorse complicate man's attempted solutions of his problems?
3. What ways have men used to escape their basic problem rather than solve it?

OTHER SOURCES

Cherbonnier, E. LaB., *Hardness of Heart*. Garden City, N. Y.: Doubleday & Company, Inc., 1955, chaps. 6–9.

DeWolf, L. Harold, *A Theology of the Living Church*. New York: Harper & Brothers, 1953, chap. 23.

Pike, James A., *Doing the Truth*. Garden City, N. Y.: Doubleday & Company, Inc., 1955, chap. 6.

Rall, Harris Franklin, *A Faith for Today*. New York: Abingdon Press, 1936, chap. 11.

———, *Religion as Salvation*. New York: Abingdon-Cokesbury Press, 1953, chaps. 7–9.

Richardson, Alan, *Science, History, and Faith*. London: Oxford University Press, 1950, chap. 8.

Wickenden, Arthur C., *Youth Looks at Religion*. New York: Harper & Brothers, 1939, chap. 8.

16

chRist anд human ReдemptION

So far we have been thinking about our human situation, that we experience a claim upon us which we have not and apparently cannot satisfy in our present condition, and yet that the fulfillment of our lives and consequently our ultimate happiness depends on our responding to that claim. We are creatures who need to be remade. We do not have in our possession the simple possibility of turning to God. If we did, we would not be in our predicament. Something must be done for us and in us to make us right.

The testimony of Christians is that this "something" is done for them in, by, and through Jesus Christ. This is the good news to which St. Mark refers at the beginning of his gospel (1:1). The claim is evident in the familiar verse of the Fourth Gospel: "For God so loved the world that He gave His only Son, that whoever believes in him should not perish but have eternal life" (John 3:16). Or in St. Paul's words: "God was in Christ reconciling the world to Himself" (2 Cor. 5:19). Specifically, we have heard that "Jesus saves," or that "salvation is in Christ," or that "Jesus died for our sins." But such statements make little sense unless we are aware not only of the need to which they refer, but also of how they apply to that need in terms of our experience. How is it that Christ saves us?

Redemption is the term Christian theology most often uses to designate what happens to men in this experience. *Atonement* usually refers to what Christ does to make this possible. Strict logic suggests that we consider atonement first, but it may be more helpful to begin instead with our human experience.

1. What happens in redemption?

Our experience comes to us with a wholeness that defies its being broken into convenient parts for analysis. When Christians relate their experience they are apt to speak in some simple way such as "I was lost, but now I have been found." Later we shall consider some of the expressions that have been used to describe this experience and its significance. But now for purposes of clarity we shall consider our human needs that we have already studied.

a. Confrontation with reality. The first thing Christ does is to awaken men to the reality of their lives and their relation to God. Sin blinds us, preventing us from seeing life in true perspective. So long as we are certain that the world is out of joint, that every difficulty we face arises external to our control, we cannot be delivered from our predicament.

An objective appraisal of our situation might well reveal the importance of external factors—for there certainly are complications in life that prevent us from doing the best we know or that shockingly twist our best intentions to produce evil as an end result—still, the fact that we so continually seek to blame others or impersonal forces for our difficulties shows that we evade the reality of our own problem. We are convinced that had we the power to remold the universe after our hearts' desire, it could not fail to be improved.

This is the very attitude that separates us from God. Yet how can we even see this as the problem if we are sure that only others are wrong? Certainly our initial assumptions do not permit such a conclusion. But it is precisely this need that Christ meets, enabling us to see ourselves as we are. At least this is the testimony of Christians, that when denunciations and condemnations—even dire threats—failed, somehow Christ has granted them true insight. Through our self-righteousness and defensive barriers he is able to bring the knowledge of reality.

One example from Luke's gospel will illustrate this point. Zacchaeus, a local tax collector, was hated by the people of his community and counted outside the pale of Israel by the godly. No doubt he had heard more than enough admonitions about what he should do; and no doubt he assured himself that he was not so bad as many who condemned him, who were saying one thing but doing another. But when Jesus entered his home, unexpectedly asking for hospitality, Zacchaeus saw things differently: "Lord, the half of my goods I give to the poor; and if I have defrauded anyone of anything, I restore it fourfold." No wonder Jesus could reply, "Today salvation has come to this house" (Luke 19:8, 9).

This ability of Jesus to bring people to an understanding of themselves can be seen negatively in the reaction of the scribes and Pharisees to him. Perhaps the unified outlook of this group has been overdrawn, since it was of a scribe that Jesus said, "You are not far from the Kingdom of God" (Mark 12:34); and it was a group of Pharisees who warned him of Herod's intention to imprison him (Luke 13:31). Yet the New Testament represents this group as forming his principal opposition. Why this should have been so is not too difficult to see. The Pharisees represented the best of society so far as law-abidingness and earnestness of purpose were concerned. They consciously strove to do the right thing. But in this very striving they were blinded to their own imperfections. They recognized that the insight Jesus could give them would threaten their hard-won position, which they could maintain only by completely rejecting such insight. So violent was their rejection that they plotted his death (Mark 3:6).

The insight that Jesus brings men not only reveals their true status before God but opens to them the depth and pervasiveness of their own sin. True insight does not come easily because it cannot be superficial. Sometimes people are apt to think that if their acts are not the best, certainly they mean well. Yet it was questionable motives that Jesus so often had to expose and clarify. To the man complaining of the injustice of the settlement of an estate he said, "Take heed, and beware of all covetousness; for a man's life does not consist in the abundance of his possessions" (Luke 12:15). To the two disciples who sought the choice places in the Kingdom of God he spoke of service as being the true indication of greatness (Mark 10:43). Even prayer, he said, could be a means of self-glorification (Matt. 6:1).

But the clearest insight has come through the crucifixion,

because in it men's real motives were bared. It was through this experience that Peter recognized the folly of his bravado (Matt. 26:33, 74, 75), and Judas saw the hideousness of his treachery (Matt. 27:3, 4). Throughout time, Jesus' crucifixion has demonstrated how ostensibly good motives often lead to tragedy because they come short of purity.

b. *Assurance of forgiveness.* Such revelation of self-truth would be desolating were it not for the fact that at the same time, often in the same experience, Jesus has also brought an assurance of God's love and forgiveness. In fact, it may well be that it is only because there is that atmosphere of acceptance and welcome that we dare consider the truth of ourselves, putting aside our rationalizations and self-deceptions. Somehow Christ is able to create a new relationship between man and God.

If, in the relationship of sin, we are at all aware of God, we see Him as One who threatens to destroy our whole system of meaning in life, One who is set against us. Our redemption waits until we can recognize that God's activity is for our welfare, that He destroys only in order to create something better. Hence Jesus assures us that God's approach is not a curse but a blessing.

To some extent he does this by calling on our own experience: "If God so clothes the grass of the field, which today is alive and tomorrow is thrown into the oven, will he not much more clothe you, O men of little faith?" (Matt. 6:30). Seeing life maintained day after day—the sun rising on the evil and on the good (Matt. 5:45)—we should be reassured that God is not ultimately against us. Even tragic accidents, he taught, could not be explained as God's punishing unusually evil sinners (Luke 13:1–5). And if this Divine concern for us does not depend on our righteousness, then we dare be honest before God and ourselves about our lack of righteousness.

Moreover, Jesus in his ministry mediated forgiveness. One

example is that of the paralytic whose friends lowered him through the roof of a house to Jesus' feet, because the press of the crowd prevented them from bringing him in through the door. Jesus' words to the young man were, "My son, your sins are forgiven," and when some questioned his authority to forgive sin, he said, "Rise, take up your pallet and walk" (Mark 2:1–12). Another example is the story of the woman "who was a sinner," who came to him when he was dining at the home of Simon the Pharisee. Jesus did not reject her attentions, and when he was challenged by the group's condemnation of the woman, he pointed out that forgiveness and love go hand in hand, that she was forgiven much because she loved much (Luke 7:36–50). Still another example is the story that appears at times in old manuscripts of Luke, at other times in those of John—the story of the woman taken in adultery. Caught in the act, she was brought by her accusers to Jesus for his opinion of the case, since the law prescribed her death. He said nothing about the merits of the case, but only that the man without sin should begin the execution. When they all withdrew, leaving Jesus alone with the woman, he said to her, "Neither do I condemn you; go, and do not sin again" (John 7:53–8:11. The story is sometimes found following Luke 21:38).

But beyond these specific examples was his whole attitude of life that brought him to those who were despised by the better society of his day. There was the call to Levi the tax collector to become his disciple (Mark 2:14). There was his association with the publicans and sinners to the extent that he was charged with being a drunkard and glutton himself (Matt. 11:19). There is his statement that the sick need the physician and that, therefore, he had come to call not the righteous but sinners to repentance (Matt. 9:12, 13).

But more important than all these was his attitude as he approached his death on the cross. Had he died bitter and vindictive, it would have been understandable in the light of the treachery, faithlessness, and sheer cruelty that he was forced to undergo. But he was not vindictive. And his prayer, "Father, forgive them; for they know not what they do" (Luke 23:34) has always indicated to Christians that the firmer one's loyalty to God, the closer to this attitude toward life one will come.

The action of Jesus cannot be separated from the purpose of God in Christian thought. St. Paul, after commenting on the fact that seldom will one man willingly die for another, though occasionally for a truly good man "one will dare even to die," says, "But God shows His love for us in that while we were yet sinners Christ died for us" (Rom. 5:8). So just as Christ's role in bringing us knowledge of ourselves centers in the cross, so also does his assurance of forgiveness.

c. Mediation of power. Christ makes available and mediates a power by which we can organize and live life by a new principle. Again, this may be seen in the assurances he gave people during his ministry. "If you have faith as a grain of mustard seed, you will say to this mountain, 'Move hence to yonder place,' and it will move; and nothing will be impossible to you" (Matt. 17:20).

Even more important was the effect of his fellowship on his followers. With him people did the most extraordinary things— not miraculous, necessarily, but extraordinary. Levi left his job as tax collector, Zacchaeus gave back money he had stolen, Mary of Magdala began a new life, Peter and his fishing companions launched a world mission, and even Thomas whom tradition has called "the doubting one" said, "Let us also go, that we may die with him" (John 11:16). It was his continuing presence which he promised the disciples that strengthened them in their mission (Matt. 28:20).

Power is always related to motivation. We can do many things under proper motivation that would otherwise be impossible for us. A physically weak mother will display amazing strength to save her children if they are in danger. Christ inspired the motivation of gratitude in his followers—not only those who were directly associated with him in life, but those who heard from others about him. And here again, just as in his revealing our true situation and God's forgiveness, gratitude for him centers in the cross. St. Paul could say, "The life I now live in the flesh I live by faith in the Son of God, who loved me and gave himself for me" (Gal. 2:20). Or from 1 John, "We love, because he first loved us" (4:19).

But beyond even the motivation of thankfulness, the New Testament indicates that through Christ, God's power is now available to us. "The law was given through Moses; grace and truth came through Jesus Christ" (John 1:17). Its potency is to be seen supremely in Christ's resurrection. St. Paul prays that his readers might have some conception of the "immeasurable greatness of His power in us who believe, according to the working of His great might which He accomplished in Christ when He raised him from the dead" (Eph. 1:19, 20). He speaks of his personal weakness as being the occasion for the manifestation of God's power: "I will all the more gladly boast of my weaknesses, that the power of Christ may rest upon me" (2 Cor. 12:9).

2. The meaning of atonement

Thus far we have thought in terms of what Christ does to redeem men, in the sense of bringing them insight, forgiveness, and power. But another question often asked is whether he must also do something for God to make divine forgiveness possible. This question is raised by two different groups of people: the first think of God primarily in terms of justice, while the second think in terms of all that is involved in genuine forgiveness.

Those who stress the unremitting justice of God generally conceive of justice as retribution with "an eye for an eye" as the general pattern if not the ideal. For example, if a man steals, it is thought that he "deserves" to be punished; and although a prison sentence or perhaps a fine is substituted for the seizure of his goods, the length of the sentence or the amount of the fine is in some way made to correspond with the seriousness of his offense as well as his motivation. When his punishment has balanced his offense he has discharged his "debt" to society and may be allowed to take up his regular life again. He can now be forgiven.

If this concept of justice is predicated of God, it is thought that something must satisfy God in the "eye for an eye" pattern in order that forgiveness shall be possible. God, in other words, cannot forgive until something has made up for man's sin, until the scales of Divine justice have been balanced. This approach has led to the various "substitutionary" views of the atonement: in order to overcome sin and reconcile man to God, Christ had first to take such punishment on himself as men deserved because of their sin. These views have varied from the position that in his death on the cross Jesus experienced the entire wrath of God toward the whole human race, to the position that God as supreme Governor of men decides what satisfaction He shall receive for all affronts to His dominion, and so is able to substitute one man for all humanity, a substitution we would not normally consider strict justice. Cruder expressions have spoken of the blood of an innocent victim as God's price for forgiveness. The death of Christ on the cross has been seen as the offering of such a victim. It is recognized that Christ does not work independently of God—there being no conflict of their wills—still, the death of Christ in some way reveals the struggle of God's love and, consequently, His desire to redeem men, with His justice that demands their death.

The other approach is through an awareness of all that is involved in forgiving. To forgive, it must be remembered, has as its object persons rather than acts. It is not the same as to ignore. If a friend has done something to hurt us, we cannot ignore it. We might not be at all bothered had a stranger done the same thing to us. What matters is that someone close has violated the mutual relationship of trust and concern. This violation of the personal relationship brings us hurt or pain— not of a physical, but of a spiritual, sort. The closer the relationship, the more intense the hurt, and the more difficult is dealing with the rupture.

Moreover, there are aspects of such an experience that cannot be balanced out by justice of the retributive sort. A friend may be able to pay back a sum that he stole from me, but this does not remove the original breach of trust. I, in turn, may give him a sound scolding, but again this does not eliminate the original hurt. I may get rid of the hurt by ceasing to care about him, because the alternative to forgiveness is to allow the person who was so close to become no more than a "heathen and a publican" (Matt. 18:17). But the only positive way I can maintain the relationship is to "absorb the hurt" [1] of its violation myself. And if my friend also wants the relationship maintained, he must swallow his pride, which makes him unwilling to accept my forgiveness without "meriting" it. The closer our relationship, the more my friend and I will understand what it means to absorb the hurt. And appreciating this through our experience, we will be drawn even closer together.

In order to continue our thinking about Christ and our redemption we must understand how Jesus approached his death as the climax of his entire ministry. According to the New Testament, Christ never regarded his death as merely the result of human wickedness. He saw it as his vocation. He regarded it as somehow "necessary" because of his intention to fulfill his own ministry of reconciliation rather than to suffer a martyr death at the hands of the secular and religious authorities at Jerusalem.

Following Peter's confession that Jesus was the Christ, Jesus,

[1] This suggestive phrase is from Pike, *Doing the Truth*, p. 86.

says Mark, "began to teach them that the Son of man must suffer many things, and be rejected by the elders and the chief priests and the scribes, and be killed, and after three days rise again" (Mark 8:31). When Peter rebuked him for saying this, he replied, "You are not on the side of God, but of men" (Mark 8:33). Again in 9:31 and 10:33 are references to his coming death. Then in 10:45 is another interpretive statement of the events that lay ahead: "For the Son of man also came not to be served but to serve, and to give his life as a ransom for many." Later Jesus' parable of the vineyard which had been let out to tenants who killed the owner's servants and finally his own son, who had been sent to assert the owner's authority, is intended to refer to his approaching death (12:1–9. The parable corresponds to that in Isa. 5:1–7). Two more indications of this same thought are in the gospel: at the institution of the Lord's Supper he said of the cup of wine, "This is my blood of the covenant, which is poured out for many" (14:24); and in his prayer in Gethsemane, "Abba, Father, all things are possible to thee; remove this cup from me; yet not what I will, but what thou wilt" (14:36).

Throughout the book of the Acts are references to the suffering and death of Christ as being predicted by the Old Testament prophets: "What God foretold by the mouth of all the prophets, that His Christ should suffer, he thus fulfilled" (3:18); ". . . I stand here testifying both to small and great, saying nothing but what the prophets and Moses said would come to pass: that the Christ must suffer . . ." (26:22, 23). Another reference to the prediction of the prophets regarding the suffering of Christ is found in 1 Peter 1:11. But what is it to which these passages refer?

Their reference is indicated in the opening chapter of Mark's gospel in the voice Jesus hears at his baptism: "Thou art my beloved Son; with thee I am well pleased" (1:11). The first part of this is a quotation from Psalm 2 which traditionally had been related to God's receiving the king of Israel into the special relation of Divine Sonship and which may also have been connected with God's anointed one or special agent (Messiah). The second part is from Isaiah 42:1 which refers to God's servant. This theme of God's servant is unique to the second part of Isaiah, reappearing in succeeding chapters and reaching its poignant climax in chapter 53. The idea expressed is that instead of being welcomed when he comes to men, God's servant is reviled, abused, and finally killed as a criminal. But instead of lashing back in revenge, the servant takes the abuse on himself even in death. God vindicates his faithfulness, however, because this obedience brings those who persecuted and abused him to repentance. "He shall see the fruit of the travail of his soul and be satisfied; by his knowledge shall the righteous one, my servant, make many to be accounted righteous; and he shall bear their iniquities" (Isa. 53:11). That Jesus had this passage in mind is indicated by his statement recorded in Mark 10:45.

What this points to is that Jesus somehow saw himself as fulfilling the role of God's servant in absorbing all the hurt of human sin which is necessary for forgiveness. If we keep in mind the supremely personal factors involved in our own experience of forgiveness and forgiving we see here the importance of two points: (1) personal relationships, not merely specific acts, are involved, and (2) the closer the relationship is, the more serious any violation of it. Christ in his dedication, expressed so unforgettably in his willingness to be obedient even to death, shows us the depth of the concern of God—the seriousness with which He regards our alienation because of His great love, and at the same time demonstrates His willingness to take on Himself that hurt, made more intense by His concern, in order to forgive. Forgiveness comes only at great cost, but not at a price that can be calculated. Christians have somehow seen this in the life, but supremely in the death, of

Christ which in one moment bound up the meaning of his entire ministry.

But the love of Christ that committed him to his mission and his willingness to take on himself all the hurt and meanness of sin are not that of a Prometheus who defies the hostile gods on man's behalf, but rather the very love and will of God, Himself. Jesus' life was his own choice, but the choice was to fulfill God's will. In other words, here is where the God who gives life meaning declares Himself. It is in Christ that we see God's purpose revealed in the only way we could hope to see and to understand it. In short, "God was in Christ reconciling the world to Himself" (2 Cor. 5:19).

In seeking to understand what the Christian means by atonement, then, four points must be kept in mind. First, through Christ men have actually found their way to God by discovering forgiveness for their sin and power to live by faith. If it were not for this experience, there would be no doctrine of the atonement. Since Christ, men have known a different relationship with God. Second, it was Christ's specific intention, an intention expressed throughout his ministry but particularly in his sense of the necessity of his death, to reconcile men with God. Third, true reconciliation can never be had by making light of sin. It can never be an escape from judgment but must lead to redemption through judgment. Fourth, the activity of Christ was no independent action on his part, but was his commitment to the will of God Whose purpose was to redeem men.

The attempt to express these four points in an over-all picture is made in several ways in the New Testament by references to some other human experience akin to the restoration of the Divine fellowship. One of these ways is expressed in the term *ransom* or *redemption*. The imagery is obvious: a ransom is the price set for the freedom of a slave. Jesus used this term about himself (Mark 10:45), and the word is found again in 1 Tim.

2:5, 6. In 1 Peter 1:18, 19 the ransom price is said to be not gold or silver but the very blood of Christ.

Another expression is found in the idea of sacrifice. This was only natural since Judaism provided the pattern in the animal sacrifices performed at the temple in Jerusalem. It may be this reference which lies behind the phrase "the lamb of God" used in John 1:29. St. Paul uses the theme in Ephesians 5:2, and at times specifically refers to blood as the focus of sacrificial thought (see Col. 1:14, 20). But the theme of sacrifice is given its principal treatment in the anonymous Letter to the Hebrews. Here the Jewish cultus is seen as a prototype of the final and perfect sacrifice which Christ made both as high priest and as the victim. A brief outline of this is found in Heb. 9:11–14.

Some have found another expression in the idea of substitution—that somehow Christ received in himself the evil effects of sin, so freeing us. St. Paul speaks of Jesus "who was put to death for our trespasses and raised for our justification" (Rom. 4:25). A less ambiguous reference is found in 1 Peter 3:18: "For Christ also died for sins once for all, the righteous for the unrighteous, that he might bring us to God, being put to death in the flesh but made alive in the spirit."

Many have questioned, however, the use of the substitutionary idea, because a wider reference to vicarious suffering—that Christ suffered in our behalf, even giving his life for us, not in the sense of substitution but rather in the sense of complete self-giving—is much more apparent in the New Testament. If a man should die trying to save his family from their burning home, for example, we should speak of his dying for them, but not necessarily that his life was substituted for theirs. It is more in this sense that St. Paul writes, "But God shows His love for us in that while we were yet sinners Christ died for us" (Rom. 5:8). In the Fourth Gospel Jesus speaks of himself as the good shepherd who gives his life for the sheep (John

10:11), and the author of the First Letter of John writes, "By this we know love, that he laid down his life for us" (3:16).

It has been largely as expansions of these ideas that the traditional doctrines of the atonement have been developed. Many times, however, in trying to absolutize concepts originally meant metaphorically, theologians cheapened the principal theme. For example, using the ransom imagery to explain how Christ brings men back to God, some insisted that a real transaction took place, and that a price had to be paid to the devil for men's freedom. (Only, in the resurrection, which the devil had not at all anticipated when he first struck the bargain of the soul of the Son of God for the souls of all humanity, Christ was lost to the powers of hell.) Others insisted that the price was paid to God, because man, through his sin, had put himself in debt to God: God could never in any sense be in debt to the devil.

It was from this second approach that most of the substitutionary views of the atonement developed, each repeating the pattern that a substitute had to be found to take the burden of a punishment of death that otherwise would have fallen on mankind. Some stressed the element of punishment, emphasizing the suffering Christ endured, and religious art as well as literature has magnified the theme of the agonies of Christ. Some, drawing also on the sacrifical imagery, stressed the purity of Christ as being the only possible substitute for an impure humanity. Many times the implied idea of sacrifice was more akin to the pagan idea of attempting to placate God, rather than the Hebrew idea that God provides the sacrifice as a means of reconciling men and renewing the covenant relationship, that the sacrifice is in no real sense a substitute for those who offer it. Others have stressed the obedience of Christ as substituting for the universal disobedience of mankind. As we have already noted, substitutionary views usually sought to defend God's justice. If justice means that the guilty one, and not some innocent party, pays the price equivalent to his wrongdoing, then substitution is not justice. Moreover, a price once paid means a transaction completed with no further obligation, yet this is scarcely the meaning of the Christian experience. In fact, it has been in reaction to the problems involved in substitutionary theories that a completely different approach has been made. Called "moral influence theories," they usually emphasize Jesus' perfect example of obedience and faith as a stimulation to men's own finest living. Christ becomes the hero to be emulated, not a substitute to excuse one from living that quality of life.

The fact that no one such theory has become official for the Church indicates how difficult a matter it is to say with sympathy, precision, and comprehensiveness exactly how Christ redeems men. The reality of the experience challenges both our attempts to give it expression in words and our easy ridicule of such attempts that have been found to be so painfully inadequate.

We must not think, however, that Christ's role in redemption was confined to his earthly career in the first century. His is a continuing reconciliation. On the one hand there is a once-for-all-ness about it, so that what happened in first century Palestine is pertinent to our own situation today. A good share of the work of the Church is to acquaint men with the historical facts of Jesus' life and the theological interpretation that sets that life in the context of God's eternal purpose. On the other hand there is a continual newness about it: what we experience is not merely teaching about the past but a fresh moment of decision with its opportunity of a new relation to God and, consequently, new life in the present.

QUESTIONS FOR DISCUSSION

1. What considerations must be included in the attempt to explain what is meant by "Jesus died for our sins"?

2. What evidence is there that Jesus did not regard his death as the triumph of wickedness?

3. Why is Christian redemption not to be regarded as an escape from life's problems?

OTHER SOURCES

Anderson, Bernhard W., *Rediscovering the Bible*. New York: Association Press, 1951, chap. 8.

DeWolf, L. Harold, *A Theology of the Living Church*. New York: Harper & Brothers, 1953, chap. 31.

Filson, Floyd V., *Jesus Christ the Risen Lord*. New York: Abingdon Press, 1956, chap. 6.

Finegan, Jack, *Beginnings in Theology*. New York: Association Press, 1956, chap. 15.

———, *Rediscovering Jesus*. New York: Association Press, 1952, chap. 17.

Hamilton, William, *The Christian Man*. Philadelphia: The Westminster Press, 1956, chap. 3.

Harkness, Georgia, *Understanding the Christian Faith*. New York: Abingdon-Cokesbury Press, 1947, chap. 5.

Houf, Horace T., *What Religion Is and Does*, rev. ed. New York: Harper & Brothers, 1945, pp. 303–11.

Lyman, Mary Ely, *Jesus*. New York: Asociation Press, 1937, chaps. 3, 4.

Miller, Alexander, *The Renewal of Man*. Garden City, N. Y.: Doubleday & Company, Inc., 1955, chap. 3.

Rall, Harris Franklin, *A Faith for Today*. New York: Abingdon Press, 1936, chap. 13.

———, *Religion as Salvation*. New York: Abingdon-Cokesbury Press, 1953, chap. 10.

Spurrier, William A., *Guide to the Christian Faith*. New York: Charles Scribner's Sons, 1952, chap. 9.

Tilden, Elwyn E., Jr., *Toward Understanding Jesus*. Englewood Cliffs, N. J.: Prentice-Hall, Inc., 1956, chap. 23.

Whale, J. S., *Christian Doctrine*. New York: The Macmillan Company, 1941, chap. 4.

Wickenden, Arthur C., *Youth Looks at Religion*. New York: Harper & Brothers, 1939, chap. 7.

Wolf, William J., *Man's Knowledge of God*. Garden City, N. Y.: Doubleday & Company, Inc., 1955, chap. 8.

17

the reality of redemption

The key to the human problem, in the Christian view, is sin, which is the violation of the relationship between God and man brought about by man's disobedience and idolatry. The problem is thus both falling away from God and substituting a false god for the true one. The opposite of sin is not so much objective goodness but faith—the relationship of trust. *Redemption* quite simply means that we are brought into the relationship of faith from the broken relationship of sin. But the change from sin to faith is not the simple thing that it appears to be on the surface. We cannot trust or commit ourselves to another merely by a process of will. We must first be convinced that the other is worthy of our trust, that it is safe for us to become so involved. And yet our existence in sin prevents this very thing because it has destroyed the relationship in which alone we can see that it is safe to rest our lives in God's hands.

Hence, if we were to reduce to its simplest terms the effect of Christ on us, we could say: Christ makes faith possible for us. What this means is that we change our whole perspective so that everything in life, everything in our experience takes on a different appearance because now it is seen in relation to God, in Whom alone we can find the meaning of life, a meaning that embodies our own best welfare even though it may run contrary to our current plans. We have already tried to see what is involved objectively—how it is that Christ can bring about such a change. Words have failed Christians just at this point. But the reality is undeniable: Christ does make faith possible.

This change from sin to faith is what Christians call *salvation*. For purposes of our discussion it may be well to divide this into steps, provided we realize that the firsthand experience does not necessarily move by steps. Traditionally these have been termed *awareness, repentance,* and *conversion,* or *the new life of faith.*

1. Awareness

Awareness is the ability to see things in their true light. It has two foci: ourselves and God, and the new insight is related to both. It is because we see God as He is that we can see ourselves as we are, and it is because we are willing to accept the truth about ourselves that we can see God for what He is. Instead of thinking that God is against us, we recognize that He is and always has been for us, and that what we have interpreted as our greatest threat has instead been our greatest potential blessing. Evil results of our sinful lives we may have regarded as the arbitrary punishment of a God who could not tolerate human independence. Now we are enabled to see them as a merciful warning of a way of life that could end only in utter self-destruction.

But we are also enabled to see ourselves as we are. The depth of the illusion that we are not at fault is hard to plumb. It is seen on a national basis in the facile assurance that every threat to peace stems from wicked warmongers who control other nations and never from our own national policies that we are certain are formulated according to strict justice. Consequently, much of our time is spent in parading our self-righteousness before others who, in turn, may look at us with the same view we hold toward them. Even when we do look at our nation's position with a critical eye, noting features that ought to be changed, we usually conclude that others must make the change, that interests contrary to right are bending government policy by their influence, that because the ideas and goals of our group are not finding expression, the welfare of our nation—in fact, of the whole cause of righteousness—is threatened. Analysis of national problems leads therefore to the conviction that the greed of labor is to blame, or the dominance of capital, or the overexpansion of government; but always it is some group other than our own. Even when we turn to consider the failure of the church to influence society as it ought, we think in terms of those who fail to respond according to our understanding of the Christian message, or those who do not take their faith as seriously as we think we do.

And in the same way our personal problems are all seen as arising from something others have done or are doing. We think it is because of others' decisions that opportunities are closed to us, or because of others' snobbishness that we are excluded from certain groups. Particularly, though, in religious matters we think it is because of other people that we cannot understand or, understanding it, cannot fulfill God's claim upon us. We are apt to blame the past instruction we have received ("my parents forced me to attend church as a youngster") or the complexity of the social scene in which we must live ("of course, if everyone were Christian it would be possible for me to obey Christ"). Through all this camouflage we now see things as they are, including our own responsibility and failure and even duplicity.

Part of this is due to our new understanding of the forces that led to Jesus' crucifixion. So long as we think of it as being caused by unusually wicked people making obviously wrong choices we can assure ourselves that this event has nothing really to do with us. But when we recognize from the gospel accounts that this stark tragedy occurred because people were acting on the same principles that guide our daily lives, we can be more honest with ourselves. We recognize that we are capable of just this sort of act; in fact, that in our own way we have done it. As far as we are concerned, the crucifixion is more than an historical event which can be dated sometime in the first century. Through the proclamation of the Gospel it becomes contemporary with us, making us search our motives just as it made Jesus' companions search theirs. There is a depth in this awareness that goes beyond the glib, "I ought to change my ways." It is rather the awareness that we have played fast and loose with eternal things: "Against Thee, Thee only, have I sinned, and done that which is evil in thy sight" (Ps. 51:4).

Older revival techniques separated awareness of God's love from awareness of human sinfulness and strove for a "conviction of sin." Since a person could be ignorant of the fact that he was doing wrong, emphasis was placed on the preaching of the law—what God expects of men. Only after he had been thoroughly convinced of his sinfulness could he then be offered the mercy and forgiveness of God found through the Gospel. It was felt that there was no use to speak of redemption unless people were first aware of the need for it. Perhaps this approach is correct—logically. Yet the awareness of that radical misorientation of life—sin—cannot come apart from the knowledge of God as He is. Sin is not the less terrible because it is thrown against a God of love rather than a forbidding deity. Sin in its true dimension can be seen only when, at the same time, we recognize God for what He is. So St. Paul could say that it is God's kindness which is really meant to lead men to repentance (Rom. 2:4).

2. Repentance

Repentance is our positive response to awareness. It is this new insight put into action. It has, therefore, both a backward and a forward reference. Its dimension of aspiration toward something positive separates it from mere regret or remorse. St. Paul distinguishes between a worldly and a godly grief for sin (2 Cor. 7:10). Worldly grief is simply the feeling of remorse and guilt. It is the painful consciousness that we are the sort of people who can do despicable things. Consequently it entails a feeling of shame and dirtiness. Such a sense of guilt can dominate our whole lives. Since it can do nothing to change the past, it is essentially destructive. By focusing our attention on what is hopelessly unchangeable, it incapacitates us. It therefore leads to death. Godly grief, on the other hand, does not merely mourn for the past, although this is involved. It resolves that what has happened in the past through sin shall not have only a negative effect on life, but shall be turned to a positive purpose. So it looks to God in faith for genuine meaning even in past sin.

Repentance is more profound than the superficial idea that at any time we can turn a new leaf, utterly forsaking the past and so be completely separated from all that has gone before. Repentance is not the same as a series of New Year's resolutions. It involves not merely what we have done, but what we are as well. And it recognizes that our past is nevertheless a part of us and shall always continue to be so, only that in relation to God through faith it can have a new and positive meaning.

For this reason the Christian life is more than balancing "good" deeds against "bad" ones. It is not so much specific deeds of life that are the problem, but the principle giving rise to them. Even relatively good deeds can be improperly motivated. Moreover, good deeds in themselves have no power to remove guilt or to alter the past and its inevitable outcome in the present. Repentance goes much deeper than the distinction between good and bad deeds.

It is only because of faith that we can look at the past and not be overwhelmed by it. Repentance, in other words, can never be stimulated merely by fear or regret. It must originate in a new understanding of God and a new relationship to Him. For this reason an individual who is dissatisfied with his past, not merely in the sense that it makes his present inconvenient, but in the sense that he truly detests it, may be close to what the Christian calls redemption even though he may not so interpret his experience. Dissatisfaction with ourselves that is in any sense significant can come only because of an awareness, however fleeting, of a possible new and higher quality of life. The Christian experience of redemption is not totally foreign to ordinary human experience. Sometimes an individual who is unable to understand or appreciate the Christian Gospel needs first to follow up these threads of his own experience to see where they lead.

The term *conversion* is used to apply to the change of life principle from sin to faith. It has, however, an ambiguous meaning. It refers to the change in a man as a result of repentance: a man repents, and he is converted. But so often people think of it in terms of the change from virtual godlessness to the full Christian life. Consequently, they are apt to wonder just how it applies to the person who has been raised in a Christian environment and for the most part accepts the standards of this environment for his own life. They think it may mean disowning the value of such training and background.

Each person must interpret his own experience; however, if we are going to use the term *conversion* as equivalent to *redemption,* in most cases it would not mean such a complete about-face that implies the past had nothing of Christian value. It does mean, though, that when the conscious choice presents itself for our decision—the choice of basing our lives on faith or on idolatry of some sort—we give our first loyalty to Christ. What before may have been implicit is now made conscious and explicit. Only when one is conscious of his faith can he examine it and weigh decisions by it. Neither repentance nor conversion means that Christian nurture is useless. Nor are they stimulated only by revival techniques. Repentance is involved whenever we decide that the foundation of our lives shall be God and His will, and if this is a new decision on our part, we are converted in the making and following up of it.

Is repentance a once-for-all matter? If we are thinking in terms of the major direction of life, it is perhaps a single event. This is not a matter for daily revision. In this sense, conversion and repentance are equivalents. But if we are thinking of the appropriate attitude toward God, knowing our many shortcomings—both willful and inadvertent—then repentance is the basic Christian approach to life, appropriate to every stage. Because of its element of aspiration it refers not only to the turning from gross sins as society is apt to define them, but to the continual recognition that in God alone can our lives be fulfilled.

Repentance, then, is action on the new basis of faith. Consequently, it is central to the Christian message. In the first chapter of his gospel, Mark, for example, writes, "Jesus came into Galilee, preaching the Gospel of God, and saying, 'The time is fulfilled, and the Kingdom of God is at hand; repent, and believe in the Gospel'" (1:14, 15). So also, following Peter's sermon on Pentecost when those who heard asked what they should do, the answer was, "Repent, and be baptized every one of you in the name of Jesus Christ for the forgiveness of your sins" (Acts 2:38). Repentance involves our committing ourselves to God in faith.

3. The life of faith

We have said that the three traditional "steps" of salvation are awareness, repentance, and conversion, but that *conversion* has ambiguous meanings. Sometimes it is applied to the specific change involved in repentance, and at other times it is used to refer to the whole re-ordering of life on the basis of faith. We shall speak of the "life of faith" as the rounding out, the completion of what the Christian means by salvation.

a. Forgiveness and justification. It is only as we recognize our utter dependence upon God that we can approach Him in faith, for on any other basis we come as bargainers who think we have something to exchange for God's love and forgiveness. Faith involves accepting God's forgiveness not as those who have come to merit it, but as those who cannot merit it, because it is impossible to make complete amends for the past.

We have already considered what it means to forgive—the willingness to absorb the hurt of a broken trust—and that forgiveness must be motivated by concern and love. But if forgiveness is to achieve its goal of the restoration of the personal relationship, it must be accepted by the one forgiven. The acceptance of forgiveness means a forthright recognition of the impossibility of ever making things right. All possible restitution must be made, but restitution cannot banish the original hurt, nor can it banish the guilt associated with it. In accepting forgiveness we admit this, and swallowing the pride of wanting to stand in debt to no one, we allow the other person to bear the hurt and enter into the new relationship that this opens to us.

Forgiveness, then, brings about a new situation which is itself creative. In his letter to the Colossians, St. Paul writes, "And you, who were dead in trespasses and the uncircumcision of your flesh, God made alive together with him [Christ], having forgiven us all our trespasses, having cancelled the bond which stood against us with its legal demands; this He set aside, nailing it to the cross" (Col. 2:13, 14). Forgiveness generates thankfulness in the person who accepts it, motivating him not so much to pay back the forgiver, but to live consistent with the new relationship now established. Forgiveness establishes a bond between people that probes the depths of their personalities: it is not merely the relationship of doing each other favors. To forgive and to be forgiven are alike hard because they are creative. Apart from this there is only shallow bargaining. Forgiveness demonstrates that relations between persons must be more than this—in fact, there must be a complete self-giving on both sides.

Forgiving and forgetting are sometimes confused. Forgetting stems only from indifference or poor memory. But one who truly forgives cannot remember the cause of estrangement as only estrangement, else he shows his forgiveness was not genuine. True forgiveness means that nothing is held against the person who is forgiven, but what has gone before is not forgotten: it is transformed. The unfaithfulness of a forgiven friend is remembered not as the source of bitterness, but as the provocation for establishing the relationship at a greater depth. Now it can be recalled not with shame and guilt but with gratitude. "I am the foremost of sinners; but I received mercy for this reason, that in me, as the foremost, Jesus Christ might display his perfect patience for an example to those who were to believe in him for eternal life" (1 Tim. 1:15b, 16). So Paul could remember his former life when he had persecuted the Church.

It is this acceptance of God's forgiveness on our part that traditionally has been called "justification by faith." The meaning of the phrase can be understood readily by considering what is involved when we try to justify ourselves for some past action. We give reasons or excuses to demonstrate that we were unblamable in doing what we did. Because of circumstances, or other people, or even human nature we had to do this, we say. In repentance, however, we recognize that we cannot bring adequate excuses to God, that our past alienation has been caused by attempting to do just this.

The dependence of faith on the recognition of this inadequacy explains why so often true faith is more apt to be generated in the person who is painfully aware of his inability to claim moral respectability rather than in the relatively righteous person. Jesus told the Pharisees that tax collectors and harlots, who at least were aware of their shortcomings, would enter the Kingdom of God before them (Matt. 21:31, 32). The same point is brought out in the parable of the Pharisee and the publican who prayed in the temple (Luke 18:9–14). True faith means that we approach God not because of our respectability, but because of what God is in Himself. Our trust is in God, not in what we are or can do. Here is the recognition that we do not justify ourselves but that God justifies us—that is, because of Who He is He accepts us as we are. All that we have to offer is our trust, our faith that Christ has made possible. Hence, we are justified by faith.

We need to make clear, however, that the forgiveness of which we speak is not one relevant only to the obvious sinner. It is not that publicans and harlots needed forgiveness while Pharisees did not. The Pharisees failed to recognize their need.

Nor does this mean that the only way to God is through dissipation and fast living. The decision of faith is open to anyone who recognizes his situation in relation to God and responds positively to it. The Apostle Paul is an example that a Pharisee could make this decision (Phil. 3:5) as well as a thief in the hour of his execution (Luke 23:39–43). Forgiveness is relevant, whether one is a bum or a clergyman, an illiterate savage or a university professor, a new convert to Christianity or an established church member.

Faith then is opposed to human pride. Pride asserts its own status before God. Faith admits that it has, and can acquire, no such status. But at times this teaching has been called immoral because in refusing to state requirements for the approach to God it is said to discourage moral earnestness. To the extent that one's concern with morality is only with its outward appearances, this may be so. But to the extent that one is concerned with what is fundamental to true morality—the right relation between a man and his God, apart from which nothing can be right—to this extent the objection misses its point. When a person regardless of his adherence to, or deviation from, conventional morality recognizes his true relation to God, then for the first time he is confronted with reality and is responding validly to it. It is from this position of humble dependence, of accepting forgiveness that the Christian life begins.

Two examples from scripture will illustrate this. The first is from the lips of Jesus himself: the well-known parable of the prodigal son, or rather of the two sons (Luke 15:11–32). It is when the boy who left home comes to himself—when he recognizes that he was not created to fulfill his life feeding swine and coveting the husks that they ate—that he returns to his father, not as an equal who will claim favors, but as a son who needs nothing else so much as the love and acceptance of the father. And the father in turn receives the boy as a son who has recognized his need. The boy has learned reality. He does not need further punishment in order to be taught. He can be restored to the fellowship of the family because now he honestly can accept that fellowship. And the elder brother of the parable, the son who stayed home to perform his duty, keeps himself outside that fellowship because he still is not willing to live in the proper relation to his father although his life may have been more acceptable morally.

The second example, drawn from St. Paul's Letter to the Romans, is expressed in the language of the courts and, consequently, may be more difficult to understand. Lying behind his thought is the procedure of a judge "justifying" one of the contestants in any litigation: that is, one man was declared to be in the right and the other in the wrong. The man declared to be right was said to be justified. In the closing portion of chapter 3 of the letter, St. Paul says that God has a new way of dealing with sin. He justifies men on the basis of their faith. When they turn to God in utter trust and commitment, then God treats them as, if they were righteous. He holds nothing more against them, but takes this as the foundation of a new life. Paul draws his primary example from the story of Abraham who simply trusted God's promise to him and for whom God reckoned that trust as true righteousness (Rom. 4:3; Gen. 15:6). It is Christ, according to Paul, who makes it possible for us to approach God in such trust.

b. Sanctification. But it is when we consider what follows on justification that the charge of immorality against such teaching is countered by a new and positive emphasis. The relationship to God in faith puts all of life on an entirely different basis. In other words, when we come to trust God, accepting our limitations and our responsibilities, we are free to develop life on a sound foundation, or rather, we are free to live guided by a new principle. The basis of our daily action is no longer a false meaning of life, but the true one. Such a radically new orientation is bound to have pervasive effects. So again in

Romans, St. Paul speaks of the continuing influence of Christ—
not just to reconcile us to God when we were enemies of His,
but to save us following that reconciliation (Rom. 5:10).

Our difficulty in understanding all that is involved in Christian salvation may lie partly in the terminology used. Many
people speak of themselves or others as "saved" following the
conversion experience. It implies some sort of permanent status
which one has acquired. Actually this expression is seldom
used in the New Testament. The usual reference is "we *are
being* saved" which implies a continuing process extending
throughout life. If conversion is understood as an event, it must
be regarded as a beginning, not an end. And this process of re-
ordering life on the new basis of faith is called *sanctification.*

Just what is involved in sanctification or "being saved" is the
subject of the subsequent chapters of Romans. In brief, negatively, it means "dying" to everything that has sin as its foundation; and, positively, it means living by faith as both motivation
and guidance. In fact, this new basis of life is so genuine that
New Testament people can explain it in no other way than
that God's Holy Spirit, or Jesus Christ himself, takes up abode
in the controlling center of individual personalities. "For the
love of Christ controls us, because we are convinced that one
has died for all, therefore all have died. And he died for all
that those who live might live no longer for themselves but for
him who for their sake died and was raised. . . . Therefore if
anyone is in Christ, he is a new creation, the old has passed
away, behold, the new has come" (2 Cor. 5:14, 15, 17). Or
again, "I have been crucified with Christ; it is no longer I who
live, but Christ who lives in me; and the life I now live in the
flesh I live by faith in the Son of God, who loved me and gave
himself for me" (Gal. 2:20).

The new foundation of life releases a new power in living.
What before was impossible because of the control of sin now
becomes truly possible. The reformation that the law could not

accomplish is effected by God (Rom. 8:2). The book of Acts represents Jesus' last promise as the assurance of power (1:8), and throughout the New Testament there is ample testimony to its reality: "But to all who received him, who believed in his name, he gave power to become children of God" (John 1:12); "I can do all things in him who strengthens me" (Phil. 4:13). The Letter to the Hebrews enumerates many of the heroes of old Israel, explaining the source of their strength: ". . . who through faith conquered kingdoms, enforced justice, received promises, stopped the mouths of lions, quenched raging fire, escaped the edge of the sword, won strength out of weakness, became mighty in war, put foreign armies to flight"; and continues that God had foreseen something even better for us (Heb. 11:33, 34, 40).

But the change from the old basis of sin (defiance of God) to faith (trust in God) is indicated not so much by a white and black distinction but by a growing and maturing obedience to the new principle. "If the Spirit of Him who raised Christ Jesus from the dead dwells in you, He who raised Christ Jesus from the dead will give life to your mortal bodies also through His Spirit which dwells in you" (Rom. 8:11). The idea has a similarity in the situation a naturalized citizen of this country faces. His allegiance to the government of his old homeland has been broken: it has no claim upon him. He is now a citizen in the fullest sense here. But his old customs and thought patterns and most obviously, perhaps, his native tongue will remain with him. Yet to the degree that he gives himself to the life of his new home, these older habits will give way to new ones. He will learn a new language and new customs. So with the man who changes the basis of his living from idolatry to genuine faith: old habits may continue by sheer inertia, yet as time goes on they will be replaced by new ones in keeping with life's new orientation.

The New Testament has various ways of stating this change.

We have already used the language of the synoptic gospels that speak of repentance, of a turning from former life to a new type of living. St. Paul, whose thought we have also considered, speaks metaphorically of men as being slaves, either to sin or to God (Rom. 6:17–19). He also speaks of the life in sin as death and that of faith as resurrection, comparing our experience here with the death and resurrection of Christ, a comparison made more vivid in the symbolism of immersion baptism (see Rom. 6:3–11).

Another expression of the same reality is found in the Letter to the Hebrews. We have, according to this author, the possibility of two different citizenships. We can be citizens of this world, completely at home in it, satisfied with what it has to offer. But Christ opens to us the possibility of citizenship in God's Kingdom. If we respond in faith and obedience we become citizens of this new order, but consequently we continue our life in this present world as aliens. This does not mean that our life is unhappy here. It does mean that we recognize that nothing here can permanently satisfy us. Abraham is the example of the man whose true citizenship belonged to heaven and who therefore could not be satisfied with even the earthly land of promise. "For people who speak thus make it clear that they are seeking a homeland. If they had been thinking of that land from which they had gone out, they would have had opportunity to return. But as it is, they desire a better country, that is, a heavenly one. Therefore God is not ashamed to be called their God, for he has prepared for them a city" (Heb. 11:14–16).

The Fourth Gospel uses the concept of a new birth. According to this thought we are all born into a physical, fleshly existence. In fact, we may live our whole lives on that plane. But through Christ there is opened to us a higher quality of life on the spiritual plane. When, in response to Christ's challenge we come to believe in him, we are born into this spiritual life that has its own purpose, its own motivation, and its own reward. "That which is born of the flesh is flesh, and that which is born of the Spirit is spirit" (John 3:6). We are all challenged, therefore, to be "born again," not into the old world of flesh, but into the new realm of the spirit. Apart from this new birth we cannot even see, much less understand, the Kingdom of God (3:3).

The newness of life organized on the basis of faith as against idolatry is crucial, but we must note in what this newness consists. It is not a severing of all connection with the past. That is, effects of sin, especially those of a physical sort, cannot suddenly be negated. A drunkard, for example, may be given a new "heart" but not a new liver. The conversion of a murderer will not restore the life of the person he has killed nor eliminate the complications that have followed on his act. And the conversion of the ordinary person will not remove entirely the patterns established in the past, the commitments that have been made, and the effects of them on his life. Conversion does change the meaning of these, however. Things which were purely negative now assume a positive significance because in them, as in all other aspects of life, God is trusted. At the very least they become instruments of discipline and learning in the new life of faith.

c. Christian love defined. If we ask what it is that characterizes this new life and if we look for something more definite than a greater attractiveness of those who respond to God in faith, the answer is love. Unfortunately, in English the word is so ambiguous that it has lost any specific Christian content that it might have had. The unique New Testament word is *agape* (ah-GAH-pay) which is to be distinguished from two other Greek words for love: *eros* and *philia. Eros* is the love that is generated in a person by the desirability of its object. Sexual attraction, for example, is of this nature, as our word *erotic* from the same root indicates. *Philia* is the mutual love between brothers or friends. *Agape,* however, is not generated by the desirability of its object, but by the nature of the subject who loves. God's love for us is *agape* in that He loves us not because we in our sinfulness are so attractive that He cannot help desiring us, but rather because it is His nature to love. In other words, He loves because of Who He is, not because of what we are. But in our relation to God in faith, we too are enabled to love with this Divine quality of love, for God's love is "shed abroad in our hearts" (Rom. 5:5). It is this new type of love that characterizes the Christian life. This is the outward indication of our redemption. "We know that we have passed out of death into life, because we love the brethren" (1 John 3:14).

Such love has two foci: first, love of God Who has made it possible; and second, love of our neighbor. Our love of God must be complete. Nothing can vie with it. It requires all our heart, soul, and mind. We love our neighbor, however, not the same way we love God, for this would be idolatry, but as we love ourselves (Matt. 22:37–39). Yet the love of neighbor is in no sense antithetical to our love of God, because love of God cannot exist apart from it (1 John 4:20). Our love of God is seen in our loving whomever God loves. It is only through such love that human community which sin has broken can be restored. Love, in other words, creates a new community, the Church (see Part Six).

Because Christian love has this origin and this nature, it extends to those who, humanly speaking, are unlovable. That is, this new type of love is under our control (or perhaps we should say, "under the control of Christ"). It is not merely our reaction to what we find already desirable: it is determined not by something external to us, but rather by what we have become through faith. Consequently, it can be extended even to those who do not appreciate and return it. Forgiveness has its origin in such love, for it alone can stimulate the person who has been wronged to set things right (Matt. 5:23–24).

It is extended to enemies, as well as to those whom society

usually passes by—the publicans and sinners whom Jesus sought out or the exasperatingly pagan people who made up the early church (Matt. 5:43–48; Rom. 12:20). But such love is not exhausted in a personal feeling of good will toward others. It must become a determiner of action. So we read, "But if anyone has the world's goods and sees his brother in need, yet closes his heart against him, how does God's love abide in him?" (1 John 3:17).

The real definition of *agape* is given only in Jesus Christ, in his words, but supremely in his life. The quotation he took from Isaiah for the theme of his ministry pointed toward it: "The Spirit of the Lord is upon me, because He has anointed me to preach good news to the poor. He has sent me to proclaim release to the captives and recovering of sight to the blind, to set at liberty those who are oppressed, to proclaim the acceptable year of the Lord" (Luke 4:18, 19). The meaning of love is further borne out by his teaching. In the Sermon on the Mount, for example, he stresses the return to the original purpose of the Old Testament law which can be fulfilled not just by refraining from murder, adultery, and false oaths, but only positively in respect for other people, in a genuine appreciation of the role of sex in life, in a devotion to truth that need not be established by appeal to some external guarantee of veracity. His emphasis on service is primary: "Whoever would be great among you must be your servant, and whoever would be first among you must be slave of all" (Mark 10:43, 44). His own ministry of service, seen in the compassion which prompted his healings, again qualifies the meaning of love.

But the supreme manifestation was seen in his redemptive death. "In this is love, not that we loved God but that He loved us and sent His Son to be the expiation for our sins" (1 John 4:10). "Greater love has no man than this, that a man lay down his life for his friends" (John 15:13). "Walk in love, as Christ loved us and gave himself up for us, a fragrant sacrifice and offering to God" (Eph. 5:2). "He saved others; he cannot save himself" (Mark 15:31). "Have this mind among yourselves, which you have in Christ Jesus, who, though he was in the form of God, did not count equality with God a thing to be grasped, but emptied himself, taking the form of a servant, being born in the likeness of men. And being found in human form he humbled himself and became obedient unto death, even death on a cross" (Phil. 2:5–8).

It is this self-giving of Jesus, then, that becomes the pattern and goal of all Christian love. It is from his life that St. Paul draws the qualities expressed in the incomparable thirteenth chapter of 1 Corinthians: patience, humility, joy in the right, endurance even beyond death. Moreover, the practical admonitions that are found in Paul's letters may be best understood as attempts to apply love as the final arbiter and determiner of action in the problems with which he was confronted. To those in the church at Corinth who boasted of their knowledge and who consequently were splitting the church into factions, Paul emphasized the service aspect of love, its primary concern for others: "knowledge puffs up, but love builds up" (1 Cor. 8:1). For those who were expressing their new freedom in ways destructive of the fellowship, he pointed to the love of Christ that enabled him to use his freedom through obedience, thus redeeming both Gentile and Jew (Rom. 15:8–9). To those who were so sure their position alone was right that they condemned every one else, he insisted that each lives to Christ and no longer to himself, the very essence of *agape* (Rom. 14:5–9).

d. The ethics of love. Instead of a new code of rules, then, to govern the life of faith, there is only the commandment to love (John 15:12), the definition and example of love in Jesus Christ, and the power to live by it given in the presence of the Holy Spirit. St. Paul can summarize Christian ethics in a sentence: "For you were called to freedom, brethren; only do not use your freedom as an opportunity for the flesh, but through love be servants of one another" (Gal. 5:13). This means that the emphasis of the Christian is not on stereotyped and routine behavior governed by rules. The emphasis is rather on the free expression of a new spirit, defined in Christ and applicable to the unique situations in which each person finds himself. Hence the question to be asked in each situation is "How can I express the love of God as Christ revealed it?" Paul does add two lists characterizing two different orderings of life: living by the flesh brings "immorality, impurity, licentiousness, idolatry, sorcery, enmity, strife, jealousy, anger, selfishness, dissension, party spirit, envy, drunkenness, carousing, and the like"; but living by the Spirit produces "love, joy, peace, patience, kindness, goodness, faithfulness, gentleness, self-control" (Gal. 5:19–23). The same thought is embodied in the Johannine writings as "He who says he abides in him [Christ] ought to walk in the same way in which he walked" (1 John 2:6).

What this means is that in the Christian life there is never a time when Christian love is not relevant, though the situation to which it must be related may be far from perfect. To attempt to express Christian love in absolute rules which do not correspond to a nonabsolute existence leads inevitably to despair. Some who take the commandment against killing as absolute, for example, find difficulty in seeking to relate it to a world of war and brutality without attempting in some way to escape the world. There are those, too, who reject the commandment because the world is not perfect, because they think such laws were meant only for a Utopian situation. The main line of Christianity, however, following the teaching of the New Testament, has always tried to apply love in the prevailing situation even though it was not an ideal one.

An example of this can be found in the Galatian letter. Love strives for perfection, and yet it has significance for the imperfect. "Brethren, if a man is overtaken in any trespass, you who are spiritual should restore him in a spirit of gentleness"

(Gal. 6:1). Love, in other words, creates a community of love; but if one does fail this community, love means reaching out to save him.

The popular book by Charles M. Sheldon, *In His Steps,* took for its principal character a man who always asked himself, "What would Jesus do in this case?" There are those who will say that Jesus would not find himself in some situations. It is hard to conceive of a situation where his way would not be relevant, however. War is certainly not his way, and yet even in a war in which we may feel helplessly embroiled, love can direct whatever choices we are able to make. We may be part and parcel of an economic system that is not patterned on love, yet within that system we can express our love and concern toward others. Of course there is the wider issue of whether war ought to be abolished and economic systems made more Christian. There can be little dispute at this point. The Christian must give himself to this activity as well. What we are stressing here is simply that love does not wait for a perfect situation to be put into practice. Whenever a choice presents itself to us for our decision, love suggests an answer which may not be perfect but which will be the best under the circumstances that prevail.

Jesus' famous parable of the Good Samaritan (Luke 10:29–37) is to this point. When the Samaritan found the wounded man on the roadside, the question at immediate hand was not one of changing the racial feeling between Jews and Samaritans, nor of ridding the country of thieves, nor of effecting a better distribution of national wealth so that people would not be tempted to rob others. The immediate question was what could be done for the man, and the Samaritan responded to it in love. Perhaps in a different situation—as a state counselor hearing reports of bandits harassing strangers, for example—he would have done something else.

When each man is responsible for his own way of expressing Christian love, there will be differences of opinion about what should be done in particular cases. This is often disturbing to people who tend to think in terms of absolutes—right against wrong. And church history abounds in cases where the will of the majority was forced on all dissenters. St. Paul, in dealing with this problem, reminds us of several important considerations. None of us is infallible, consequently, we cannot properly judge others, particularly in relation to our status before God. We do have responsibility for each other, and we must look not only to our own satisfaction but to the welfare of all. Finally, the community of love does not depend on absolute uniformity: we must not think that because another disagrees with us his own Christian commitment must be deficient (see Rom. 14).

e. The cross. But love dare not be identified with the negative resolve not to hurt anyone's feelings. It does not mean this in God's dealing with us. The love of God is not such amiability that would prevent evil results following sinful choices. God's love for us does not mean that we shall not be hurt if we live contrary to His will. There is a rigor of discipline about love. "God is treating you as sons; for what son is there whom his father does not discipline?" (Heb. 12:7).

In our relation with others, love can never be defined in the negative form: "Do not do to others what you do not want them to do to you." Love means treating another person as a child of God who can respond to God in faith even when he would rather not be so treated. And there is no illusion in the New Testament that love means the absence of conflict: "For we are not contending against flesh and blood, but against the principalities, against the powers, against the world rulers of this present darkness, against the spiritual hosts of wickedness in the heavenly places" (Eph. 6:12). Only love does not seek to destroy its enemies: it must win them.

The role of love in a world which obeys another law, however, means suffering or the way of the cross. Hence Jesus' words to his disciples, "If any man would come after me, let him deny himself and take up his cross and follow me. For whoever would save his life will lose it; and whoever loses his life for my sake and the Gospel's will save it" (Mark 8:34, 35). To those in our day who identify the Christian life of love with outward success and social adjustment, the New Testament's emphasis on suffering as a disciple can only be embarrassing. And it is an emphasis. "Do not wonder, brethren, that the world hates you" (1 John 3:13). "Therefore let us go forth to him [Jesus] outside the camp, bearing abuse for him. For here we have no lasting city, but we seek the city which is to come" (Heb. 13:13, 14). "For it has been granted to you that for the sake of Christ you should not only believe in him but also suffer for his sake" (Phil. 1:29). "You will be hated by all for my name's sake. . . . Do not think that I have come to bring peace on earth; I have not come to bring peace but a sword" (Matt. 10:22, 34). These passages are taken from scattered parts of the New Testament to illustrate how widespread a theme it is.

One whole book, 1 Peter, is given to the problem of the suffering of Christians. Not only is there the warfare of the two principles of flesh and spirit within the individual (2:11), but there is suffering caused by the misunderstanding and misrepresentation of non-Christians (2:20). When one suffers not because he has done wrong, but because he has done right, he can be sure he is participating in Christ's own experience (2:21), and the example of faithfulness and patience gives him a pattern for his own action. Moreover, the sufferings of Christ had a redemptive effect, "For you were straying like sheep, but have now returned to the Shepherd and Guardian of your souls" (2:25). Consequently, the Christian must remain faithful to Christ and be prepared to suffer when the principle of his loyalty conflicts, as it surely will, with the rest of the world (3:15, 4:1, 2).

The life of love is not enjoined with any foolish expectation that all will work out well, that others will immediately respond to love's overtures, and all will be peace and tranquility. The Christian life is not generated by any Utopian scheme, nor was it meant to create a Utopia, though this has sometimes been confused with its object, the Kingdom of God. The Christian life is a response in obedience and faith to God: it is living according to God's will as set forth in Jesus Christ. And it finds its vindication not in its success, judged by worldly standards in a world which does not wholly acknowledge Christ as Lord, but in the power of God and the redemption given in Christ.

Summary

Redemption is, in simple terms, the changing of life's orientation from sin to faith; *sin* being the determination of life's meaning and course by something other than God, and *faith* being the response in obedience and trust to God. The possibility of this change is somehow found in the life, death, and resurrection of Jesus Christ. Far from its being our accomplishment, to benefit from it we must acknowledge our impotence and receive the forgiveness of God which creates a new relationship and gives us new insight into ourselves, our relations with other people, and the problems which sin has left us.

The redeemed life is lived with Christ as its center of loyalty ("Jesus Christ is Lord") and is characterized by love in its full Christian sense, a love unmistakably defined by God in Christ. This love provides a guide for action relevant to every decision we make and a power to act accordingly. Although it means living by God's will, it also involves warfare with any other principle of life, a warfare that involves suffering both as discipline and as a badge of honor.

QUESTIONS FOR DISCUSSION

1. What is the principal difference between the Christian and the non-Christian life?
2. Often it is said that Christian love cannot be reduced to a code of rules because it is defined in a person. What does such a statement mean?
3. Read 1 Cor. 8 and 10. How does St. Paul deal with the question of eating meat that had been sacrificed to idols? From this discussion, what general principles can be derived for resolving conflicts of opinion on the application of love to a given situation?

OTHER SOURCES

Caird, G. B., "The Truth of the Gospel," *A Primer of Christianity*. London: Oxford University Press, 1950, Part III, chap. 9.

DeWolf, L. Harold, *A Theology of the Living Church*. New York: Harper & Brothers, 1953, chap. 34.

Finegan, Jack, *Rediscovering Jesus*. New York: Association Press, 1952, chap. 10.

Fosdick, Harry Emerson, *A Guide to Understanding the Bible*. New York: Harper & Brothers, 1938, chap. 5.

Gilkey, James Gordon, *A Faith to Affirm*. New York: The Macmillan Company, 1940, chaps. 3, 4.

Hamilton, William, *The Christian Man*. Philadelphia: The Westminster Press, 1956, chaps. 4–6, 11–13.

Harkness, Georgia, *Understanding the Christian Faith*. New York: Abingdon-Cokesbury Press, 1947, chap. 8.

Lewis, C. S., *Mere Christianity*, Book III. London: Geoffrey Bles, 1952.

——, *The Screwtape Letters*. London: Geoffrey Bles, 1942.

Marney, Carlyle, *Faith in Conflict*. New York: Abingdon Press, 1957, chap. 3.

Miller, Alexander, *The Renewal of Man*. Garden City, N. Y.: Doubleday & Company, Inc., 1955, chaps. 4, 5.

Pike, James A., *Doing the Truth*. Garden City, N. Y.: Doubleday & Company, Inc., 1955, chaps. 7, 8.

Rall, Harris Franklin, *A Faith for Today*. New York: Abingdon Press, 1936, chaps. 12, 14.

———, *Religion as Salvation*. New York: Abingdon-Cokesbury Press, 1953, chap. 11.

Spurrier, William A., *Guide to the Christian Faith*. New York: Charles Scribner's Sons, 1952, chap. 12.

Tilden, Elwyn E., Jr., *Toward Understanding Jesus*. Englewood Cliffs, N. J.: Prentice-Hall, Inc., 1956, chap. 17.

Wickenden, Arthur C., *Youth Looks at Religion*. New York: Harper & Brothers, 1939, chaps. 4, 9.

Wright, G. Ernest and Reginald H. Fuller, *The Book of the Acts of of God*. Garden City, N. Y.: Doubleday & Company, Inc., 1957, part iv, chap. 5.

18

eternal life

So long as the Christian life implies a battle, even
though it be conducted by the strategy of love, so long as the
cross is a reality of experience, it cannot be completely fulfilled
in this present world order. And if the Christian is to take hope
that what he has begun shall, in fact, be completed, he will

194

have to place his confidence in the power of God, which is superior to any earthly or diabolical force. There must be a dimension of life beyond that of time as we now experience it. Eternal life refers to life seen in this larger context.

In order to understand what is involved in this term, we must clear away misconceptions that have arisen through the years. One of the most persistent and perhaps pernicious is that eternal life is significant only because it relates to some possible existence of the human personality beyond death. The signs that query, "Where will you spend eternity?" reflect this view. Associated with it is the idea that every human individual has some inherently immortal element usually called the *soul* which survives physical death.

1. Origin of the belief

Professor John Baillie has written that it is easier to understand the Christian meaning of eternal life if we trace the actual development of the concept.[1] He distinguishes between two quite different ideas which people often confuse. The first is a belief in a nonphysical aspect of man that survives death, a belief which possibly had its origin in man's dream experience, in which something of the self separated from the body to live independently. What lived on beyond death was not the whole personality, however, but only the shadow of the self. No particular religious significance was attached to the idea: "It came, if I may be allowed for the sake of vividness so to express it, *not from the priests but from the psychologists*. It was in no sense a product of ethical idealism or of religious faith and aspiration, but was merely a corollary of the ordinary lay psychology of the time and place."[2]

Moreover, just because there was no religious coloring

[1] John Baillie, *And the Life Everlasting* (New York: Charles Scribner's Sons, 1933; London: Oxford University Press, 1934), p. xi. Used by permission.
[2] *Ibid.*, p. 91. The italics are Dr. Baillie's.

attached to the idea, instead of generating hope in a future existence, it produced a dread at the thought of an inevitable continuance, not of the full self but only of a shadow lacking what we regard as essential qualities of personality. The future life was looked on as the dreary existence in something like a vast grave. And the relative uniformity of outlook over the world is remarkable. Greeks thought of Hades and the Hebrews of Sheol, but the concept was essentially the same. Hindu thought translated the idea into reincarnation, but again this was not the basis for hope. It was rather regarded as a curse and a doom.

In our time, this line of thought is continued by those who seek to establish philosophically or scientifically the existence of the soul. Plato was perhaps the first to try by logical argument to demonstrate the survival of the soul after the death of the body. His concept of the soul, however, was enriched by the second concept to which we shall shortly turn. His thought, therefore, is interesting, but to us, today, inconclusive. For many years the idea seemed virtually impossible scientifically. The close dependence of a functioning mind on a healthy brain, the fact that brain surgery could radically alter personality—such evidence seemed to make the soul little more than a figment of pious imagination. Now, however, with the increasing recognition of the control of the mind over the body and the research into psychosomatic medicine, the idea is not quite so ridiculous. Some have thought to establish the existence of the soul through research into extrasensory perception and ghostly phenomena. We cannot argue here the evidence and the reasoning based on it. But we can point out that were it possible to demonstrate incontrovertibly the existence and indestructibility of the soul, this would not "prove" the truth of the Christian idea of eternal life. "The interest of religion is not primarily in the indestructibility of the finite but in the fellowship of the Infinite, and it is only so far as the latter is contained in the former that it is interested in the former at all." [3]

The second concept is not derived from reflection on some inevitable existence of the soul, but rather from a present experience of a different and higher quality of life. It came not by speculation as to what lay on the other side of death, but by the experience of a new sort of life in the present. Professor Baillie can thus say that this concept "is no mere development of the former but that there is between the two something like a clean 'break.'" [4] Although the concept is most fully developed in Christianity, there was evidence for it in the thought of Plato and in the experience of ecstasy cultivated by the mystery religions. In Hebrew tradition it is found in the close fellowship of the prophets with God. The Christian reasoning here is quite simple: "If the individual can commune with God, then he must matter to God; and if he matters to God, he must share God's eternity. For if God really rules, He cannot be conceived as scrapping what is precious in His sight." [5] A denial of eternal life, then, must be a denial either that our present religious experience is valid or that God is as He has revealed Himself in Christ.

It is interesting that this was also Jesus' argument when he was challenged by the Sadducees in regard to eternal life. They were traditionalists, refusing to accept any doctrine not taught in the books of the Law. Jesus said that eternal life was taught in the Law, because when He made Himself known to Moses, God said, "I am the God of Abraham, Isaac, and Jacob." If He is the God of these men who had died long since, then in some way they must continue to live (Mark 12:18–27). The point here is the nature of the relationship of personal fellowship

[3] *Ibid.*, pp. 112f.
[4] *Ibid.*, p. 119.
[5] *Ibid.*, p. 163.

established by God with men, not merely the technical matter of the verb tense.

The New Testament stresses that eternal life is a present reality. "He who believes in the Son has eternal life; he who does not obey the Son shall not see life, but the wrath of God rests upon him" (John 3:36). "He who hears my word and believes Him who sent me, has eternal life; he does not come into judgment, but has passed from death to life" (John 5:24). The same point is frequently made by St. Paul who speaks of death as death to sin and resurrection as being raised into a new life of faith: "If then you have been raised with Christ, seek the things that are above, where Christ is, seated at the right hand of God" (Col. 3:1). "We were buried therefore with him by baptism into death, so that as Christ was raised from the dead by the glory of the Father, we too might walk in newness of life" (Rom. 6:4).

It is only because of the present experience of fellowship with God with its promise of continuance that we are at all interested in an existence beyond death. Wherever the idea of life after death has appeared apart from this experience of a richer quality of life, it has been regarded as a curse—in short, hell. If today the existence of the soul could be proved, but not the reality of God's fellowship, for the Christian this would point to the reality of hell, which is essentially separation from God. Whatever else eternal life means, it means life in God's presence. It is this, and not the speculation of comfort and bliss that is its significant content.

2. Resurrection

The biblical term most frequently used to refer to our participation in eternal life is *resurrection* rather than *immortality of the soul*. The reason for this is partly the difference between Hebrew outlook and that of the Greeks. The Greeks tended to think of man as an immaterial soul which temporarily inhabited a physical body. The Hebrews thought of man as a unit with body, soul (animal life), and spirit (that aspect of man which enables him to commune with God) inseparably related. Apart from the body, the soul was not the complete man. Consequently, for them the survival of the spirit would not be the survival of the full personality, but only of a shadow of it.

In stressing resurrection, then, these people were asserting that the continuing life with God is not a shadowy, partial existence, but the full life of the person. Some people today feel no difficulty in thinking of a completely spiritual existence, and thus they are more drawn to the Greek concept. But many find it hard to conceive of a full life without some "body" by which the spirit can express itself. Utterly prosaic people, however, are apt to think of resurrection in strictly flesh and blood terms, and therein lies their difficulty. When St. Paul writes of this to his friends at Corinth, he assures them that God gives them glorified bodies that can suitably serve their life beyond death. Just as a grain of wheat perishes to produce a new plant, "so it is with the resurrection of the dead. What is sown is perishable, what is raised is imperishable. . . . It is sown a physical body, it is raised a spiritual body. . . . Flesh and blood cannot inherit the Kingdom of God, nor does the perishable inherit the imperishable" (1 Cor. 15:42, 44, 50).

Resurrection also means that the future life is not something man possesses merely as a man, but something that God bestows on him. It is not our inevitable lot. We are finite creatures. Resurrection depends on the will of God.

The idea of resurrection also went through a period of development. Most of the Old Testament expresses no view of a future life other than the existence of the shades in Sheol. In early days such concepts stimulated an interest in necromancy, as the account of Saul's consulting the soul of the dead Samuel in the hut of the witch of Endor demonstrates (1 Sam. 28:3–19). The prophets fought hard against such superstition: "And when they say to you, 'Consult the mediums and the wizards who chirp and mutter,' should not a people consult their God? Should they consult the dead on behalf of the living?" (Isa. 8:19). But the prophetic longing for the day when God's righteousness would be evident on earth projected hopes to the future generation that would be alive to enjoy the blessings when God's reign should be established. Yet it was seen that something more than a hope for posterity should be the reward of those who struggled and died to establish righteousness. And when this recognition was coupled with the depth of religious experience, the idea of resurrection was born. Those who knew God in life would be raised to join the generation living when the new age was inaugurated. In many places in the writings of the period approaching New Testament times only the resurrection of the just was anticipated, but at times the resurrection of the wicked was also contemplated for the sake of a final judgment.

In the time of Christ, the Pharisees accepted belief in resurrection. The Sadducees, however, denied the doctrine. Hence it was possible for St. Paul to throw into confusion the Jewish council composed of members of both groups by suggesting before that body that he was on trial because of his belief in the resurrection (Acts 23:7).

3. The Resurrection of Jesus

Now we must turn from belief in resurrection in general to the resurrection of Jesus. The New Testament never suggests that because of the general belief, Jesus' resurrection was expected. It is always the other way around. The general belief gained acceptance because of the personal experience of those associated with Jesus.

a. Its importance to the Gospel. In our day, belief in the resurrection is often held to be an optional matter since it seems so difficult to accept. But for the Christians of the New Testament, the resurrection was not subordinate to Jesus' teachings or to some other facet of doctrine. It was central. The disciples were those who were witnesses to the resurrection (Acts 1:21, 22). It was testimony to the resurrection that was the substance of the first Christian preaching. "This Jesus God raised up, and of that we all are witnesses" (Acts 2:32). "But you . . . killed the Author of life, whom God raised from the dead. To this we are witnesses" (Acts 3:14, 15). "They put him [Jesus] to death by hanging him on a tree; but God raised him on the third day and made him manifest; not to all the people but to us who were chosen by God as witnesses, who ate and drank with him after he rose from the dead" (Acts 10:39–41). Checking the references to resurrection in a good concordance of the Bible will show how central a theme it is.

In his correspondence with the Corinthians, St. Paul demonstrated the importance of the resurrection for Christian faith. After enumerating Jesus' resurrection appearances to himself and others, "most of whom are still alive" (1 Cor. 15:3–8), he writes, "If Christ has not been raised, your faith is futile and you are still in your sins. . . . If in this life we who are in Christ have only hope, we are of all men most to be pitied" (1 Cor. 15:17, 19; see also the marginal reading). "Why am I in peril every hour? . . . What do I gain if, humanly speaking, I fought with beasts at Ephesus? If the dead are not raised, 'Let us eat and drink, for tomorrow we die'" (1 Cor. 15:30, 32). In other words, it was the resurrection that gave birth to the Christian Church, and perhaps today, as someone has said, it is the Church which is the best evidence of it.

b. The disciples' experience. Some have sought to explain the resurrection appearances of Jesus in terms of the disciples' wishful thinking. The New Testament evidence, however, is not that the disciples believed so strongly in resurrection that they convinced themselves that Jesus had to be alive. Throughout the gospels they are pictured as failing to take Jesus seriously when he spoke of it (Mark 8:32, 9:32). When the women who found Jesus' tomb empty reported their experience to the disciples, the latter considered the story "an idle tale, and they did not believe them" (Luke 24:11). When Jesus walked with two disciples, they failed to recognize him (Luke 24:16). When he appeared to the full group, "they were startled and frightened, and supposed that they saw a spirit" (Luke 24:37). The Gospel of John says that Mary Magdalene first took Jesus for the gardener (John 20:15). Thomas refused to believe the universal testimony of his fellow disciples (John 20:25). Even in the familiar haunts of Galilee they did not recognize him (John 21:4). St. Paul does not mention the empty tomb, yet it is important, for had the authorities been able to produce Jesus' body, all the new and disturbing preaching would have been silenced in Jerusalem. And though it may have been possible for the disciples to fabricate a story and corroborate it with manufactured evidence, this would have been totally out of keeping with early Christian emphasis on candidness and honesty. Accepting the fact of the resurrection is not easy, but to reject it introduces even more serious difficulties.

Yet in saying all this we must recognize that Jesus' appearances were to his followers and Saul of Tarsus, and not to the public at large. The sort of objectivity that many people have in mind when they speak of the resurrection—an appearance so concrete that had, say, Herod or Pilate been in the upper room with the disciples, they should have seen Jesus as the disciples saw him—this is not a part of the scriptural record. It would have been of the nature of a "sign" to compel assent, the sort of sign that Jesus so definitely denounced (Mark 8:11, 12). The appearances were objective, however, in the sense that they were not produced by pious imagination. Yet only those of faith saw Jesus following his death.

We need to examine carefully what we say at this point. The faith of which we speak is not, first of all, a certainty that people live on in some recognizable form after death. This may be important, but it is not the most crucial issue. It rests on a faith even more fundamental. The faith is rather a trust in God, a trust which leaves the major issues of life in God's hands, confident that they will not be betrayed. Reports of the dead having come to life cannot in themselves establish such a faith. The real point at issue is Jesus' resurrection in relation to his understanding of his life and the God to whom he committed himself. This is what is at stake. The testimony of the disciples and of the Church is that those who have ventured so to trust God have seen ample evidence to justify their commitment.

This point is further borne out by the language of the New Testament. Seldom does it say that Jesus arose from the dead. Instead the phrasing is that God raised him. The reference, thus, is not so much to Christ's nature as to God's purpose. It is this larger purpose of God that is the real subject of Christian faith and teaching (see chaps. 6 and 11).

In other words, faith did not produce the phenomena involved in the resurrection of Christ. It enabled the disciples to see and interpret phenomena whose source was elsewhere. In this sense their faith was not so much like a projector that throws on a screen the images fed into it, but more like a microscope that enables one to see things invisible to his naked eye but which are nevertheless there to be seen.

What the resurrection of Christ shows for the Christian is not the details of a future existence, but rather that his trust in God is safe and true. And that very trust carries implicitly an eternal dimension because its object is God, Who is eternally true. We can have this quality of trust only in that God to Whom we do matter eternally. This is the faith reflected in 1 John 3:2: "Beloved, we are God's children now; it does not yet appear what we shall be, but we know that when he appears we shall be like him, for we shall see him as he is."

4.   The nature of eternal life

From this central faith inherently tied in with the disciples' experience of the risen Christ, we turn to a consideration of what the future life may be like, and we turn from solid agreement to varying views. Instead of trying to establish any one of these views as the correct one, let us rather seek to understand what is involved in each of them. These views gravitate around two themes: heaven and hell.

a. Heaven. Heaven, as we have mentioned, means life in the presence of God. It means the absence of earthly frustrations that have hampered the full expression of love. It means a greater certainty of faith than this life can afford. St. Thomas Aquinas could speak of it as the vision of God that on earth is possible only by a special Divine miracle. The theme, then, of heaven is fulfillment, completion, the reaching of a promised goal.

This theme, however, is pictured differently by different people. Whatever imagery may be used, we must understand, is not meant as literal description but as stimulation to our imagination. In this usage language becomes more like a work of art that is capable of creating an over-all impression, rather than a vehicle of scientific accuracy. Pictures found in the Revelation give us assurance of its basic meaning, but do not satisfy our curiosity about details: "There shall no more be anything accursed, but the throne of God and of the Lamb shall be in it, and his servants shall worship Him; they shall see His face, and His name shall be on their foreheads. And night shall be no more; they need no light of lamp or sun, for the Lord God will be their light, and they shall reign for ever and ever" (Rev. 22:3–5). So also with the hackneyed images of harps, pearly gates, and golden streets. The theme of eternal rest so often applied to heaven had more meaning to those whose lives were unremitting weariness. For many of us, a

picture of continued personal growth and service is more in-
viting. Perfection need not be thought of as a static goal. It
can mean a maturity which is expressed in action. Christianity
has always permitted great freedom in framing such an idea.

One essential feature of heaven in Christian thought is the
preservation of individual personalities. We have discussed the
logic involved in this belief. Eastern concepts of "reabsorption"
into the one Ultimate Reality can never satisfy one whose
experience, however ethereal, remains his own, even when it
includes the Divine fellowship. It is not an impersonal "spirit
of goodness" that we love in our friends, but those friends themselves. Nor can the idea of immortality only within the memory
of the living be satisfactory. When the memory is lost something of priceless value is gone. We may cherish memories, but
a memory and a person are two different things. While many
think that the concept of personal immortality is the height of
human egoism, the Christian feels that no other theory can
adequately account for our experience of fellowship with God.
Jesus indicated what we all must surely admit, that the life fulfilled in heaven will not have the same limitations and relationships as life on earth, but that to be overly concerned about it is
to doubt the power of God (Mark 12:24, 25).

b. Hell. The idea of hell, however, has been more difficult to
understand. Here again we have mentioned that it stands for
separation from God. Some of our difficulty with the concept
may originate in the fact that several biblical ideas are combined in our usual concept of hell. Most of these were current
thought in Jesus' day. He simply used them to express his own
ideas.

One of these was the concept of Sheol which was merely the
abode of the dead. At first no thought of punishment was attached to the idea, but in later Judaism it was regarded as the
realm where men lamented their condition with weeping and
gnashing of teeth. Jesus frequently used the word *Gehenna*

(see Matt. 23:33, marginal reading). Gehenna was originally the Jerusalem city dump where perpetual fires consumed the rubbish. Another term related to it is the "furnace of fire" (Matt. 13:42, 50). In Matt. 25:41 Jesus says that the eternal fire was not meant for sinners at all, but for the devil and his angels. Some have drawn from this term the idea that hell means endless fire. Jesus may have meant, instead, the final disposition and destruction of what has become worthless. At other times he spoke of "outer darkness" (Matt. 22:13, 25:30). Apparently this carried the idea of conscious separation from life's fulfillment, or the complete subjection to hopeless remorse. Still another idea is that of eternal punishment (Matt. 25:46). Punishment, Dr. Plummer says, is not necessarily to be identified with pain, much less unending pain.[6] It may mean eternal or irreparable loss.

Many in our day insist that each of us creates for himself a heaven or a hell as a state of mind in which he lives his earthly days. There is much to be said for this idea. But the traditional ideas of heaven and hell serve to indicate that eternal destinies are at stake in this life. Jesus taught that a man himself is responsible for his existence in hell. If one makes his decisions, constantly refusing to respond to the highest he knows, he is something less than a man as God created him. Perhaps hell can best be defined as the loss, the eternal loss, of the unique qualities that make us men.

5.   Are all men saved?

By now we should be able to see that when the Christian speaks of eternal life he is not thinking primarily in terms of its duration. Perhaps it is unfortunate that the word *eternal* is frequently translated "everlasting." Actually, it comes from the

---

[6] Alfred Plummer, *An Exegetical Commentary on the Gospel According to S. Matthew* (New York: Charles Scribner's Sons, 1909), p. 352.

same root word as *eon*. It means the life characteristic of the age to come, or the life of the Kingdom of God.

But it is when *eternal* is linked with the idea of everlasting torture that most trouble arises in people's minds. Punishment that has as its goal the reclamation of a person is understandable and desirable. But punishment as some sort of nonending vengeance is beyond our sympathy and comprehension. We could find it easier to understand hell if there were the possibility that those existing in it might repent, and we could understand the eternal love of God more easily if we could think that in whatever eons might lie ahead, God would be just as interested in man's redemption as He is to send Jesus Christ to earth.

Three principal views of the final disposition of mankind in eternity have been formulated: universalism, conditionalism, and eternal life and punishment.

a. Universalism. Universalism is the view that ultimately God's love will prevail and all men will inherit eternal life. This does not discount the importance of moral earnestness or the reality of life and death issues that demand our decision. It means, however, that God does not admit defeat of His love, that He will continue striving with men until all are won.

There are some scripture passages which give support to this view. "Then as one man's trespass led to condemnation for all men, so one man's act of righteousness leads to acquittal and life for all men" (Rom. 5:18). "For to this end we toil and strive, because we have our hope set on the living God, who is the Savior of all men, especially of those who believe" (1 Tim. 4:10).

b. Conditionalism. Others, holding that eternal life is definitely a positive quality which must be appropriated when the opportunity is presented to us, regard it as conditional—that those not responding simply cease to exist at death, and that only those who have found eternal life on earth will live on.

Many regard this as basically more kind than eternal and unremitting punishment, and still a serious enough result of sin.

And again biblical texts can be produced to support the view. "He who hears my word and believes Him who sent me, has eternal life; he does not come into judgment, but has passed from death to life" (John 5:24). "The dead in Christ will rise first; then we who are alive, who are left, shall be caught up together with them in the clouds to meet the Lord in the air" (1 Thes. 4:16, 17). The book of the Revelation, although it speaks of the resurrection of all for final judgment, also speaks of a "second death" for those not included in the "book of life" (Rev. 20:14, 15).

c. Eternal life and punishment. The view with which we are likely most familiar is the one that accepts the continuing existence of all men: the righteous in heaven and the wicked in hell. Those who hold this view regard it as the only one which can explain and support the crucial nature of our life on earth. The life we now lead is "for keeps," and eternal destinies are determined by it.

And again there is biblical evidence to support the view. At the conclusion of the parable of the last judgment Jesus says of those who have not served him, "They will go away into eternal punishment, but the righteous into eternal life" (Matt. 25:46). The same thought concludes the parable of the wheat and the weeds (Matt. 13:36–43). St. Paul speaks in similar terms in 2 Thes. 1:5–11.

Actually, all three views have something important to say, and perhaps all three are needed to express, however haltingly, the significance of the theme. The traditional view emphasizes the absolute importance of faith and obedience in this life, the fact that there may well come the time when the opportunity of decision is lost forever. (See Jesus' parable of the wise and foolish maidens, Matt. 25:1–13. Hell, incidentally, can be understood as the loss of free choice.) The conditional position again emphasizes the loss of a wasted humanity and takes account of the recognition that we cannot think of a realm of evil symbolized by hell as being in perpetual opposition to God. And the universalists emphasize the continuing love and mercy of God. It is hard to see how a God Who would give "His only begotten Son" should ever cease to care for men, even in their most blatant sin. And yet, surely even God cannot save against his will the man who will not be saved, at least so long as human freedom has any meaning.

Summary

Although the subject of eternal life taxes our reason and imagination, it is important to the Christian understanding of man. It asserts that the issues of life are not finally settled on earth and that one must look beyond physical existence if he is ever to understand the meaning of physical existence. It further asserts that the fullness of life is not a stage to which we all shall inevitably progress, but one which calls for our conscious choice, with entailed renunciations. And finally, it asserts that our fellowship with God, including all its ramifications in our relations with our fellow men, is the only enduring value because it is beyond the limitations of time.

QUESTIONS FOR DISCUSSION

1. Why is not the survival of the soul the primary concern of the Christian?
2. For what realities do heaven and hell stand? How might they be described in contemporary terms?
3. By what reasoning does the Christian support his belief in personal immortality?

OTHER SOURCES

Anderson, Bernhard W., *Rediscovering the Bible*. New York: Association Press, 1951, chap. 9.

Baillie, John, *And the Life Everlasting*. New York: Charles Scribner's Sons, 1933, chaps. 3–7.

Caird, G. B., "The Truth of the Gospel," *A Primer of Christianity*, London: Oxford University Press, 1950, Part III, chap. 8.

DeWolf, L. Harold, *A Theology of the Living Church*. New York: Harper & Brothers, 1953, chaps. 26, 27.

Finegan, Jack, *Beginnings in Theology*. New York: Association Press, 1956, chaps. 9, 16.

Fosdick, Harry Emerson, *A Guide to Understanding the Bible*. New York: Harper & Brothers, 1938, chap. 6.

Gilkey, James Gordon, *A Faith to Affirm*. New York: The Macmillan Company, 1940, chap. 9.

Harkness, Georgia, *Understanding the Christian Faith*. New York: Abingdon-Cokesbury Press, 1947, chap. 10.

Marney, Carlyle, *Faith in Conflict*. New York: Abingdon Press, 1957, chap. 4.

Pratt, James Bissett, *Can We Keep the Faith?* New Haven: Yale University Press, 1941, chap. 11.

Rall, Harris Franklin, *A Faith for Today*. New York: Abingdon Press, 1936, chap. 28.

——, *Religion as Salvation*. New York: Abingdon-Cokesbury Press, 1953, chap. 28.

Richardson, Alan, *Science, History, and Faith*. London: Oxford University Press, 1950, chap. 10.

Shinn, Roger Lincoln, *Life, Death, and Destiny*. Philadelphia: The Westminster Press, 1957, chaps. 1 to 3.

Spurrier, William A., *Guide to the Christian Faith*. New York: Charles Scribner's Sons, 1952, chaps. 8, 10.

Whale, J. S., *Christian Doctrine*. New York: The Macmillan Company, 1941, chap. 8.

Wickenden, Arthur C., *Youth Looks at Religion*. New York: Harper & Brothers, 1939, chap. 10.

{ five }

god and the world

19

CReation

We began our study with an attempt to understand the nature of religion and what is meant by God. Then we turned to Christianity specifically with its proclamation of the Gospel or good news of what God has done for man. We examined the implications of this for our understanding of God and men and the relationship of faith. We noted that this understanding of the human situation depends on the subjective experience of human life—that is, as seen from within.

Now we must turn to another aspect of the relationship of God to our experience, the objective aspect denoted in the expression, "God and the world." In using *world* as we are here, we mean more than our planet the earth. We mean more than the complete astronomical universe. We are referring to the objective content of our experience—our fellow men, the natural order, all that we include in physical existence. Whereas we have been considering God's relation to us as subjects, we now consider His relation to the objective aspects of our experience.

Yet even in such a consideration as this we do not move outside the context of faith. We do not suddenly dismiss our entire understanding of God that is found in our subjective experience. We seek rather to relate it to the world about us. The Christian affirmation is that there is but one God, and that the same God we meet in our own experience is the Creator of all that is.

1. The meaning of creation

The Christian understanding of this relation of God to the world is given in the term *creation*. The word is used at the very beginning of the Bible: "In the beginning God created the heavens and the earth . . ." (Gen. 1:1). What is it then that the doctrine of creation implies about the relation of God to the world?

In the first place it indicates that the world contains within itself no explanation or cause for its own existence. Whatever we find in the world is contingent. It ultimately depends upon something else. A tree, for example, cannot be accounted for in itself but depends on seed, atmosphere, and soil, and each of these factors in turn is contingent upon something else. The seed requires another tree to produce it, and the soil is derived from rock through erosion. And again, the rock and the erosive process are contingent upon other things. Nothing within the world as we find it is ultimate: it is all dependent upon something else.

In the second place, the doctrine of creation states that the world is ultimately dependent upon God and nothing else. This is what is meant by the mysterious phrase *ex nihilo* (from nothing). It does not mean that God took nothing as His raw material and from it fashioned the world. It does mean that the ultimate ground of the world's existence is found in God alone. This means that the world in the most important sense is unified: it has a rational structure and can be understood adequately only as one coherent system.

But in the third place, the doctrine states that God is not the world, but in important ways is over and against the world, or *transcendent* to it. This means, for one thing, that our search for the meaning of life cannot be completed within the natural order. It also means that the relation of God to the world is one of freedom and not necessity. Therefore, although the world expresses a rational order, that exact order cannot be derived merely from first principles by logical necessity (which, incidentally, was the goal of Greek science), but must be discovered empirically through observation and experimentation. God is not completely contained within the natural order. He stands outside of it so that it must conform to His will, and not He to it.

Finally, the doctrine of creation indicates that the world is basically good since its origin is in God and He has expressed Himself within it. The word used for this aspect of the relationship is immanence: God is *immanent* in the world insofar as it reflects His character and purpose. (Note the distinction between *immanent* and *imminent*, which means impending, or *eminent*, which means famous.) The biblical story of creation emphasizes this when God is seen surveying His work and pronouncing it good (Gen. 1:31). Within the world, then, we should expect to find evidences of the nature of God.

Although many people are likely to see in the term *creation* only another way of accounting for the origin of all things, a way that is directly opposed to scientific attempts to understand the beginning of the universe, its real meaning is more profound. *Creation,* as we are using it, is not a scientific term. The natural events attendant on the emergence of the physical universe are properly the study of science. What we are speaking of, however, is the present relation of God to the world, a relation that, of course, implies a certain understanding of natural origins, but a relation which is fundamentally a religious, rather than a scientific, concern.

2.   Creation compared with other concepts

We will find it easier to understand this meaning of creation if we compare it with other concepts of the relation of God to the world rather than with scientific theories of the origin of the natural order. Our religious concepts must be related to scientific data and theory (and we shall try to do just this presently), but not in the sense that only one of the two can be the "true" account of the same events. As we noted in chapter 3, religious questions and scientific questions are two different inquiries.

The first concept of the relation of God to the world that we shall consider as an alternative to creation is found in *pantheism.* Perhaps it is an oversimplification to say that the pantheist holds that everything is God, and yet this is the essential content of the concept. God, in other words, is in no sense other than this world. All of us, all the components of our environment are simply parts of God. The material and the process of nature are God.

Pantheism is typical of such religions as Hinduism, and it was important to several Greek intellectual systems. It has fatal inadequacies, however, in spite of the attraction of its meditative simplicity. For one thing, if everything is God, nothing is God. That is, if we say everything is God we are adding nothing to our understanding of the world or of God. Then, too, pantheism does not account for our clear recognition that nothing in this world is ultimate. Everything we see and know gives no accounting for its existence. This fault is often obscured in the naturalistic forms of pantheism which equate the "world-process" with God. But the "world-process" is no more self-explanatory than the various elements that constitute it. And finally, pantheism gives no accounting of our religious experience that we are more than "natural" creatures, that an absolute claim is laid upon us which both challenges and judges us.

The problems of the relation of God to the world involved in pantheism often lead people to assert its opposite, *deism*. Deism, which was never more popular than in the seventeenth and eighteenth centuries when the impact of a mechanistic world view was making itself felt in religious circles, holds that God was related to the world only at its inception, that natural laws have since carried it along totally divorced from any supernatural "interference." The picture most frequently given in illustration is that of the watchmaker who builds his machine, winds the spring, and then leaves it to tick out its life.

The attraction of deism probably depends on the atmosphere of natural law defined by natural science. Everything increasingly can be described in terms of definable laws, and while natural piety may revolt at complete atheism, God thought of in terms of a supernatural agency loses His relevance except as a possible initiator of the whole process. Much of our discussion of deism therefore will have to wait for our consideration of the cosmological argument for God—that all things demand a "first cause." But at this point we can note that the chief problem of deism is that it ignores the very question it seeks to answer—God's present relationship to the world. Seventeenth

and eighteenth century deists believed firmly in Divine righteousness. But this belief required for its support belief in a
future life in which earthly injustices would be rectified. But if
God has no relation to the world, there is absolutely no ground
for these beliefs, or for the experiences giving rise to them for
that matter. Deistic concepts, then, are inconsistent with themselves, and deism becomes impossible when these inconsistencies are recognized. A God unrelated to the world cannot be
a judge of human activities within the world.

A third concept of the relation of God to the world is found
in the various dualistic systems. We are not concerned primarily
here with the dualism of good and evil, although this eventually does become involved, but with that of material and mind
or spirit. All things, according to dualism, can be traced to two
ultimates: God and some more or less recalcitrant material with
which He worked. The view has been perennially attractive.
Plato gave it classic expression in his picture in the *Timaeus* of
the Demi-urge imposing form on formless matter over its resistance. It has some popularity today with uncritical minds
who radically divorce the world of material from the world of
spirit. The difficulty is that it leaves open to question what is
ultimately dependent on the material principle and what is
dependent upon God and how the two are related.

The concept of creation means that the world of our experience is essentially unified because it is dependent on one source.
This world is not ultimate and its meaning is not contained
within itself. It is the creation of God Who not only made it
but continually makes it. Consequently, it can never be understood apart from God.

QUESTIONS FOR DISCUSSION

1. Why is the concept of creation more than simply a theory about
   the origin of the earth?

2. What makes the concept of creation essentially contrary to the view that the world is basically evil?

OTHER SOURCES

Barth, Karl, *Dogmatics in Outline,* trans. G. T. Thompson. New York: Philosophical Library, 1949, chap. 8.

Burrows, Miller, *An Outline of Biblical Theology.* Philadelphia: The Westminster Press, 1946, chap. 5.

DeWolf, L. Harold, *A Theology of the Living Church.* New York: Harper & Brothers, 1953, chaps. 11–15.

Farmer, Herbert H., *God & Men.* New York: Abingdon-Cokesbury Press, 1947, chap. 5.

Finegan, Jack, *Beginnings in Theology.* New York: Association Press, 1956, chap. 5.

Lewis, C. S., *Mere Christianity.* London: Geoffrey Bles, 1952, Book II, chap. 1.

Mascall, E. L., *Christian Theology and Natural Science.* New York: The Ronald Press Company, 1956, chap. 4.

Pratt, James Bisset, *Can We Keep the Faith?* New Haven: Yale University Press, 1941, chap. 7.

Rall, Harris Franklin, *A Faith for Today.* New York: Abingdon Press, 1936, chap. 8.

Whale, J. S., *Christian Doctrine.* New York: The Macmillan Company, 1941, chap. 1.

20

the rationality of creation

Christianity conceives of the relation of God to the world in terms of creation. But is this only a religious concept that bears no reference to the world of our daily experience as it is described by science, or is it consistent with this world? It is important that we ask the question the way that we have in-

220

stead of the familiar but misleading way: "Can the existence of God be proved?" It makes clear to us that we do not know God only as an inference from our knowledge of the world. What we seek to do is to examine a relationship.

But the question has not always been discussed in this temper. Usually the line of thought has been to develop an argument so convincing that one could do nothing but accept the reality of God's existence. This has the tendency to make of God nothing more than an inference from our knowledge of the world. And the God Who confronts men through the Bible is not One Whose existence must first be established by some other more fundamental and reliable evidence.

So far as recorded thought goes, it was probably Plato who first produced "proofs" of God. His purpose was to answer those whose appearance was new to the religious scene—those who disbelieved in God not because of some moral perversion but for intellectual reasons. And Plato sought to establish even more cogent reasons for belief.

1. The cosmological argument for God

Plato's first argument was derived from a study of motion. According to the concept of motion current in his day (and one which continued to be held until the time of Galileo), a body would continue to move only so long as a force continued to act upon it. He could therefore distinguish between communicated motion—that is, motion given to a body by another agent—and self-caused motion, which was characteristic only of soul-possessed or living things. Tracing the course of motion and participating in the general Greek abhorrence of infinite series, Plato showed that ultimately all motion in this world is of the communicated sort derived from souls and the absolute beginning of it all must be a supreme soul which is God.

Present-day formulations of the cosmological argument for God are not drawn up in terms of kinetics, but usually in terms of the causal sequence studied by the sciences. Since science seeks to determine the cause of any event in terms of previous related events, this sequence is seen to lead back to the original or "first cause" of the whole series which is identified with God.

How valid is this argument so far as scientific thought is concerned? For centuries it was regarded as indisputable. But with the advent of a mechanistic concept of the world, the necessity for a beginning of all things began to be questioned. That is, if the world did not have a beginning but is itself eternal, there is no need to speculate about a first cause. Hence instead of submitting in belief to this argument, men queried further, "What caused the first cause?" And so long as the first cause was thought of as being essentially of the same order as the succeeding causes, the question was perfectly valid even though it was disconcerting.

More recently, however, the idea that the world is timeless has met serious challenge. Several lines of evidence seem definitely to date the universe, although the exact age can only be estimated within the period of one to ten billion years. The first of these is the known rate of disintegration of radio-active elements. That they exist at all shows that they must have had a beginning; and working from the rate of their disintegration as well as the proportion of their active amounts to the products of their decay, one can arrive at the length of time they have been in existence. A second line of evidence is developed from the fact that spiral nebulae apparently are moving away from our own part of the universe at an ever increasing rate. At some time in the past they must have been closer together, since the expansion cannot have gone on forever. Computations based on observation of the movement can establish, again approximately, when the whole process began. A third line of evidence is based on a statistical analysis of properties of stars found in star clusters. All three lines of evidence establish the age of the universe at approximately four billion years. Various speculative pictures of the "beginning" have been formulated by scientists to relate these facts, one of which, theorizing the condensation of a neutron gas cloud, has been developed by Dr. George Gamow in *The Creation of the Universe*.

This recent challenge to the idea of the timelessness of the universe on the part of scientists is not introduced to silence all discussion of the matter and thereby prove the Christian doctrine of creation, because other equally competent scientists give other explanations of the same phenomena. The thought is introduced, however, to point out that the concept of creation in terms of a beginning is not incompatible with the world of science.

But we may take another approach to the problem, not by asking whether the cosmological argument proves the existence of God, but rather by noting what it indicates about the relation of God to the world. The answer we receive from this approach is that it shows that what is spoken of as the "first cause" cannot be of the same order as the second, third, fourth, and subsequent causes in the chain of cause and effect. If it is of the same order, we are justified in asking, "What caused it?"

Hence the distinctively Christian formulation of the cosmological argument does not seek to demonstrate the necessity of a first cause but of an unconditioned ground of existence. The argument is from the contingency of the natural world. That is, nothing in this world can bring itself into being. It cannot give itself existence. Existence can be communicated but not originated. Yet something outside the world must continually bestow existence upon it. Hence there must be a genuine Creator. And this argument does not depend on a specific beginning of the world to be valid. It is in connection with these considerations that Dr. E. L. Mascall asks, "If we are *not* already convinced of God's perpetual activity, why is the first moment of the world's existence a sign of his activity *then?*" [1]

[1] E. L. Mascall, *Christian Theology and Natural Science* (New York: The

Some of the difficulty in recognizing this in the past has been due to thinking of creation as a process already within time. In fact, Newtonian physics posited an infinite extension of space and time. The universe was thought to be created in space and at a particular moment. Recent developments in physics, however, have demonstrated that space and time are both dimensions of relationship and have no "absolute" reality. In this sense time begins and space comes into being when the world is created. To think, therefore, of what came prior in time to the creation of the world is to confuse our concepts.

For the Christian, the Greek concept of a "prime mover" or a "first cause" is a misnomer, for the first cause used in this sense does not lie at the beginning of the causal sequence but underlies the whole process. It must be genuinely other than that process. This is one of the points in the doctrine of creation—that the world is dependent upon God but in no sense actually is God.

Another consequence which may not be so obvious follows from this argument. The very nature of Creator (falsely called "first cause") precludes its being discovered by the scientific study of natural cause. The scientific concept of cause is that of a related event of the same order as the one in question, in other words, one which is itself caused. A cause which underlies the whole basis of scientific work because it underlies the whole world is not an object of scientific study. When the scientist, working back to ever more fundamental aspects of nature, comes to a question mark which indicates the limits of his study within his present abilities, this question mark is by no means the Christian God. God is not to be identified with what is unknown scientifically; else as our scientific knowledge expands, God is found to recede and perhaps eventually to disappear.

Ronald Press Company, 1956; London: Longmans Green & Co., Limited), p. 148. Reprinted by permission.

It is because of this problem of terminology and concepts that we must think carefully about the relation of science to religion. To ask the religious question about the relation of God to the world is not the same as to ask the scientific question about the origin of the world. The scientific question cannot be answered with piety's simple affirmation "God," and the religious question cannot be answered with a scientific tracing of the chain of cause and effect. This is really what the cosmological argument indicates—that the ground of the world's existence cannot be a stage, even the first stage, within that existence. It points clearly to the transcendence of God.

2. The teleological argument

Plato's second line of argument was drawn from the field of astrophysics and was supposed to clinch the first. He noted that the movement of the heavenly bodies except for that of the planets (called *wanderers*) was not random but rather in a circular pattern. Since the circle symbolized perfection to the Greeks, the circular movements of the stars were thought necessarily to be governed by Divine purpose. The teleological argument is that the world as we know it is organized in a pattern that only an intelligent designer could have devised. The apparent ordering of the world by a purpose is seen as evidence of God who has formulated that purpose and carried it out.

In our time the emphasis has since been transferred from astronomy to biology. Instead of an explanation involving the movement of the heavenly bodies that seem to us so tightly controlled by clearly definable but impersonal natural laws, the evidence for Divine purpose has more easily been seen in the development of living organisms. A favorite example is the human eye, whose intricacy defies any explanation in terms of mere chance. In the retina alone, 137 million seeing elements must function together, and the total number of delicate adjustments—any one of which could prevent sight were it not correct—is almost beyond a tally. Only a supreme artificer, it is said, could have formed a structure so complicated as the human eye and so perfectly adapted for the function of sight. Of course many other examples of remarkable adaptation of a living organism to its environment could be given.

The teleological argument retained its convincing power until the mid-nineteenth century when Charles Darwin submitted his theory of natural selection, attempting to account for the same phenomena in a different and nontheistic way. The offspring of any organism, he suggested, vary slightly from the parent organism. Some of these are better able to cope with their environment than others and hence will outlive the others, producing offspring with their own superior characteristics. What we are likely to interpret as the work of some great purposer is really the result of natural selection operating through countless ages.

This reply to the teleological argument was for a time almost completely devastating, but second thought has restored much of its importance. For one thing, the course of evolution when seen as a whole has moved in a direction that evidences consistent progress. Its results have been cumulative. Second, purposiveness is definitely observable in the behavior of individual organisms: their parts do not act as they would separately but work collectively for the well-being of the whole. Finally, since it is no longer possible to assume an infinite age for the world, the entire evolutionary development must be crowded into the total period that life has been on this earth. The mathematics of probability of the concurrence of suitable variations runs into astronomical figures.[2] Often it is said that to account for the phenomena we have mentioned as the result of the conscious purpose of God is mere anthropomorphism—thinking of God

[2] For more complete treatment of these reasons see Arthur F. Smethurst, *Modern Science and Christian Beliefs* (New York: Abingdon Press, 1955; London: Nisbet and Co. Ltd.), pp. 118–29. Used by permission.

in human terms. But of course the concepts of mechanism and natural law are just as anthropomorphic as teleology.

Probably the most convincing presentation of the teleological argument does not depend on the single example approach that we have given, but on the whole range of our interrelated experience. Thus Professor Peter Bertocci enumerates seven links in what he terms the *wider teleological argument:*

> Link One: The Purposive Interrelation of Matter and Life.
> Link Two: The Relevance of Thought to Reality.
> Link Three: The Interrelation of Moral Effort and the Order of Nature.
> Link Four: The Interrelation between Value and Nature.
> Link Five: This World as Good for Man.
> Link Six: The Significance of Aesthetic Experience.
> Link Seven: Religious Experience as Confirmatory [of the whole].[3]

But so far as proof of God's existence is concerned, the teleological argument is inconclusive. It is perfectly proper to argue that a complicated piece of machinery implies a human mind that has designed it (because every piece of machinery that we have known in our past experience has had a human designer and fabricator), but we cannot argue except by analogy to a creator of the universe. We have known no other universes in relation to their creators from which we can generalize with any logical certainty.

Of course the argument from analogy does have cogency. But as Immanuel Kant pointed out long ago, the teleological argument for God implies the ontological (which we shall presently discuss): we must begin with some knowledge of God, so that we can relate the evidence of purpose to God to Whom such purpose is relevant and pertinent. Hence Professor Herbert H. Farmer at the outset of his Gifford Lectures remarks, "If the reasonings of natural theology [the attempt to present Chris-

---

[3] Peter Anthony Bertocci, *Introduction to the Philosophy of Religion* (Englewood Cliffs, N. J.: Prentice-Hall, Inc., 1951), pp. 331f. Reprinted by permission.

tian theism as the most reasonable world view] convince a man at all, they always draw some of their power to do so from the fact that something of natural religion or natural religio-theism is concomitantly active in his mind." [4]

To recognize this is not to discredit utterly the teleological argument. Just as we had to ask to what the cosmological argument really pointed in the relation of God to the world, so we need to ask it in this case. And the answer is that it indicates the immanence of God. In other words, the world as we know it gives us some indication of the nature of its Creator. While the cosmological argument points to God's transcendence—His being "other than the world"—the teleological points to God's making Himself known within the world.

We have noted, however, that both arguments are in themselves inconclusive. Working *merely* from them, one would not, necessarily, be led to a belief in God. And yet through the ages people have found them convincing. Thus Professor Farmer continues:

We conclude, then, that the degree in which a reasoned case for theism carries conviction (coercive logical demonstration not being possible) depends on the degree in which there is already present in the mind a disposition towards theistic belief; or, in other words, natural theology can only make progress towards its desired haven when it allows its sails to be filled in part by the wind of natural religion. It does not, however, follow from this that the presentation of such a reasoned case is of little importance. On the contrary, it is of great importance, in three ways at least.[5]

And he lists these as enabling us to grasp the unity of the world, disciplining and developing the content of our theistic belief, and calling forth the religious response on a deeper level.[6]

[4] Herbert H. Farmer, *Revelation and Religion* (London: Nisbet and Co., Ltd., 1954), p. 9. Reprinted by permission.
[5] *Ibid.*, p. 13.
[6] *Ibid.*, pp. 13–15.

3. The ontological argument

It has been the investigation of what Professor Farmer calls the "wind of natural religion" that has led to the formulation of the ontological argument for God. In brief it is that the concept of God is prior to our thought about Him, that we have direct knowledge of God which we may seek to clarify through the process of reasoning.

Like the other arguments, this one has a venerable history reaching back into the Greek period to the Stoics. Equating reason with the nature of all things and thus ultimately with God, they argued that since man already possesses reason, he need not investigate the outside world to find God but, rather, needs to turn to the introspection of his own mind. We know God in much the same way that we recognize axiomatic truth. If one does not believe, for example, that quantities equal to the same quantity are always equal to each other, it would be impossible to prove it to him. Any number of particular cases bearing it out could be cited, but one cannot formulate a universal truth absolutely true from a number of particular cases. This proposition is simply "self-evident." And ultimately all our reasoning depends upon some such directly known truth for its validity.

The classical formulation of this line of thought into a specific argument was made by St. Anselm, Archbishop of Canterbury in the eleventh century. Anselm was asked by his monks to give them an argument for God that would be conclusive in itself—that is, would require no external evidence. He began by saying that what we mean by God is the perfect being. Since an existent being is more nearly perfect than only an imaginary one, God cannot be thought of as not existing. In this bald form the argument may seem quite specious. But if a person objects by saying that he can conceive of such a God as not existing, the answer is that he is simply not talking about the same God. The true God, in other words, cannot be thought of as nonexistent.

How can we distinguish between this argument applied to God on the one hand, and to, say, a purple unicorn on the other? Two things can be said here. First, while we can conceive of a purple unicorn, we can, without contradiction, conceive of it as a purely imaginary beast. We cannot, however, without contradicting ourselves conceive of the ground of existence as not existing. Second, the purple unicorn combines our experience of a horse or pony, a cone-shaped horn, and the color purple. Certain features of our concept of God may be similarly explained, but the idea of God underlying all these cannot be thus accounted for. We cannot, for example, reach the concept of infinity merely by totaling finite numbers, for infinity is a quantity so large that it is undiminished regardless how large a specific number is taken from it. Therefore, while part of our concept of God may involve projection of our earthly experience and dreams, the eternity and infinity of God cannot be thus explained.

But the real importance of Anselm's thought is not his argument which gives us at best only the bare existence of God, but rather his recognition that faith is prior to understanding. What he was looking for was not so much an argument to justify his belief, but one to clarify the inner logic of that belief. Unless one has the faith, he cannot hope to understand the faith, for he will not know what he is talking about. Hence, all the argument can do is show that we already believe in God because we engage ourselves in the process of clarification.

It is this line of thought that explains such credibility as the other arguments might have for us. Our attempts to demonstrate God's existence do not begin with our experience of the world and so wind their way toward God. Plato was in no sense surprised by new information when he completed his two lines of reasoning. They were rather begun with the end clearly in sight. We do not attempt to prove totally unknown things. We argue only about things that somehow have found a place in our experience. We may thus argue about certain qualities of God attributed to Him by various religious groups, but to deny God utterly requires a prior affirmation.

If the ontological argument, then, cannot establish the existence of God in the full Christian sense, what is its value? Here again we need to take the same approach that we have to the other arguments and ask what it actually indicates about the relation of God to the world. The answer is that it points to the dual relation of immanence and transcendence, for God could not be known to us at all were He not in some degree immanent; and on the other hand, the fact that our thought about Him is so elusive, that it gives us only a bare "that He is" and not a complete "Who He is," indicates His transcendence.

Summary

We have been examining the relation of God to the world implied in the Christian doctrine of creation. This is a much wider subject than the mere beginning of the world, the sort of thing investigated by physics, paleontology, and astronomy, but it must bear relation to the knowledge obtained through these scientific disciplines. This relation is explored in the three classical arguments for the existence of God: (1) the cosmological, which points to God's transcendence, (2) the teleological, which points to His immanence, and (3) the ontological, which points to both as they are given in our knowledge of God prior to our attempt to understand Him. Although these do not "prove" God, they are important in helping us to clarify our thought of His relation to the world.

QUESTIONS FOR DISCUSSION

1. Why is it that the attempts to prove the existence of God are always less than absolutely convincing?

2. Of what value to Christian faith are the arguments for God's existence?

OTHER SOURCES

Baillie, John, *Our Knowledge of God*. London: Oxford University Press, 1939, chaps. 3, 5.

DeWolf, L. Harold, *A Theology of the Living Church*. New York: Harper & Brothers, 1953, chaps. 5, 6.

Farmer, Herbert H., *Towards Belief in God*. New York: The Macmillan Company, 1943, chaps. 2–11.

Harkness, Georgia, *Understanding the Christian Faith*. New York: Abingdon-Cokesbury Press, 1947, chap. 4, parts 1, 2.

Horton, Walter M., *God*. New York: Association Press, 1937, chap. 3.

Houf, Horace T., *What Religion Is and Does*, rev. ed. New York: Harper & Brothers, 1945, chap. 10.

Hutchison, John A., *Faith, Reason, and Existence*. New York: Oxford University Press, 1956, chap. 5.

Jenkins, Daniel, *Believing in God*. Philadelphia: The Westminster Press, 1956, chap. 2.

Mascall, E. L., *Christian Theology and Natural Science*. New York: The Ronald Press Company, 1956, chaps. 3, 8.

Rall, Harris Franklin, *Christianity*. New York: Charles Scribner's Sons, 1940, chap. 12.

Wolf, William J., *Man's Knowledge of God*. Garden City, N. Y.: Doubleday & Company, Inc., 1955, chap. 11.

21

the problem of evil

So far we have approached our study of God as the search for the meaning of our total experience, although we have noted that this search, unlike others, involves our being found as well as our finding. We have considered God's relation to us in the subjective aspects of our experience, and we have

233

sought to relate this to our objective experience of the world. For the Christian, this relation is defined in the concept of creation. But there are elements that refuse to be fitted into one over-all pattern of meaning for life—in fact, that are destructive of any attempt to establish meaning. If we are to be honest in clarifying the relation of God to the world, we must turn to consider the problem of evil.

1. The meaning of evil

In simple terms, the problem of evil involves aspects of our experience that do not make sense.

The problem of evil arises for the Christian out of the meeting of three beliefs: that God is good, that God is almighty, and that evil is real. We may avoid the dilemma of the Christian by denying any one of these propositions. But the curious fact is that, no matter which one we deny, evil ceases to be the grim reality we all know it to be.[1]

We must recognize this at the outset, lest we despair over our inability to understand what, by definition, defies meaning. The phenomena of evil are frequently divided into two categories, natural evil and human or moral evil.

a. Natural evil. As the name implies, natural evil originates in what can be called "the amoral character" of nature. One may consider this as nature's indifference to human dreams and achievements. A tornado strikes a community, for example, and buildings are destroyed, whether they are empty garages or inhabited houses. A flood indiscriminately ruins the property of a philanthropist, miser, good citizen, and recluse. An earthquake cracks and makes useless a costly dam intended to supply water for irrigating acres of wasteland that would have increased human food supplies. One aspect of natural evil, in other words, includes all that is destructive of human meaning and accomplishment.

[1] G. B. Caird, "The Truth of the Gospel," *A Primer of Christianity* (London: Oxford University Press, 1950), Part III, pp. 71f. Reprinted by permission.

Or one may consider as natural evil those aspects of nature which, though not directly related to human welfare, are contrary to all human values. Here are the "blind alleys" of evolution, such as the dinosaurs, which have perished completely. Or here are the various creatures that prey on each other, maintaining themselves only at the cost of other living things. This process may be justified when it is the lower form that is sacrificed for the higher; but when it goes in the opposite direction, it is sheer evil. Dr. Mascall, summarizing Sir Charles Sherrington's description of the life of the liver-fluke writes:

The liver-fluke starts life from the egg as a small pondworm which bores its way into the lung of a water-snail and turns into a bag which feeds on the snail's blood. There its cells become separate individuals, which bore their way out into the body of the snail and live upon it, skilfully preserving their food as long as possible by starting with the less vital parts. They breed in the body of the dying snail, and finally the young ones bore their way out and settle down in an encysted form among the green leaves at the edge of the pond. They are swallowed by a browsing sheep or ox, the cyst is dissolved in the animal's stomach, and the liver-flukes thus released swim from the stomach to the liver, where they suck the animal's blood and mature. The animal is then suffering from "sheep-rot." After three months the mature flukes produce eggs which pass down the animal's liver-duct and escape to the wet pasture; thence as free larvae they reach the pond and look for another water-snail. And then the whole story begins afresh.[2]

In other words, here is a picture of worm life being supported at the cost of higher creatures.

Still another facet of natural evil is the problem of pain, both animal and human. While we readily admit the necessity of pain for the maintenance of our life and safety, we can see no reason why it should continue after it has served its alerting function. If I have tight-fitting new shoes, I may be glad for the warning of pain before a serious blister or abrasion is produced. I am glad that pain makes me jerk my hand away from the hot toaster before my skin is burned. But pain continues long after its warning function has been fulfilled and in diseases

[2] E. L. Mascall, *Christian Theology and Natural Science*, pp. 296f

such as cancer, until its victim is released only by death. Many people are even more awed by pain suffered by animals who, unlike men, cannot use it as stimulation for programs of medical research.

This, then, is the picture of natural evil: those aspects of nature over which we have no real control and which are totally contrary to our view of the meaning of life found in relation to God its Creator.

b. Human evil. The other type of evil is that resulting from human choices. Its relation to natural evil may be more or less apparent. Destructive floods, for example, can often be traced to the exploitation of forests and fields by an earlier generation. Or it may seem to be confined within human affairs. War is perhaps the best example of this. Even though natural factors such as population pressure may help set the stage for war, actual hostilities depend on a highly organized human endeavor. But along with any possible worthy objectives (such as the attainment of freedom or the protection of a homeland) come hosts of evils—mass killing, wholesale destruction, and the personal and social problems that war leaves in its wake.

War is a good example, but perhaps it is overly dramatic. The man who, ignoring a highway stop sign, involves innocent parties along with himself in an auto accident is another example. Still another is the person who merely leaves the lid off his garbage can and thus plagues his whole neighborhood with flies. And with the current interest in psychological problems, one need only mention the complications involved with a domineering parent or a personally insecure leader.

We must note carefully, however, what the problem specifically is. The human origin of the problem may blind us to the problem itself, which is that effects arising from human choices extend beyond all intended bounds to affect people who are themselves in no way responsible for those choices. Members of a family can be injured because of the carelessness of a driver they have never known. Thousands of lives are blighted by a war which they in no sense instigated.

This, then, is the problem of evil—the blind, meaningless chaos that refuses to conform to the pattern we should expect if this is a world of God's creation.

2. Some attempted solutions to the problem

So long as man has pondered his experience, he has sought to wrestle with the problem of evil, precisely because it is contradictory to the balance of his experience. And this point may well be emphasized: The problem is with these evil aspects of life. Occasionally someone will surrender to skepticism or nihilism, but most people assume on good evidence that life as a whole makes sense. The pattern of meaning takes shape, and these things of which we now speak contradict it. The over-all impression is not that they prevent any formulation of meaning. But the attempt to impress a pattern of meaning on every fact of life without considering it fully gives rise to partial or fallacious answers to the problem of evil.

a. Evil defines the good by contrast. This answer is suggested by those who feel that good and evil are only relative judgments and consequently a contrast is needed in order to know either one. One's appreciation of love is increased if he has also known faithlessness. One's enjoyment of a good apple is augmented by his having eaten a rotten one. It has even been suggested that the saints' bliss in heaven could not be complete unless they could also be aware of the torture of the damned in hell!

Of course we may well question whether the good can be known only by contrast with evil. We do not have to eat good and rotten apples alternately in order to appreciate wholesome food. But aside from arguing this issue, the question at hand is whether every evil can be explained as a necessary contrast to good. A twinge of toothache may give me a momentary appreciation of sound teeth, but it surely is not good sense to say that a person must be helplessly crippled by disease in order to appreciate good health. And if we even concede that one person's suffering may increase the enjoyment of others who participate in it only vicariously, we have the additional question as to why the individual reaping the benefit does not also pay the price. This answer, containing some measure of truth, is not adequate.

b. Evil is instrumental to good. We all know that to achieve certain goals in life, we must also endure inconveniences. Few would hold that musical practice in itself is a good, but it is necessary to the development of adequate performing ability, which is good. New roads are certainly important to highway safety, yet their building entails awkward detours, the appropriation of choice farm land, as well as the hazards of the construction process. And in order to develop qualities of character —patience, courage, faithfulness—one must live through situations in which these can be expressed; hence, personal hardship is training for higher character values. So, it is said, all evil is simply the "inconvenience" necessary to the achievement of the best things in our own lives and in God's total purpose in creation.

But the trouble is that while this may well account for some things we regard as evil, it does not explain everything, especially when we are totally unaware of the good ends to be achieved by the evil we now experience. And it has nothing to say about the reality of present evil. Temporary inconveniences may be necessary to achieve certain ends, but this does not alter the fact that they are inconveniences. It simply goes against the grain of our experience to say that all evil is in some way instrumental to good.

c. Evil results from a short-range view. Another partial answer, closely related to this, is that we judge things as evil because we cannot see the whole picture of the world as God sees it. Things which to us are terrible, in the light of the ages become meaningful. It is only our limited viewpoint which prevents us from seeing all evil as really good. When the boll weevil moved into southern cotton fields, the destruction it wreaked was regarded as unmitigated evil. But when the farm situation improved because of diversified cropping which the weevil forced on the area, the insect was seen as something of a blessing. A statue was even erected to it! Disastrous floods have forced flood control measures benefiting communities far more than merely providing respite from destruction. The military exploits of Alexander the Great brought untold hardship, as all military campaigns do. Yet as a result a common language was spread over the known world of that age, making a degree of peace possible and enabling early Christian missionaries to be understood wherever they went. Seen from their total results, Alexander's conquests were a good thing, it is said.

Particularly in looking back over his life one is apt to recount how events that at first seemed pure liabilities have later been seen to contribute to good. Radical changes of plans dictated by accidents later appear to have been the wiser course. And sometimes severe personal calamity for the first time will arouse an individual to the reality and importance of the spiritual dimension of life.

The trouble with this proposed solution is two-fold. In the first place, it is an argument from ignorance. "If you could only see things in the long view" means little because none of us has that span of vision. If we did, we might possibly conclude that things are much worse than they seem, that what appears to be good in the present will ultimately be seen to be evil. To argue from ignorance leads nowhere. In the second place, this does not really deal with the fact of present evil. For human beings whose earthly life, at least, is not set in the dimension of ages but rather of decades, the "temporary inconvenience" is of major importance.

And yet, as with the other answers, there is here a modicum of truth. People maintain a relatively hopeful outlook over-all, because life does give that impression. But to recognize this is not the same as to say that everything we experience as evil is really not evil because we are unable to view it within an eternal perspective.

d. Evil is punishment for sin. Particularly in organized religious groups has this answer constantly recurred. Of course there is some truth in it. Sin does lead to evil results which are by no means confined to the inner life of the sinner. There are those who would account for all the chaos of nature, all the cruelty and frustration of life as the direct result of the sin of the first man. But this—though it may still be questionable—is far different from saying that all evil we experience today is punishment for our sin.

According to this view, the good man prospers and the evil man suffers. And when circumstances arise apparently contradicting this maxim, they are explained as indicating the hidden sin of people which otherwise would have gone undetected. Thus when tragedy strikes an acknowledged "good" family, their goodness is said to be only superficial and not genuine. The same outlook is expressed by people who ask, "What have I done to deserve this?" when trouble comes.

But the Bible, while admittedly giving this answer in various places, also refutes it. Job, for example, is the story of the blameless friend of God who suffered the loss of everything including his own health. His friends, however, insisted against his protests that he was really guilty of some secret sin, and when he in all honesty could not accept their exhortation for him to repent, they charged him with imaginary sins, so reluctant were they to surrender their answer to the problem of evil. In the lifetime of Jesus, when people asked whether a boy or his parents sinned, because the boy was born blind, Jesus answered that it was neither (John 9:3). So also he said that the workmen killed during the construction of a certain tower were in no sense worse sinners than the balance of the population (Luke 13:4).

In other words, while sin brings evil, all evil cannot be traced to the sin of the people affected by it. The answer, again, is only partial.

3. Attempts to include irrationality in meaning

Accordingly, then, since these have proved futile attempts to fit evil into a system of meaning that essentially denies its irrationality, other views have been proposed which would in some way include this element.

a. Evil is the work of demons. One of the most popular answers, by no means confined to Christianity, is that evil is due to the work of a whole host of perverted spiritual beings consciously trying to defeat God's purpose. The leader of the rebellion is usually some figure such as Satan; and although in the end God is seen to be victorious over him, during our life he is able to twist God's good creation to produce genuine evil. Elaborate demonologies have been conceived. The New Testament, reflecting the first-century cosmology, is full of such thought. The lower atmosphere was believed to be inhabited by disembodied spirits who sought to possess men and thereby wreak their havoc in disease, insanity, and social chaos.

But there is more to the idea than ancient superstition. Those currently attracted to it are generally overwhelmed by the seeming organization of evil, the fact that it is so diabolic. Not only are there storms which destroy people and their property, not only are there the possibilities for irresponsible actions, but there is also the most subtle perversion of the best things. Spiritual pride, for example, can infect the heart of the saint in his most lofty meditations. Human love can easily and all too unknowingly degenerate into vicious possessiveness. Hence many are drawn to the conclusion that this cannot be accidental but is rather the result of a conscious warfare between transcendent spiritual beings, God and the devil.

There are difficulties with such a view. One of the most obvious is that it is so hard to correlate with the scientific picture of the world, with the modern medical approach to disease. And yet at times even psychiatrists speak of mental illness almost in terms of "possession," reflecting the idea that "something" has seized control of a person to warp hopelessly his life responses. Another objection is that the concept of a devil in no way accounts for the problem. It recognizes an interrelatedness in the realm of evil, but it does not explain the origin of Satan or the origin of the temptation to pride that in the traditional view made the angels fall. It does, however, acknowledge the basic irrationality of evil to which St. Paul referred as the "mystery of iniquity" (2 Thes. 2:7).

b. *God is limited.* Another answer, out of the main course of tradition, but recently stressed by Professor Edgar Brightman of Boston University is that God is limited. He is good, but He is unable to make His good will always prevail.[3] On the surface this sounds much like Plato's concept of the Demi-urge, struggling to impress form on recalcitrant matter. But Professor Brightman insists that the limitation cannot be something outside of God, since everything has its origin in God alone, but rather something within God which He is seeking to overcome. For one thing, the whole rational order is seen as a limitation on God's work, which He did not create but to which He must conform. Even God cannot make a square circle or a round triangle, nor can He make unequals equal, or truth false, even to save human lives. Consequently, while God would freely will the end of all earthly evil, this cannot be destroyed without also destroying the possibility of good. Unfortunately, the limitation of God is such that the possibility of achieving the good means

[3] Edgar Sheffield Brightman, *A Philosophy of Religion* (Englewood Cliffs, N. J.: Prentice-Hall, Inc., 1940), pp. 336–40.

also the possibility of evil. God nevertheless struggles to over-come evil by forever creating new values.

Here again much is to be said for the idea. It is hard to think that a God Who could do something about suffering would re-fuse to do so if His power were truly unlimited. Yet again, this only lays the problem within God and does not solve it. It re-asserts the irrationality of evil, but only by putting that irra-tionality within God. Many would insist that the God they have known has not been subject to limitations other than those of His own choosing.

c. Evil is delusion. Still another answer, perhaps the ultimate so far as evil's irrationality is concerned, is that it is a delusion. Typically pantheistic religions that make everything God tend to view the material world as something less than real. It is only the inner spiritual consciousness which is real. Since evil is so integrally related to the material world, it is looked on as a delusion from which one can escape by concentrating on the inner life. In other words, this view goes beyond the idea that in the long run evil will be seen to be good. The problem here is human apprehension. We are deceived. Unless we train our-selves through certain spiritual disciplines, we do not see things as they are. This is a genuine human shortcoming, and so far as it affects our lives, it is evil. But there is no objective reality to evil as such. The irrationality is fundamentally unreality.

As we have noted, there is something to be said for the general outlook that recognizes a difference between things as they are and as they may appear to us with all our limitations. But this view gives us no answer to the present problem of evil, other than to assert against our experience that it does not mat-ter. Nor does it enable us to distinguish between delusion and reality: if evil is unreal, perhaps the idea that all is resolved in God is also unreal.

d. Evil originates in the will. It is misleading to speak of *the* Christian answer to the problem of evil, for two reasons. First,

Christians have never been unanimous in their philosophical analysis of life's problems. Second, Christianity gives us less of an answer to the problem than a way of dealing with it. Traditionally, however, Christians have held that evil cannot be attributed to God, nor can it be attributed finally to an independent spiritual being opposed to God. Essentially, evil is unreality, not because it is an illusion or because it does not matter, but because it means a falling away from God, Who alone is the source of reality.

For this reason St. Augustine, for example, located evil in the will (the wanting, desiring part of man) and refused to offer an explanation for its corruption other than the will itself. His reasoning is simple. Temptation has no influence on a pure man but only on one who to some degree already desires evil. Even the suggestion of the Serpent to Eve, in the Genesis story, that disobedience to God would mean becoming like Him would not have appealed to her had she not first considered the desirability of becoming like God. And even if evil is traced beyond mankind to the fall of angelic beings through pride, the same difficulty presents itself. We are confronted with an evil will that can be explained in no other terms precisely because a free choice is free when it is not determined by something else. The will is the locus of evil's fundamental irrationality.

But the nature of evil, St. Augustine insists, can be nothing positive in itself. It is a falling away from God. There is no "efficient cause" of evil but only a "deficient cause." [4] Any failure to adhere to God produces evil and corrupts the natural order that God created good, because created from nothing and therefore subject to change, it is perverted when directed away from God. Gold is never in itself evil, but man's greed and miserliness can make it produce evil. Sex, too, is good, but evil desires can pervert it.

[4] Augustine, *The City of God*, XII–7.

Does this give an adequate account of what we regard as evil in this world? Probably not, for if past human experience holds any lesson, there is no final answer. Christianity indicates how evil could have entered the world, but not why. The Genesis account represents man's sin as corrupting the whole natural order because it was created to be subject to man. While he still maintains dominion, it is won only at the price of pain and frustration. But science makes it difficult for us to conceive of the world with man at the center. Natural processes are seen to run their course whether or not men are even around to benefit or to suffer from them. And the idea that natural catastrophes are punishment for sin is hard to accept even though we take it, as the earlier Christian theologians did, as referring to a general, corporate human sinfulness and not the particular sin of the individual or community stricken.

Probably all that can be finally said is that while evil remains a mystery, we know enough to attribute it neither to God Who alone is good, nor to some power that exists independently of God. Ultimately evil means the perversion of what is basically good, perversion through its willful misdirection away from God for Whom all things exist.

4. The practical approach to evil

All of the positions we have so far considered have been attempts to bring evil into some total system of meaning, either by denying its irrationality, as in the partial answers we have looked at, or by attempting to incorporate such irrationality somehow in one's total world view. But there is another approach to the problem which is essentially practical rather than theoretical, and it is this which more nearly characterizes the Christian attitude toward it.

a. Conditions necessary for freedom. We have said that the uniquely human characteristic is the ability to make decisions which, along with our natural endowment, shape our destiny.

We are creatures who can obey God not merely mechanically like the rest of creation but of our own volition. But certain conditions must prevail to make freedom possible. What are they? First, there must be a dependable, stable environment in which, and to some extent against which, our choices can be made. Second, there must be sensitivity to this environment. Third, our choices must have genuine results brought about by them. Finally, there must be a real community of persons responsible to each other.

This is a picture of the world as it is. We find it stable and dependable. The natural movement of air currents normally brings the alternation of rain and sunshine, but under certain conditions it can produce a tornado. If such regularity were interrupted to prevent the tornado, the stability of the world on which we must rely would also be gone. Our choices could have no meaning if today a dropped brick fell to the ground but tomorrow it would be as likely to soar into the air. Decisions require a stable background.

And of course no person could depend on his environment unless he were sensitive to it, not just in a broad sense, but sensitive to the slightest differences. A man's sense of smell may be inferior to a dog's, and his sight not so keen as a bird's, but his combination of senses, along with his capacity to remember and to anticipate, gives him unsurpassed sensitivity. But sensitivity sufficiently stimulated means pain. To eliminate pain, one would have to eliminate sensitivity that enables us to respond as men.

If there is to be genuine freedom, the choices we make must have definite consequences. Decision would mean nothing if, regardless of what we decided, everything turned out just the same. When I regard another person as someone to be exploited for my own gain, my relation with him cannot be the same as if I consider him a friend who is worthy of my concern for his own sake. But this means that if a wrong decision is made, then its results must be endured—if right choices are to have any significance. One of the most important consequences linked with decision is the matter of human ignorance. We do not know everything and we do not learn what we need to know unless we decide to investigate. Learning is itself a choice for which the alternatives are knowledge and ignorance. But if learning is an achievement, and essentially a cumulative achievement of mankind, this means that at times we must act in ignorance with the attendant possibility of evil. Yet apart from this possibility decision and freedom could not be real.

The importance of community may not be so readily apparent, yet we know from sociological studies that to be a human being in the full sense means to live in community. The capacities for decision are developed only in some type of society. A child would not learn to speak and communicate apart from the fellowship of other people. Apart from human society we certainly could not learn the meaning of love, upon which some of our most significant decisions are based. Yet this very fact that, like it or not, we are bound to each other produces conditions under which the innocent can suffer. Not only in the complicated social orders of our civilization but in any simpler pattern of organization people are affected by each other's decisions. Yet this is simply the obverse side of the fact that humanity also means society.

These four things—the stability of the world, our high degree of sensitivity, the genuine consequences of human decisions, and the interrelatedness of all men—make possible the highest reaches of the human spirit in response to God and the world by providing the context for freedom, but at the same time they open the possibility of evil. We are humans because we can make decisions, but to decide involves the danger of real alternatives: not all ways are the same, nor do they have identical consequences. This is what is involved in the statement that although evil is in no sense good, it is good that there is the possibility of evil. Why this is so we cannot say. But that it is so, and that it is necessary to our development as men, we know quite well. Christianity thus begins where we are.

b. Eradication of evil. The Christian attitude toward evil is not to ignore it, or to deny it by attempting to force it into some total pattern of meaning, but rather to eradicate it. This approach is indicated in several ways in the Bible. In Genesis, for example, God is represented as giving man dominion over the earth for his welfare. This does not mean, of course, that man can exercise that dominion independently of God. But it does mean that when, say, natural disaster strikes, the reaction ought not to be to placate the storm gods, but to exert such measures of control as are feasible. The general attitude toward the natural world which characterizes our Western civilization has essentially this religious origin. It marks the difference between Greek science, which sought to understand nature through universal principles arrived at through reasoning processes alone, and modern science, which seeks to control as well as to understand nature. Apparently, then, part of the Christian answer to the problem of evil is the activity of men who are guided by their religious faith.

The mission of Jesus as it is presented by the gospel writers is the struggle with demonic forces and victory over them. Thus are people restored to sanity and health by the superior power of God (Luke 11:14–23), and the disciples are commissioned to this same work (Mark 6:7). For the Christian there is only one ultimate power who is at work to defeat evil, bringing suffering to an end. Because of this the human struggle against evil is given meaning.

Moreover, if, as St. Augustine says, the ultimate evil is the evil will, then the defeat of evil somehow rests on the redemption of man. And here is where Christianity centers the problem. Nature may be amoral, but men are given dominion over nature as part of God's over-all plan for good. Much more serious than the amorality of nature is man's perversion of his dominion when he directs it away from God. The cure for that can be only the remaking of men, and here again the attitude toward evil found in Christianity is apparent.

Evil is real, but not final. In the "end" it will be defeated by God. From Isaiah's picture of the latter days when war will be abolished and even wild animals will no longer prey upon each other (Isa. 11:6–9), to John's vision of the victory of the heavenly host over all evil including death (Rev. 21:1–4), men of biblical faith have taken heart in their struggle to achieve meaning in life.

c. *Endurance in faith.* But while eradication of evil is the long term answer, something still must be said for those who are called on to endure it in the present. The final answer to war, for example, is a radical change in human relationships, a change which Christians must seek to bring about, but something is needed for those who suffer its ravages without a practical hope for its elimination. Here Christianity says that the endurance in faith of evil that cannot be eradicated at the present time can itself become good.

It is difficult to express this idea without misrepresenting it. Certainly the endurance of evil is not a good for its own sake that would in any way compete with the good of eliminating evil. And yet anything that provides the context in which one can exercise faith can, in a sense, be called "good." To some extent, faith must always be exercised in spite of outward appearances: the declaration of the meaning of life comes in the face of denials of its meaning. But enduring evil with faith that God is supreme over it gives life a quality it otherwise could not have had. While the warfare against evil continues, those who endure it in the faith that even this apparent meaninglessness can be given meaning—they, themselves, become agents in the creation of meaning. So St. Paul can say that for those who love Him, God works in all things for good (Rom.

8:28), and he assures his readers that nothing can separate them from the love of God (Rom. 8:38, 39).

Summary

The question of the relation of God to the world is in large degree the question of the meaning of the world in our total experience. While so many aspects fit into the total pattern—the pattern implied in creation—some do not, and to these we give the name *evil*. Often people refuse to acknowledge its presence, denying those facts that are not consistent with their scheme of meaning. Still others respond by incorporating some measure of irrationality in their total world view.

To an extent, Christianity does the latter in its refusal to attribute evil to either God or some opposing spiritual power that, like God, is ultimate, and in its continuing recognition of the fact of evil. But, positively, it holds that evil is to be fought and eliminated because the ultimate power and reality are God's alone. To those, however, who are called to endure the struggle, it offers the transformation that faith can effect: evil endured in firm trust can actually become the avenue of good.

QUESTIONS FOR DISCUSSION

1. Why is evil a problem for the Christian particularly?
2. Why does the attempt to explain evil also explain it away?
3. How does Christianity retain evil's irrationality in relation to its conviction that the world is a rational order because God created it?

OTHER SOURCES

Bertocci, Peter Anthony, *Introduction to the Philosophy of Religion*. Englewood Cliffs, N. J.: Prentice-Hall, Inc., 1951, chaps. 16, 17.

Brightman, Edgar Sheffield, *A Philosophy of Religion*. Englewood Cliffs, N. J.: Prentice-Hall, Inc., 1940, chap. 8.

Caird, G. B., "The Truth of the Gospel," *A Primer of Christianity*, London: Oxford University Press, 1950, Part III, chap. 5.

DeWolf, L. Harold, A *Theology of the Living Church*. New York: Harper & Brothers, 1953, chaps. 17, 18.

Farmer, Herbert H., *Towards Belief in God*. New York: The Macmillan Company, 1943, chap. 13.

Finegan, Jack, *Beginnings in Theology*. New York: Association Press, 1956, chap. 8.

Fosdick, Harry Emerson, *A Guide to Understanding the Bible*. New York: Harper & Brothers, 1938, chap. 4.

Harkness, Georgia, *Understanding the Christian Faith*. New York: Abingdon-Cokesbury Press, 1947, chap. 4, part 3.

Jenkins, Daniel, *Believing in God*. Philadelphia: The Westminster Press, 1956, chap. 5.

Lewis, C. S., *The Problem of Pain*. London: Geoffrey Bles, 1940.

Mascall, E. L., *Christian Theology and Natural Science*. New York: The Ronald Press Company, 1956, chap. 8.

Rall, Harris Franklin, *Christianity*. New York: Charles Scribner's Sons, 1940, chap. 18.

——, *A Faith for Today*. New York: Abingdon Press, 1936, chap. 9.

Richardson, Alan, *Science, History, and Faith*. London: Oxford University Press, 1950, chap. 10, part 1.

the doctrine of the trinity

Christianity sought a statement that, in condensed form, would convey the reality of the Christian experience of God—both personally and in relation to the world. It settled on the doctrine of the Trinity. The statement that one God exists in three persons has often been dismissed as another product of theological speculation. Yet it contains in essence the unique insights of the Christian revelation. In order for us to understand the doctrine, it will be necessary for us to examine the experience giving rise to it and to define the terms in which it is traditionally expressed.

1. The experience behind the doctrine

The early Christians interpreted their experiences in terms of their own religious heritage, just as we all do. Even in the Gentile world where Greek culture prevailed, the inseparable relation of the Gospel to Judaism was evident. What was it that Judaism provided these Christians for their understanding of God? For one thing, they knew from their heritage that the whole natural order was God's creation. Moreover, He was related to them not merely as original source of their being but as Lord of both nature and history. He had led their ancestors out of Egypt, had guided Israel's destiny, had spoken through His prophets. And just as the tales of the heroes of the American revolution become in a real sense the common heritage of the most recent immigrant as well as the proudest descendant of a Mayflower family, so Gentile Christians regarded God's activity in Israel as their own history (see Eph. 2:19–22; 1 Cor. 10:1–13).

The development of the monotheistic belief in one God within Judaism was not philosophical. It was no search for the "unconditioned ground of being." The approach was moral. That is, while the question of the existence of other gods might remain open—even St. Paul (1 Cor. 8:5) can speak of gods many and lords many—there was no question that God alone was to be obeyed (Exo. 20:3; 34:14). It was from this approach, then, that the recognition came: "I am the Lord, and there is no other" (Isa. 45:6c; see also 43:10–12; 44:6–8; 44:24–45:8). God held all nations in His hand, making Himself known in judgment and redemption. He had entered into covenant with

Abraham, and He would fulfill His promise then made to bless the whole earth through Abraham's descendants.

It was with this understanding of God as Creator, Judge, and Redeemer that Christians interpreted the role of Jesus. If the gospels are at all accurate, Jesus interpreted his own mission in this context. He was sent from God, he came to fulfill God's will, his work was to do the will of Him Who sent him. In other words, Jesus' life and death and particularly his resurrection could not be accounted for merely in terms of human initiative. In this life God Himself was continuing His purpose begun centuries before—in fact, with creation itself.

In our day this inference is often denied. The issue, it is said, is not that of Divine initiative in human affairs, but merely that Jesus taught a new concept of God. But if Jesus is right in what he taught about God, then it follows that God Himself must somehow be active in the work and teaching of Jesus. To what man on earth would we give the title Father who waited for his children to "discover" him before reaching out to them in concern and fellowship? The issue therefore is not settled only by the thinking of the disciples but by Jesus' intention as well; and apart from thinking in terms of God's activity in Christ, our attempts to make sense of it all come to nothing.

But this was not all, for the experience did not end when Christ left his disciples. They had not just a fond memory of the richness of their past experience, but the continuing reality of his presence. And even beyond that, at their preaching the Gospel, the same thing happened to other people as had happened to them in Jesus' company. This they described not in inadequate and vague terms of inspiration, but in terms rather of God's giving and their receiving His own Holy Spirit.

To have the Spirit (note the definitive use of the capital letter) was to have the capacity to act as Christ did: to love with his quality of love, to obey God with his unflinching obedience, to be tied to their fellow Christians as the various interfunctioning parts of the human body—in short, to live "in Christ" or to be possessed of Christ. And all this was unexplainable in terms of their previous knowledge or capacities. Jesus' work on earth, related as always to God's eternal purpose, was continuing even though he was not physically present.

2. The development of the doctrine of the Trinity

Here, then, was the basis of what later became the doctrine of the Trinity—the knowledge of God as Creator and Lord of history, the knowledge of Christ as the fulfillment of God's purpose, and the experience of the Holy Spirit of God continuing the work of Christ. So long as the Gospel remained only on Jewish soil, the relation was taken for granted. Hebrew theology was much more concerned with the action of God than with speculation about His Being, and the simple terms of God and His Son or Servant the Christ sufficed. But when the Gospel moved into the wider world of the Jewish Diaspora, and when it claimed those who were trained in Greek philosophical thought, the expressions that had been adequate were now seen to be lacking. Particularly as the expounding of the Christian theme introduced ideas essentially alien to its central message did it become necessary to give firmer definition to what was meant.

For example, some spoke of Jesus' relation to God as that of an adopted son. Jesus' obedience was so perfect, it was said, that God claimed him for His Son. But this did not do justice to the certainty that the activity of God was more fundamental than a mere adapting to circumstances, that the obedience of Christ had a deeper meaning than mere human achievement. A further development, then, was what is called "logos Christology." *Logos* is the Greek word for "word," or "wisdom." It had been used in relation to Divine activity in both Jewish and Greek thought. In Jewish thought it referred to God seen in His activity: the world was created through His word, His purposes were carried out through His word. In Greek thought it meant the rational principle of all things that itself was Divine. The Christian experience of God's presence in Christ was accounted for as the incarnation of the *logos*, its appearing in human flesh. But this again raised questions about the relation of the *logos* to God. Was it subordinate to God, like the rest of the created order, or was it truly God Himself, and did it therefore have what we today would likely call a "personality"?

During the third and fourth centuries these questions were debated and discussed by the scholars of the Church. Their work culminated—not without serious disagreements and ruptures—in the formulation of the Nicene Creed by the first ecumenical council, with some alterations made by succeeding councils; and for practical purposes this creed came eventually to be definitive for the Church. It affirms belief in one God, maker of all things; in one Lord Jesus Christ, the only-begotten Son of God, of one substance with Him, incarnate for our salvation; and in the Holy Spirit who proceeds from the Father and the Son and is worshiped together with Them.

This terminology may be difficult to comprehend, yet it is simply the attempt to express in language the relation of the Christian certainties. In Jesus Christ we meet God Himself as He has made Himself known through His activity in history. Whereas before He was known partially, now He is seen in His fullness, because only a person can reveal the depth and mystery of what is fundamentally personal. In other words, Christians reject any hierarchical scheme of spiritual beings that was so typical of other religions of that day and which has not since lost its attractiveness although its expression may be more subtle. It was God—not some part of Him—Who had acted in Christ. And it was God giving Himself in His Holy Spirit, not some inferior emanation of Himself that could be exploited independently of Christ's Lordship. While there are subtleties in the doctrine of the Trinity that theologians would want to expound much more carefully, this outline of thought should suffice for our purpose.

The best known wording of the doctrine is the phrase made familiar through liturgy and hymn: one God in three persons. The victory of Jewish monotheism was complete. There was no question about a plurality of gods. But this one God makes Himself known to us in three ways. The word *person* as it is used in the doctrine did not originally mean a separate center of self-consciousness. *Persona* was the mask an actor wore in ancient dramatic productions. Hence we might think of "God in three persons" as God appearing in three forms: the Father, the eternal Son—God in history, incarnate in Jesus—and the Holy Spirit, so long as we remember that these forms are not successive, that God is known in all three at once, and that there is no fourth party—God—underlying the three manifestations.

Explanations of the Trinity in more popular terms generally take one of two lines. Sometimes the approach is called "modalistic," as when we think of the same person as being, say, a father, a son, and a professor at the same time. Sometimes it is social, as when we think of Tom, Dick, and Harry as separate individuals but each of them participating fully in a common humanity. This latter approach, however, runs the danger of lapsing into a belief in three gods (tritheism) instead of one God in three persons. Certainly this is so if we confuse our present idea of person with what is meant in the doctrine. So easy is this confusion that Dr. Karl Barth, one of the most famous of contemporary theologians, would have us abandon the term *person* because of its ambiguity.[1]

The doctrine of the Trinity, however, is not so much an explanation as a succinct statement of the Christian experience of

[1] Karl Barth, *Dogmatics in Outline*, trans. G. T. Thompson (New York: Philosophical Library, 1949, London: The Student Christian Movement Press, Ltd.), p. 42. Used by permission.

God. And it will no doubt remain central for the Church because it is the serious recognition of all that is involved in God's
making Himself known. It does not sacrifice relevance or comprehensiveness for superficial clarity and simplicity.

One more question, however, which we can take note of is
whether the doctrine of the Trinity has to do only with our
ways of experiencing God or whether it says something about
what God is in Himself. Our first reaction is probably to say
that we can speak only of our experience and not of what God
might be in Himself. But the question is whether our experience of God would be such as it is if there were not something "in God" corresponding to it. Could love, for example,
exist in human society or between men and God, could God
love us with *agape* love if love were not first in Him apart from
physical creation? Some theologians speak of the "social life" of
the Trinity, meaning by this something corresponding to the
fullness of life we experience only in fellowship with others.
Christians certainly do not think of God creating men because
He was lonely in Himself and needed companionship. It was
not out of His emptiness that He created, but out of His fullness. Hence the doctrine of the Trinity is not merely representative of our experience but reflective of some of the fullness of
God which must underlie our experience.

It is significant that the interest in the study of human personality had its origin in the attempt to explain the Christian
experience of God—that is, how in any sense God could be
three in one. There are not three personalities in God but one.
Recent theological thought has pointed out that our normative
concept of personality is not something we obtain from the
observation of ourselves or other people. In these cases we find
only imperfect personalities which we clearly recognize as imperfect because we have some knowledge of the standard of
perfection. "He who knows the poverty of his own personality
knows it only because there has first been revealed to him the

perfect personality of God." [2] Dr. Barth speaks the same way about our concept of fatherhood: it is found first in God Himself and then derivatively among men.

We might go on in a similar vein with the various "attributes" of God: His omnipotence, omnipresence, infinity, goodness, and love. But most of such discussion assumes a much more philosophical bent than our present need requires. Although Christianity is deep enough to contain any philosophical probings, the more normative Christian position is that these qualities are best found not in some abstract dialectic, but as God makes Himself known in history and supremely in Jesus Christ. Love, for example, is not so much defined as expressed in human redemption. Accordingly, this book omits a chapter on the nature of God, for the nature of God is discovered through the response of faith to the proclamation of the Gospel, and that we have been considering continually.

3. The doctrine of the Person of Christ

We have considered briefly the meaning of the doctrine of the Trinity, and we have noted that it grew out of the Christian experience of finding God's purpose fulfilled in Christ. But along with the attempt to clarify what this means for our understanding of God, we must consider what it means for our understanding of Christ. After the Church had decided, for all practical purposes, the doctrine of the Trinity, the question of the relation of God and man in Jesus Christ continued to be debated until it, too, was relatively settled in the deliberation of the Council of Chalcedon in 451. And that now brings us to a study of the doctrine of the Incarnation or of the Person of Christ.

The problem involved was not introduced by the theological activity of the first few centuries. It is so central to the essential

[2] John Baillie, *Our Knowledge of God* (London: Oxford University Press, 1939), p. 251. Reprinted by permission.

Christian proclamation that we can virtually say that the conviction that "God was in Christ" is the *sine qua non* of Christianity. Of it Dr. Barth writes: "The Church is not 'of the opinion,' it does not have 'views,' convictions, enthusiasms. It *believes* and *confesses*, that is, it speaks and acts on the basis of the message based on God Himself in Christ." [3] There simply is no period in Christian history that the conviction was not stated as the essence of faith. It is found throughout the New Testament. "In him all the fullness of God was pleased to dwell" (Col. 1:19). "In the beginning was the Word, and the Word was with God, and the Word was God. . . . And the Word became flesh and dwelt among us, full of grace and truth; we have beheld his glory, glory as of the only Son from the Father" (John 1:1, 14). "In many and various ways God spoke of old to our fathers by the prophets; but in these last days He has spoken to us by a Son, whom He appointed the heir of all things, through whom also He created the world" (Heb. 1:1, 2).

But the question we should like to have answered is what this means. Jesus, of course, was a man in the full sense of the word. He was born of a human mother, he hungered, thirsted, slept, enjoyed friends, made enemies. He died. What can it mean to say that in him, in some unique sense, God was incarnate?

Professor Donald Baillie rehearses some of the common misconceptions of what the Church is saying in the doctrine.[4] It does not mean that Jesus was a god instead of a man. This would be a denial of both his humanity and monotheism as well. Nor does it mean that Jesus was a being intermediary between God and man. It does not mean that God inhabited a human body for a number of years, that Jesus' body was human but his mind or spirit Divine. It does not mean that Jesus was

[3] Karl Barth, *Dogmatics in Outline*, p. 87.
[4] D. M. Baillie, *God Was in Christ* (New York: Charles Scribner's Sons, 1948; London: Faber & Faber Limited), pp. 80–82. Used by permission.

first a man and then became Divine. "In the world of the New Testament, even though it is written in Greek, the word God is a proper name, and no one could be Divine except God Himself." [5] Finally, it does not mean that God changed into a man.

The doctrine of the person of Christ states that Christ was at the same time fully God and fully man. He was not more God by being less man, or less Divine by being more human. His humanity was genuine and complete. The Fourth Gospel speaks of the Word becoming flesh, meaning all that is distinctively human, passions and appetites as well. Nevertheless we find God fully revealed in him. In Christ we have not merely an indication or sign of something else, but the real thing.

To misconceive this relationship leads to the various attempts to divide Christ's life into a human portion and a Divine portion. And it leads to hasty definitions of what actually constitutes Divinity. Some, for example, would insist that Jesus was Divine because he did extraordinary things. Their reasoning would go like this: what we mean by God is the supernatural, and the supernatural is seen in whatever happens without natural explanation and cause—in other words, miracles; Jesus worked miracles, therefore he must have had supernatural power, and therefore he must have been Divine. Others would base their conclusion on the Virgin Birth, insisting that this made Jesus different from all other men.

But the doctrine of the person of Christ is much more profound than any such attempt to separate aspects of Jesus' life, calling one group Divine and the other merely human. Jesus was not Divine in his ability to do miraculous things and only human in his capacity for friendship. The Incarnation does not mean that some additional quality of Divinity was "added to" Jesus' humanity, but rather that the Divinity was expressed through the humanity. While the miracles of Jesus did hold a teaching value for the disciples, they did not define his Divinity.

[5] *Ibid.*, p. 82.

It was his decision to obey God to the death, giving his life as a ransom for many, that made those followers see there was something Divine in all that he was.

To a degree, the relationship we are seeking to explore regarding God and man in Christ is akin to that of the relation of God and nature in any happening. We have spoken, for example, of the wind that parted the sea for the Israelites fleeing from Egypt, and we also said that to them this meant the intervention of God on their behalf. It is not that the Israelites thought that God took the place of the wind but rather that God was working His eternal purpose through this whole event. In a sense, too, the relationship is similar to that of our own Christian experience where our decisions and lives are our own, and yet we know that God is working in us and through us to produce a quality of life impossible to us otherwise. These two examples may give us a sort of key to the type of relationship involved between God and man in Christ.

With Christ we have a man making decisions as other men, living supremely by faith. And yet this life must also be seen in relation to God Who is active in history, Who works through men and human affairs as well as in nature. The child Jesus was born, but this was surely more than an accident of human intercourse, for we cannot understand this life unless God were present at its inception. So theology has spoken of the Virgin Birth. We need not argue the biology of this, either for or against it; we need to understand that the most important aspect of the doctrine is theological. What is at stake, really at stake, is not the how of physical conception (though this may be important in its own right) but its meaning. Christianity declares the supreme meaning is that here God enters human life, that the coming of Christ belongs to the eternal purpose of God.

So also we must look at the life of Jesus. His decisions were his. His loyalty and faithfulness were his. "If the life of our

Lord is to be conceived as a truly human life, subject to the hazards of all human life on earth, we must indeed say that the Incarnation of the Divine Word in Him was conditioned by His continual response. If it was a real Incarnation, not to be explained away in the docetic [6] manner, it depended in a sense upon His free human choice from moment to moment." [7] But again in these decisions God was at work. His life was not merely "of himself" but of God.

And so also we might look at his death. We can trace the tragic course of human events—the corruption of religious leaders, the jealousy of Roman power, the general fickleness of mobs. We can say that on such-and-such a day a certain man was executed. But this is not to explain the event. It could not satisfy the centurion in charge who had seen other men die. "This was a son of God," the gospels report him as saying, and Christians were clarifying that when they said that God did not spare His own Son but freely delivered him up for us all.

And in his life following his resurrection, Christians insist that the same relationship of God and man continues. It is not that Christ's manhood is now surrendered and he becomes God simply, but rather that his resurrected life is in its appropriate form a continuation of the Incarnation. This is what the teaching of the ascension of Christ means theologically. And this is why Christians regard the Incarnation as a once-for-all-time matter. Christ's final word at his crucifixion, according to the Fourth Gospel, was "It is finished" (John 19:30). Something took place here that like all events in history was unique and unrepeatable.

Other religions, particularly Hinduism, speak of incarnations, and some people like to think of all great religious leaders as incarnations of God. Such use of *incarnation* is decidedly differ-

[6] *Docetism* was the belief that Jesus' humanity was not real but only an appearance.
[7] D. M. Baillie, *God Was in Christ.* p. 149.

ent from the Christian use. To say that Buddha or Gandhi is an incarnation of God is perhaps to say something very fine about these men, but it is not to say anything very profound about God. The reaction to such statements may be acquiescence or perhaps questioning, but certainly not the probing, "What must I do to be saved?" precisely because it is not seen in the context of God's wider purpose.

In other words, the Christian would say that such usage does not take incarnation seriously. God is God, immanent in a sense in all creation, but nevertheless transcendent. He is not known in general. In order for us to know Him as He is, He must enter human life, not as a chance visitation but to become man, not to take on outward appearances, but to become man in reality. Christianity asserts that this has taken place in Jesus Christ and continues to take place in him. Professor Farmer writes:

Christianity's insistence on the uniqueness of the Incarnation and its preoccupation with history are inseparably bound up together; for history is essentially the sphere of the singular, the unique. In other words, the Christian belief in *the* Incarnation is not really in any sense at all parallel to the oriental belief in avatars, and it is dangerously misleading to assert that it is: for it is belief in the "inhistorisation" of God, if I may coin such a word, whereas the latter belief . . . has no sense of the significance of history at all.[8]

The Incarnation is genuine. It is in Jesus' humanity that God is seen. And in the doctrine of the Person of Christ the Church has tried to say this without succumbing to the temptation to oversimplify and thus falsify. The question of how this could be said waged on after the matter of the Trinity was settled. It was all too easy to make Christ a Divine figure at the cost of making his humanity only stage play, for the world of that time had no difficulty in conceiving quasi-human Divine manifestations. It was all too easy to say that in Jesus a human body and a Divine soul were joined, but to be human is more than to have a human body. It was too easy to say that in some in-

[8] Herbert H. Farmer, *Revelation and Religion*, p. 195.

definable way and to some indefinable degree—thereby avoiding the issue—Jesus was "like" God but no more. But while the formulation of the doctrine did not result in a completely straightforward expression, it was honest to the mystery of the relation we have been discussing. The official position was that two "natures," the Divine and the human, were joined, but not confused, in one person: Jesus Christ. His humanity was real in every sense of the word, except as that may imply sin. And his Divinity was real as well—no mere "pointing toward" something else not there contained, but God Himself present for man's redemption. But while man and God can never be confused with each other, Christ was not torn by two motivations. His personality—to use a hackneyed phrase—was integrated.

Hence, perhaps we can do no better than to clarify what is involved and recognize the implicit mystery. Yet it is not mystery in the sense of being something spooky, nor in the sense of being so sacred that we dare not question and examine it. But it is mystery in the same sense that our own Christian lives defy cold analysis, for we recognize that to be truly free means to be inseparably bound with God.

Before we close this discussion, however, we must remind ourselves that ultimately the doctrine of the Incarnation says more about God than it does about Jesus. The question is not merely whether Jesus Christ is that Incarnation, but Who God is. To accept the Incarnation, therefore, is to accept the God of Jesus, not merely to acquiesce in some statement about his person. It means that God is no aloof "prime mover" but One who seeks men and thus makes possible men's search for Him. As Professor H. R. Mackintosh has put it, "Faith, as a self-renouncing trust in the Highest, is an attitude I can take solely to a Being of whom I can predicate a living interest in my lot." [9]

[9] H. R. Mackintosh, *The Christian Apprehension of God* (New York: Harper & Brothers, 1929; London: Student Christian Movement Press), pp. 119f. Reprinted by permission.

4.   The doctrine of the Holy Spirit

What we have said about God the Father and the Son is no doubt familiar to those acquainted with Christianity, but this familiarity cannot be assumed for the doctrine of the Holy Spirit. For one thing, the concept has been so watered down by the ill-considered application of the word *spiritual* to all sorts of experiences that it has lost definitive meaning. We speak glibly about joining in with the spirit of a group, about having a spiritual feeling, or about a spiritual person, or even about participating in some indefinite way in the Spirit of God. But the doctrine of the Holy Spirit is more concrete and important than this.

First of all we can say that the Holy Spirit refers to God's activity within us. That is, if the Incarnation of God the Son in Jesus Christ can be spoken of as objective, then our appropriation of it is subjective. While God on the one hand does something for us, on the other hand He does something within us. One aspect of this, to which we have already referred, is the recognition of the Bible as God's word to us. The Bible may well be the record of God's past revelation to men, but it becomes actual living revelation to us when we are convinced that here God is addressing us personally and we must pay heed. "For as God alone is a sufficient witness of Himself in His own word, so also the word will never gain credit in the hearts of men, till it be confirmed by the internal testimony of the Spirit." [10]

So also our turning to Christ in faith, while it is our decision, rests on a conviction that such faith is right and ultimately safe, and again, this conviction is God's work within us. This is the experience to which St. Paul referred as the testimony of the Spirit: "When we cry, 'Abba! Father!' it is the Spirit himself

---

[10] John Calvin, *A Compend of the Institutes of the Christian Religion*, ed. Hugh Thompson Kerr, Jr. (Philadelphia: Presbyterian Board of Christian Education, 1939), p. 16. Reprinted by permission.

bearing witness with our spirit that we are children of God" (Rom. 8:15, 16).

And if it is the Holy Spirit who gives witness to us of God's claim on us, then in a sense it is the Spirit who creates the fellowship of the Church and is responsible for its life. St. Paul speaks of the gifts of the Spirit—different capacities of different people—given for accomplishing God's purpose through the Church (1 Cor. 12:4–13). What binds Christians together, in other words, is not their natural cameraderie, nor their human determination to cooperate—their "spirit of unity"—but their sharing in the unity of God's Spirit. So also the Spirit produces the change in life in us from sin to faith. St. Paul speaks of "living by the Spirit" (see Rom. 8), for the resource of Christian living is not stoical grit but the Spirit of God.

It is the relation between inner witness of the Spirit and the outward Lordship of Christ that links the Spirit inseparably with God and Christ. No one led by the Spirit can say, "Jesus be cursed"; and obversely, it is only by the Spirit that one can say, "Jesus is Lord" (1 Cor. 12:3). The Spirit is as free and perhaps as unpredictable as the wind (John 3:8), but his character is that of Christ. The Spirit, in other words, is not an indefinable, impersonal force which people feel. He is a continuation of Christ in the world and attests His Lordship. So real is this relationship that the Fourth Gospel says the Spirit could not come to men until Christ was glorified (John 16:7–15), and St. Paul can use Spirit of Christ and Holy Spirit almost interchangeably. This means that the Spirit has Christ's personality, and although that character is established, he cannot be exhausted by pat human formulas.

And this is why the Spirit is included with the Father and the Son in the Trinity. The Church never did give the Spirit the careful consideration given the relation of Christ to God, and the bareness of the creeds at this point reflects that neglect. But it has insisted that the Spirit comes from the Father and the Son (at least in the Western part of the Church) and that God is known in these three persons.

It has been the failure to recognize the mutual relation of the Father, Son, and Holy Spirit that has caused trouble not only in the Church but in society as well. When the Spirit is dissociated from the whole Christian understanding of God, people exploit their own feelings. This happened with St. Paul's converts at Corinth who brought with them into the Church largely pagan concepts of spirituality. They came to regard "speaking in tongues" (which we would probably call gibberish or ecstatic speech caused by intense emotional stimulation) as the choice manifestation of the Spirit, and they took pride in their ability thus to speak in tongues. St. Paul declared, however, that the Spirit, being the Spirit of God and of Christ, is not given to men for their personal exploitation, but for accomplishing God's purpose. So while the Apostle did not forbid speaking in tongues, he did insist that this was decidedly subordinate to the welfare of the Church and its mission (see 1 Cor. 14).

Similar misunderstanding of the role of the Spirit is found today among those whose religious testimony is always to their own feeling. Of course they do not divorce these utterly from new life in Christ, but the emphasis is placed on their personal experience rather than on Christ. Traditionally this has been called *enthusiasm* (note the technical difference in meaning from the typical use of the word in everyday speech) which concentrates on "religious experiences" and is apt to evaluate them from the standpoint of their intensity. Those who fail to relate the Spirit to Christ often succumb to the most unchristian conduct in the belief that it is "Spirit-led." The New Testament warns that "spiritual influences" must be evaluated: only those are from God which corroborate the work of Christ (1 Cor. 12:10; 1 John 4:1–3).

Summary

Such a brief treatment of the doctrine of the Trinity is apt to be unsatisfying, for that doctrine has concerned the theologians of the Church for centuries. But any attempt to understand it must begin with the full Christian experience of God as the Father, as the Son incarnate in Jesus Christ, and as the Holy Spirit bearing witness in us of the Lordship of Christ; and yet in these three: one God with one purpose, one will, one concern of love. Professor Donald Baillie thus concludes his discussion of the Trinity:

> Therefore it seems to me that the Trinitarian approach to God must always be important for Christian worship, as a safeguard against our worshipping an idol of our imagination instead of the true God. . . . I do not see how this doctrine, with its symbolical expressions, can be fully rationalized and conceptualized and worked out into a philosophical theology. But it seems to me to be an indispensable summing-up of the Christian Gospel for the life of worship. . . . To those who know and accept the whole Christian story, this doctrine is a symbolical epitome of the truth about God, and its constant use in our worship helps to secure that we are drawing near to God as He really is—the God who was incarnate in Jesus Christ.[11]

QUESTIONS FOR DISCUSSION

1. What understanding of God and His relation to men underlies the doctrine of the Trinity?
2. What is the practical importance of the doctrine for Christian life and worship?
3. What fundamental convictions concerning God are expressed in the Formula of Chalcedon (see Appendix)?

OTHER SOURCES

Baillie, D. M., *God Was in Christ*. New York: Charles Scribner's Sons, 1948, chap. 6.

Barth, Karl, *Dogmatics in Outline*, trans. G. T. Thompson. New York: Philosophical Library, 1949, chaps. 6, 12, 21.

Burrows, Millar, *An Outline of Biblical Theology*. Philadelphia: The Westminster Press, 1946, chaps. 3, 4.

[11] D. M. Baillie, *God Was in Christ*, pp. 155f.

Caird, G. B., "The Truth of the Gospel," *A Primer of Christianity*. London: Oxford University Press, 1950, Part III, chaps. 6, 7.

DeWolf, L. Harold, *A Theology of the Living Church*. New York: Harper & Brothers, 1953, chaps. 30, 32.

Farmer, Herbert H., *God & Men*. New York: Abingdon-Cokesbury Press, 1947, chap. 6.

Filson, Floyd V., *Jesus Christ the Risen Lord*. New York: Abingdon Press, 1956, chaps. 7, 8.

Finegan, Jack, *Beginnings in Theology*. New York: Association Press, 1956, chap. 12.

Fosdick, Harry Emerson, *A Guide to Understanding the Bible*. New York: Harper & Brothers, 1938, chap. 1.

——, *The Modern Use of the Bible*. New York: The Macmillan Company, 1924, chap. 8.

Harkness, Georgia, *Understanding the Christian Faith*. New York: Abingdon-Cokesbury Press, 1947, chap. 5.

Lewis, C. S., *Mere Christianity*. London: Geoffrey Bles, 1952, Book IV, chaps. 1–3.

Rall, Harris Franklin, *A Faith for Today*. New York: Abingdon Press, 1936, chap. 7.

——, *Religion as Salvation*. New York: Abingdon-Cokesbury Press, 1953, chap. 14.

Richardson, Alan, *Science, History, and Faith*. London: Oxford University Press, 1950, chap. 7.

Spurrier, William A., *Guide to the Christian Faith*. New York: Charles Scribner's Sons, 1952, chaps. 6, 7.

Tilden, Elwyn E., Jr., *Toward Understanding Jesus*. Englewood Cliffs, N. J.: Prentice-Hall, Inc., 1956, chaps. 24, 25.

Welch, Claude, *In This Name*. New York: Charles Scribner's Sons, 1952.

Whale, J. S., *Christian Doctrine*. New York: The Macmillan Company, 1941, chap. 5.

SIX

the church and the
christian hope

23

the possibilities
of history

From considering the relation of God to man and to the world, we turn now to look at how Christianity sees God's purpose carried out within the world. There has been reason for our taking this course. It is only God, being transcendent, Who can provide life with a meaning broad enough to include all facets of human experience. And it is only through incarnation that God can be known by us and that meaning learned. We have noted briefly the historical significance of the Incarnation. Now we must examine more closely the Christian interpretation of history relative to the fulfillment of God's purpose.

1. The meaning of history

It would be redundant to say that history has meaning. It is the pattern of meaning that distinguishes history from mere chronicles. The chronicler attempts to record everything without indicating what it all means or to what it might point. The historian, on the other hand, working from the raw material of the chronicler, and distinguishing the important facts from the unimportant, traces a pattern of significant events. Thus the historian will tell us about Columbus' discovery of America but not the color of the stockings Columbus wore on his twenty-first day at sea. Obviously, what the historian considers important influences all the history that he writes, for he cannot give us all the facts, nor could we assimilate them if he could.

To write significant history, therefore, is to be able to find meaning in human events. Civilizations may keep records even though they do not regard human events as ultimately significant, but the records are not history. Whenever people think that Reality is completely beyond the human order, they are likely to view human affairs as merely another example of the essentially meaningless cycle apparent in the rest of nature: nothing "gets any place" but just goes around in circles. Meaning, in such a world view, can be found only as one escapes from this physical realm to the purely spiritual realm where all is ever the same.

But with Judaism, and more particularly with Christianity, eternal reality is not found apart from human events but within them. One meets God within history, not divorced from it. God declares Himself in history in judgment and redemption, as we have noted (see chap. 10). History therefore takes on meaning because it is no longer merely distraction or illusion but the scene in which eternal destinies are acted out. But only those who share the biblical faith, recognizing the principle by which human events are to be evaluated, are those who see in history the biblical meaning.

We might take our cue to the meaning of history from the drama. A drama has both a beginning and an end usually joined by the development of a plot, within a definite setting, and with definite movement. So Christianity finds the meaning of history revealed in Christ, but the drama of history occupies the whole stage of human existence, and its conclusion will be the accomplishment of God's purpose. The conclusion is not merely a final curtain brought down at a signal from the stage manager, but rather a fitting and relevant consummation of the action of the entire drama.

2. The Church and history

To take history seriously in this sense means to attach incomparable importance to human activity. If we do not find reality by escaping from human events, then that reality is bound up in those events. This means that we learn truth, for example, not as an immediate gift from heaven, but by our association with our fellow men and the world about us. If we are denied capable teachers, or adequate facilities, or sufficient time devoid of the usual daily round of work, we shall remain in ignorance of many things. Most obviously, we build on the achievement of earlier generations.

While many are ready to acknowledge this fact in scientific pursuits, even in philosophy, they are not ready to see its relevance in religion. They cannot admit that one's relation to God might depend on more than one's own sincerity. To the question of the salvation of the non-Christian we shall return when later in this section we consider that specific problem. But what does it mean to take history seriously in regard to religious concerns? It means certainly that to some degree our knowledge of God upon which our whole response to life is dependent is mediated to us by other people. It is to this that St. Paul refers when to the Romans he writes: "But how are men to call upon Him in whom they have not believed? And how are they to believe in Him of whom they have never heard? And how are they to hear without a preacher? And how can men preach unless they are sent?" (Rom. 10:14, 15). Some have concluded from the fact that since our parents, say, teach us about God, God is no more than a creation of our parents, or of society at large. Others to counteract this often reply that our knowledge of God has nothing to do with our social heritage. Both positions are false, for although society does not create the idea of God, it may be, and is, mediated by social means.

It is therefore unavoidable that Christianity should be involved in what has been called the "scandal of particularity." That is, if God is known in history, and we take history and its limitations seriously, God must be known not in general but in particular circumstances by particular people. If God is to make Himself known to men in their affairs, He must begin somewhere at some time. The biblical teaching is that while He was always known in some way to man (for to be a man means to be capable of knowing God), the real fulfillment of His purpose began with the call of Abraham and the covenant made with him and was continued through Abraham's descendants—the people of Israel (Gen. 12:1, 2).

The choosing of Israel as a starting point did not mean any particular preference for that people above all others. It was not because of any merit on their part that God began with them, nor did this mean they were to be favored above all others. "It was not because you were more in number than any other people that the Lord set His love upon you and chose you, for you were the fewest of all peoples" (Deut. 7:7). "Do not say in your heart, after the Lord your God has thrust them out before you, 'It is because of my righteousness that the Lord has brought me in to possess this land' " (Deut. 9:4). Or in the words of the prophet Amos, "You only have I known of all the families of the earth; therefore I will punish you for all your iniquities" (Amos 3:2). Israel was God's servant through whom He could work for the salvation of all.

The Old Testament is largely the story of Israel's learning the meaning of her role through disobedience, judgment, and restoration. Often enough the nation was apostate. And from the Christian standpoint Israel's rejection of Christ meant the rejection of her unique vocation as God's people. God had brought her into existence not to be one more nation among the nations, but to be His servant through whom the world might find redemption. "It is too light a thing that you should be my servant to raise up the tribes of Jacob and to restore the preserved of Israel; I will give you as a light to the nations, that my salvation may reach to the end of the earth" (Isa. 49:6).

This of course would have meant self-renunciation. Particularly did it mean that the nation could not settle down in some static pattern, but rather had always to be willing to move ahead as God led. The rejection of Christ meant that Israel rejected God's leadership in preference for her established cultus. And the chief stumbling block at this point, as St. Paul admitted, was the cross (1 Cor. 1:23). Looking for some manifestation of power that would strengthen the role of good in the world, or rather looking for the vindication of righteousness, she could not accept the fact that this very thing would mean judgment for her. Rejecting the judgment, she rejected her vocation.

But this did not leave God without a people through whom He could work (nor did it mean that He rejected Israel). Centuries earlier Isaiah had spoken of the faithful remnant through whom God's work should be done (Isa. 6:13; 10:20–22; 11:11). Not all the nation would remain obedient, but God's work would be accomplished through those who would obey. This concept of a remnant—the "true" Israel—played an important part in the subsequent development of Jewish religious thought. And it was crucial to the founding of the Christian Church.

When Jesus met the opposition of the scribes and Pharisees who represented official Judaism, he withdrew into the wilderness with his followers and there appointed twelve "to be with him." (See Mark 3 for the story of the mounting opposition and Jesus' withdrawal and choice of his disciples.) This number is significant. It represents Israel in the traditional twelve tribes. And the implication is that here Jesus was selecting a special group which he could train to carry out God's purpose because the nation as a whole was not responding to him. There are those who deny that Jesus intended to found anything like the Church, but this would mean that all his closest followers totally misunderstood his intention.

If it was not Jesus' purpose to found the Church in this radical sense, it is hard to see much meaning in his ministry. . . . The proof that Jesus intended to found a Church lies, therefore, in the character of his ministry and in the undoubted fact that the inevitable fruit of that ministry was the foundation of the Church.[1]

With the recent archaeological investigation of the Qumran community on the shore of the Dead Sea has come an awareness of the existence of special groups within Israel who thought of themselves as the remnant of Isaiah's prophecy. It would not be unheard of for Jesus and the disciples to constitute a similar one.

But the group that Jesus called together differed in its mem-

[1] Daniel Jenkins, *The Strangeness of the Church*, pp. 37f. Copyright 1955 by Daniel T. Jenkins, reprinted by permission of Doubleday & Company, Inc.

bership from the Qumran community in that shortly after the Resurrection it was no longer one completely within Israel. It was recognized, especially under the leadership of such Hellenistic Jews as Stephen and Paul, that the real bond of the group Jesus called together was not blood but faith, and therefore its scope was the whole world. "That is why it depends on faith, in order that the promise may rest on grace and be guaranteed to all his [Abraham's] descendants—not only to the adherents of the law but also to those who share the faith of Abraham, for he is the father of us all, as it is written, 'I have made you the father of many nations'" (Rom. 4:16, 17; see also Rom. 4 and Gal. 3). Actually this development was not novel with the Hellenists. Jesus himself had carried his work into Gentile territory, largely to get away from opposition it is true; but the gospels record examples of the most profound faith among the traditional outsiders in response to him. In other words, the condition of membership in this remnant was such that it inevitably included more than Jews.

The dawning recognition of this fact precipitated a crisis in the early church. The first Christians were Jews. In an objective analysis they might have admitted that the Gospel was for the whole world, but their habitual exclusiveness made them exceedingly reluctant to extend themselves beyond Judaism. Acts, for example, speaks of St. Peter's unwillingness even to enter the home of the Gentile Cornelius until a vision repeated three times convinced him that it was God's will (Acts 10). But the crisis came at Antioch where, apparently from the first, Gentiles were included in the Christian fellowship. Trouble arose when Peter, who had been eating with these Gentile Christians, withdrew from them on the arrival of a party of stricter Jerusalem Christians. St. Paul accused him openly of trying to live by a double standard (Gal. 2:11–14). The matter was finally settled by the Jerusalem leaders: membership in the Christian community would not depend on being a Jew

(Acts 15:1–29). This meant that the community established by Jesus transcended social and national barriers to encompass all who would be brought to faith in God through Christ. And this was the group, then, through whom God would fulfill His purpose in the world.

In a sense we can say that this community is properly the meeting point of the Gospel and the world. This is how God confronts the world with the Gospel. This is His agent in history.

QUESTIONS FOR DISCUSSION

1. What significance does the conviction that God makes Himself known in history have to our understanding of the role of the Church?
2. What new insight as to the meaning of "chosen people" did the Christians come to possess?

OTHER SOURCES

Brown, Robert McAfee, *The Significance of the Church.* Philadelphia: The Westminster Press, 1956, chap. 3.

Butterfield, H., *Christianity and History.* London: G. Bell and Sons Ltd., 1950, chaps. 6, 7.

DeWolf, L. Harold, *A Theology of the Living Church.* New York: Harper & Brothers, 1953, chap. 37.

Finegan, Jack, *Beginnings in Theology.* New York: Association Press, 1956, chaps. 18, 19.

Jenkins, Daniel, *The Strangeness of the Church.* Garden City, N. Y.: Doubleday & Company, Inc., 1955, chaps. 1–3.

Moore, R. W., "The Furtherance of the Gospel," *A Primer of Christianity.* London: Oxford University Press, 1950, Part II, chap. 1.

Neil, William, *The Rediscovery of the Bible.* New York: Harper & Brothers, 1954, chap. 26.

Rall, Harris Franklin, *A Faith for Today.* New York: Abingdon Press, 1936, chap. 17.

_____, *Religion as Salvation.* New York: Abingdon-Cokesbury Press, 1953, chap. 26.

Soper, Edmund Davison, *The Inevitable Choice*. New York: Abingdon Press, 1957, chap. 3.

Wickenden, Arthur C., *Youth Looks at Religion*. New York: Harper & Brothers, 1939, chap. 12.

Wolf, William J., *Man's Knowledge of God*. Garden City, N. Y.: Doubleday & Company, Inc., 1955, chaps. 9, 10.

24

the nature of the church

So far we have been using terms such as *group* or *community* in reference to the body formed by Jesus and continued by his followers. This is the Christian Church. But now we must look more closely at this fellowship, its life and its work.

There are several hurdles we must surmount if we are truly

to understand the Church. The first of these is the idea that it is essentially a voluntary organization formed by like-minded people who find it congenial to get together to worship and to discuss their religion, but that it is an optional addition to Christianity. This misconception is probably more prevalent in America than elsewhere because in this country the multiplication of denominations and sects has inevitably led to the idea that one's church is a matter of one's own choice, and the further idea that the existence or nonexistence of a church depends on the whim of the people who constitute it. Another hurdle is the idea that the Church has an existence apart from the people who make it up, an existence that can be localized so that people speak of "going to church."

Against these ideas is the fact that essentially the Church is a community of people. It is therefore not something we go to, but a society in which our lives are set. Yet communities do not just happen. Something brings them into existence. It may be a common interest or geographical area or problem. What is it that creates this community of the Church?

1.   What is the Church?

The Church is brought together by the call of God. The Greek word for church, *ekklesia* (from which we derive our word "ecclesiastic") means "assembly." Originally it referred to the assembly of Greek citizens summoned together to conduct community business. But it was also used to translate the Hebrew word for the community of Israel brought together by the covenant with God. We have noted earlier that this marked the difference between the Hebrew concept of God's relation to men and the typical idea found in paganism that men are the offspring of God and so have some indissoluble relationship to Him.

In other words, the Church is the special people of God, the community through whom He works in the world. It is historically continuous with Israel, and in this sense it is the true Israel. But it is more. For the covenant by which the Church is called into being is different from the covenant made with Abraham and renewed with Israel at Sinai. There the covenant was ratified with the blood of sacrificial animals. The new covenant, however, is the one made by Christ and ratified with his own life (Heb. 9:15). At the Lord's Supper Jesus said of the cup, "This is my blood of the covenant which is poured out for many" (Mark 14:24). Here is the real significance of the Old and New Testaments in our Bible. Testament should be translated covenant. The two portions of scripture relate to the two covenants and particularly emphasize the new relationship between man and God established by Christ.

Professor Filson thus summarizes the implications of this covenant relation:

Since God initiates the covenant, the Church as the covenant people is not a voluntary human association or a human invention but a Divine creation. The Church is continuous with Israel, yet what God has done in Christ is so decisive and effective that the new stage of God's dealings centers faith, worship, life, and thought in Christ. It ties the benefits of the covenant to the relation of faith in Christ.[1]

And it is in this context that the Heidelberg Catechism, statement of belief of many churches of the Reformed tradition, says, "Out of the whole human race, from the beginning to the end of the world, the Son of God, by his Spirit and Word, gathers, defends, and preserves for himself unto everlasting life, a chosen communion, in the unity of the true faith." [2]

Because of this new intimate relation with Christ, the Church is called not only the people of God but the body of Christ. This means that it is the agent through which Christ can continue to work in this world. But it also means that the relation of the Church to Christ is integral, and the relation of members to

[1] Floyd V. Filson, *Jesus Christ the Risen Lord* (New York: Abingdon Press, 1956), p. 186. Reprinted by permission.
[2] Question 54.

each other is absolutely essential. In fact, here is the source of our word *member:* it originally referred to a part of the body, as an arm or a leg. Hence, when St. Paul writes that in the Church we are members of one body, he means that we cannot function at all independently of our relation to the body (1 Cor. 12:12–31). Yet the Church as the body of Christ is no substitute for him: it has no independent life, for he remains its head (Eph. 5:23).

2. Is the Church necessary?

There are those who do not accept the Church as at all essential to Christianity and so seek a Christianity unrelated to it. That one can go beyond any particular denomination cannot be denied, but we are not now speaking of this. Jesus began his work, not with isolated individuals, but with a group of disciples, and these were the core of the new community of the Church. It was only for this new community that Jesus had significance beyond that of a mere man unjustly put to death in the midst of his career. John Knox, the contemporary American scholar, speaks of Christ as the prime event in the life of the Church, and by this he means not just the facts of Jesus' life that one might expect to find in a secular history of the period but the singular interpretation of those facts as well. But it was only in the fellowship of the Church that this interpretation could be made. For the ordinary man of the world Christ had no such meaning. "The career of Jesus of Nazareth, simply as a human career, was, for all its intrinsic greatness, a relatively unimportant incident in Jewish history. The event of Jesus Christ the Lord was historically the important thing; and this event happened only in the life of the Church." [3]

In other words, it was only this fellowship that preserved

[3] John Knox, *The Early Church and the Coming Great Church* (New York: Abingdon Press, 1955; London: The Epworth Press, 1957), p. 47. Reprinted by permission.

the memory of Christ in oral and written form. There are virtually no secular records of Jesus, and the few that do exist tell us nothing new about him. It was only those for whom he mattered who prepared the New Testament. So to attempt to discover what Jesus was independent of the Christian fellowship is vain.

What was God doing through Christ? . . . Just now it is enough to say that if we may assume that God intended to accomplish what He did in fact accomplish, there can be no doubt as to what that was: He sought to bring into existence a new kind of human community—that kind of human community which the early church in the first instance and subsequently the church in all the centuries has, however inadequately represented.[4]

The New Testament does not take us beyond the life of the Church, but more deeply into it. The person who speaks of Christianity apart from the Church does not mean by it what the New Testament means.

It is hopelessly inconsistent to think of oneself as related to Christ as Lord without at the same time being related to the community which acknowledges him as Lord. Professor William Neil writes,

Personal salvation is not a private transaction with God based on acceptance of scriptural truth, but life lived in obedience to God within the Church, and illumined and sustained alike by living worship and written word.[5]

Or, more completely, again in the words of Professor Filson:

By the very nature of God's covenant, the Church is where men find God's righteous will and outreaching grace. It is the Christian's home, where he receives God's gifts, acknowledges his obligation to fulfill God's will, and finds his fellowship and place of usefulness precisely as a member of God's covenant people.[6]

[4] *Ibid.*, p. 48.
[5] William Neil, *The Rediscovery of the Bible* (New York: Harper & Brothers, 1954; London: Hodder & Stoughton, Ltd.), p. 114. Reprinted by permission.
[6] Filson, *Jesus Christ the Risen Lord,* p. 186.

3. The development of the Church

We have yet to clarify the relation of our present denominations with this community of faith of which we have been speaking. *Church* in the New Testament refers either to the whole body of Christian believers or to the Christians of a particular locality, such as "the church at Corinth." It does not refer to what we mean by *denomination*. In fact, the New Testament people would have been at a loss to understand this at all. And we shall not understand it unless we can see the development of the denominations in an historical context.

According to the New Testament records, Jesus not only called the disciples to him, but he gave them specific responsibilities to preach to others the good news of what God had done and to bring these others into the community of God's people. With a slight delay at his death, this work continued with zeal following the Resurrection. The disciples won not only Jews but Gentiles as well. New converts such as St. Stephen and St. Paul outdid the original disciples in their enthusiasm for the work, particularly with those of Greek (Hellenistic) background.

When the Gospel was preached to those who had no personal knowledge of Jesus and no real understanding even of Judaism, a new problem arose—that of instruction. Converts had to be trained in the Jewish scriptures as well as in the unique Christian message. Moreover, certain persons had to be delegated to supervise the common meal of the Lord's Supper that was central to the life of the Christian group (Acts 3:42). Hence in each church individuals were selected (probably by the missionaries who first brought the people together, along with the cooperation of the local group) for specific tasks: teaching, leading in worship, caring for the needy. Of course, a person's natural abilities influenced these choices. In fact, these abilities were regarded as gifts of the Spirit for the maintenance of the common Christian life (see 1 Cor. 12:4–11 and Eph. 4:7–14).

Contact among these various local groups was maintained by the apostles in their missionary travels—note, for example, the letters of St. Paul. When these original leaders died, this communication had to be carried on by designated officers of the local churches. As congregational needs expanded, three offices emerged, though at any particular time practice probably varied from one church to another. First, there were deacons who were responsible for the care of the poor, widows, and orphans, and who managed the financial concerns. Second, there were the presbyters (called "elders" in most Protestant churches and "priests" in others such as the Anglican and the Roman Catholic). Higher in rank, they presided at the worship services and generally were responsible for church affairs. Finally, there were the bishops. Some hold on the basis of New Testament interpretation that "bishop" was simply another name for "presbyter," perhaps for a presiding presbyter, but there is no doubt that before long the bishop was a distinct officer, the person in charge generally of the whole church. Because Christianity began in the large cities of the empire, these metropolitan churches assumed obligation for extending Christian mission work into the surrounding country. This work fell under the direction of the bishop, and although local churches multiplied, the bishop understandably came to be in charge of a geographical area rather than just one congregation. This organizational structure provided the opportunity for communication among the local groups: the bishops could correspond or even meet to conduct business on a wide basis.

Some churches today stress the antiquity of their pattern of government and its scriptural precedent; however, it is misleading to think of its being handed down by Jesus. The only genuine reference to organizational details in the New Testament is found in the Pastoral Epistles (1 and 2 Timothy and

Titus) which most scholars date, at least in their present form, early in the second century, even though there may be genuine Pauline elements in them. Practices seem rather to have developed to meet practical needs as they arose.

It is also misleading to think of a single world-wide organization of the church from the beginning. There was no over-all authority apart from the Spirit of God. The Jerusalem Christians assumed leadership, and the Apostles, but they sometimes were at cross purposes with each other. Through the years, and especially as teachings fundamentally contrary to the Gospel crept into Christian circles, Christians tried to establish a unity in order to meet such challenges. The first example of this was the development of the Catholic Church (as distinct from the Roman Catholic Church with its characteristic practices) in the third and fourth centuries. The basis of this unity was the canon of the New Testament (the list of books regarded as authoritative for the Church), statements of belief such as the Apostles' and later the Nicene Creeds, and standardized church government of the episcopal pattern (meaning "under the supervision of bishops"). But the uniformity was not absolute. The Eastern churches, for example, refused to accept the claim of pre-eminence on the part of the church at Rome. Nor were the councils of bishops summoned at various times truly representative of the entire church. From the earliest days, heresies plagued the churches, as well as administrative difficulties. The division between Eastern and Roman churches in 1054 (the Great Schism) was not so much a fracture of an established unity but a failure to achieve that dreamed-of unity.

Through the years there were disputes and separations. The Donatists in North Africa who denied fellowship to all who renounced Christianity under the pressure of government persecution, the Montanists in Asia Minor who claimed an authority of the Spirit for their views on the imminent end of the world, the Arians in the Near East and northern Europe

who held that Christ was created, not begotten by God, the
Hussites in Bohemia who denied the supremacy of the Pope—
all these are examples of the succession of disruptions. The
break best known to us is the Protestant Reformation drama-
tized by the career of Martin Luther. And here again there was
no over-all unity. That is, the Reformation began in isolated
local movements, and it was never integrated by a single
organization or program. Only recently have efforts to relate
the separate Christian movements found practical expression in
the ecumenical (meaning "the whole inhabited world") movement of the World Council of Churches which includes most
Protestant and Eastern Orthodox bodies, but not the Roman
Catholics because of their own choice. Important to the establishment of this organization was the incorporation of various
student Christian movements in the World's Student Christian
Federation. Yet even the World Council is not an organic unity
but a cooperative venture prompted by the recognition that
fundamentally the Church is one because God has called it together in the unity of the Spirit (Eph. 4:3).

4. The essentials of the Church

But this historical consideration simply emphasizes for us the
question as to the relation of these separate groups to the
unique "people of God" that we have seen called forth by the
Gospel proclamation. And yet when we come to ask what
constitutes the real Church of God, there is no universal agreement as to an answer. Three different emphases are made:
some stress the institution, others correct belief, and still others
some manifestation of God's Spirit. Any one group will maintain evidence of all three, but the major emphasis will be on
one.

For example, the groups that emphasize the institution stress
the fact that people cannot be bound together, certainly for
any concerted action, without some sort of organization to

direct group affairs. When we speak of the idealistic qualities of an American, we think largely in terms of ideals of character —such things as initiative, resourcefulness, indifference to social position. Yet when we get down to fundamentals, we recognize that one cannot be an American without owning allegiance to the government.[7] This government is essential to the nation. There could be no American nation without it.

In a similar way, then, according to this line of thought, the essential thing about the Church is its organization, an organization established by Christ when he gave authority to his disciples. The disciples, in turn, delegated their powers to others who succeeded them. So the line has continued through the centuries, and it is this continuing organization which is really the Church. If one is not related to this institution, he does not belong with the fellowship of apostles, martyrs, and saints. For practical purposes, this makes the Church principally the clergy, for it is they who are given the special powers and authority necessary to maintain the organization, power that has descended from Christ through an unbroken line of successors. Historically, the Roman Catholic Church is the prime example of this view, although it is held by some Anglicans as well, especially by those who insist on the necessity of "apostolic succession" of an organizational type for the existence of the Church. *Apostolic succession* means that the present clergy are in a direct line with the apostles, a line maintained only as one proper bishop ordains another to follow him.

In reaction to this view which to many was far too externalized to be consistent with a Gospel that searched the heart, an almost completely spiritualized concept developed at the time of the Reformation and became particularly characteristic of the Lutheran position. Luther held that the Church is essen-

[7] *American* is used here in its ordinary sense of referring to the United States rather than the Western Hemisphere.

tially invisible; that is, it is constituted by the faith of its members and is a spiritual society with little need of outward forms. Organizational details are worked out as they become necessary, but the ecclesiastical institution is not Divine. The essence of the Church is the correct faith of the members.

This concept, freer than the first, left no real basis for conducting the practical affairs of church life other than voluntary cooperation as far as individuals were willing to give it. Some basis of outward union had to be established, and the tendency of churches of this type has been to identify true faith which alone brings the Church into existence with acceptance of a particular doctrinal standard such as the Augsburg Confession or Luther's Catechism. Closely akin to this position is that of many Protestant "sect" groups who stress doctrines derived from a literal interpretation of the Bible. The Church is thought to consist of those who accept these doctrines.

The third position is taken by those who insist that the standard of faith—particularly as it is expressed in creeds and confessions—is too rigid, that the essence of the Church lies in the presence and activity of the Holy Spirit. Some look to Christ-like action as evidence of the Spirit's presence—the "love, joy, peace, patience, kindness, goodness, faithfulness, gentleness, self-control" that St. Paul wrote was the fruit of the Spirit (Gal. 5:22, 23). The Quakers (Society of Friends) come readily to mind as holding this position, particularly in their ministry of reconciliation and peace-making. Others, however, look to some unique phenomenon as evidence of the Spirit's presence. Pentecostal groups who stress speaking in tongues or prophesying are an example. A more bizarre one is the snake-handling cult that occasionally makes newspaper headlines.

Crossing the lines of these three emphases are two different outlooks on the membership of churches. One of these, often called the "church" type, stresses inclusiveness. The Church so conceived is the fellowship of those who are trying to grow in their understanding of, and obedience to, the Christian life. The presence of beginners and sinners in the church is no embarrassment to those holding this view because they see the church as the society in which men are able to experience the call of God on their lives. The other outlook frequently called the "sect" type looks on the Church more as the exclusive fellowship of those who have been redeemed. Only when people have achieved certain status in the Christian life are they welcomed into membership. To put it simply, the first group would say in effect, "Join the Church that you may become a Christian in the full sense," while the second would more likely say, "When you have become a Christian, then you are ready for membership in the Church."

But just as any particular church will regard organization, faith, and living spirituality—though it will stress one of these more than the others—so it will also include elements of both the sect and church outlooks, though one will predominate. In general, the Roman Catholic and various Protestant state churches have taken the inclusive approach, while independent churches have been more exclusive, since they were not committed to responsibilities for an entire population. And many of the larger Protestant denominations that began with the exclusive pattern have widened their concerns through the years to become inclusive.

In considering the relation of churches to the Church, many would seek first to determine which of these views is the true one. There are those who insist that the true Church is found only with them and that all others have no justifiable claim to the title. Thus the Roman Catholic Church designates all Protestant denominations as sects, not truly parts of the Church at all. Though it would be dishonest and foolish to say that all Christians basically agree on the concept of the Church and that the differences we have discussed are unimportant, we must ask if there is not something held in common here that would link Christians together regardless of their emphasis in their concept of the Church, in contrast to those who are non-Christian. This would need to be more than some highest common factor analytically determined, more than similarly high moral standards which may be held by those who have never heard of Christ. Professor Knox writes that there is such a factor:

> If, for example, we mean by "church" the many actual groups in various lands organized and conducting their affairs in various ways, then the church is certainly not *one* and has never been; but if, when we speak of the Church, we are speaking of the particular kind of shared experience that at least to some degree is characteristic of these various groups—if by "Church" we mean the distinctive common life—then the Church is one, indivisible, and everywhere the same. Since it is this shared experience, this community, which really constitutes the Church, the Church is eschatologically (or, if one prefers, ideally) all but identifiable with the community, and we can make such statements as, "Let the church be the Church"; that is, "Let the church fully realize and express the community which makes it the Church." [8]

And he goes on to say that the distinctive aspect of the Church is the sharing of the common memory of Christ and the common Spirit of God.[9]

The common memory of Christ is, of course, the historical circumstances of the life of Jesus: he can be located at a definite time in history, he did definite things, he was associated with certain people. Because of this common memory, Christianity cannot evaporate into mere speculation, regardless of the differing emphases of the several Christian groups. Time and again in the history of the Christian community it has been this memory that has corrected and tempered the wide variety of Christian witness.

The common Spirit of God is related to Christ as the controlling factor of the Church's life, prompting members to Christ-like living. This common Spirit is not theory, but the

[8] Knox, *The Early Church and the Coming Great Church*, p. 51.
[9] *Ibid.*, p. 52.

basis of theory. He produces a new and rich quality of community life. He is the foundation for that life. To belong to the Church means to share in it. One participates in the Spirit only as one participates in the community.

The Church, then, essentially is the community which shares the memory of Christ and the Spirit of God. As such it transcends denominational lines. No single denomination is the Church. And yet denominations are not constituent parts of the Church, for the Church exists wherever there is the fellowship of believers. The Church is a society, and a society is as truly manifest in small groups as in large. Moreover, as a society it is visible, even in the context of denominationalism. The Church is always personal, not in the sense that it is entirely a matter of private judgment, but in the sense that it is a fellowship of persons. Professor Emil Brunner writes:

The Church is never, whether visible or invisible, anything other than a community of believers; it is always composed of persons, namely, human beings who are knit together through the God-man [Christ] in person. This fellowship must have all kinds of concrete arrangements, ordinances, forms of organization, offices, laws; but because it *has* all these does not mean that its essence consists in them. . . . He [Christ], in His presence with men—that is the Church; it is never anything else.[10]

Or again in the words of another author

The most distinctive thing about Christianity, the thing that marks it off from all other religions, is that it is not first of all and in essence a religion but a society of men. The Church is an article of the faith. It is unique.[11]

Because this society is created by faith, two important implications should be noted. In the first place, the society of faith transcends all boundaries of race, nationality, and class. And here it is unique among human institutions. It crosses even the

[10] Emil Brunner, *Revelation and Reason*, trans. Olive Wyon (Philadelphia: The Westminster Press, 1946; London: The Student Christian Movement Press, Ltd.), pp. 138f. Reprinted by permission.
[11] T. Ralph Morton, *Community of Faith* (New York: Association Press, 1954), p. 24. Reprinted by permission.

barrier between the Western and the Communist blocks of nations. This world-wide scope was recognized early in Christian history with the breakdown of the Jewish-Gentile separation, and its deeper ramifications were even then anticipated: "There is neither Jew nor Greek, there is neither slave nor free, there is neither male nor female; for you are all one in Christ Jesus" (Gal. 3:28). In the second place, membership in this society means a personal decision. We do not belong to the body of Christ by natural birth but by the response of faith. The Church is not synonymous with humanity.

Christians have, through the years, regarded the Church as inclusive of both the living and the dead, and it is to this that the Apostles' Creed makes reference in the phrase "the communion of saints." That is, since the response of faith sets life in an eternal context, the fellowship of faith extends beyond the limitations of physical death. Jesus himself so understood it (Mark 14:25). The Letter to the Hebrews expounds this theme when it speaks of the saints of the past as living in faith, not receiving what God had promised "that apart from us they should not be made perfect," and continues with the picture of the "great cloud of witnesses" that constantly surrounds us (Heb. 11:40; 12:1). In other words, the fellowship of the Church is such that it transcends both time and space, and this is true only because God Who is eternal has called it into existence.

Summary

Because God makes Himself known in human affairs—in history—Christianity regards history seriously, as the drama in which eternal destinies are determined. If God's will is to be accomplished in human affairs, He must work through a people who will respond in obedience to His call, and this very response creates the community of faith. Covenant is the characteristic bond of such a group: it was through a covenant that

Israel was constituted. But when that nation refused its vocation, God worked through the faithful remnant until a new covenant was established in Christ.

This new covenant created not merely the "true" Israel, but the "new" Israel that should transcend all national and racial lines—the Christian Church. Although organizationally the Church is far from being united, it is one in sharing the common memory of Christ and the common Spirit of God. Its unity is found in the call of God that brings it into being.

QUESTIONS FOR DISCUSSION

1. What makes the Church necessary to Christianity?
2. What approach to unifying the church would be implicit to each of the three views of what makes the church the Church?

OTHER SOURCES

Baly, Denis, *Chosen Peoples*. Philadelphia: The Christian Education Press, 1956.

Barth, Karl, *Dogmatics in Outline,* trans. G. T. Thompson. New York: Philosophical Library, 1949, chap. 22.

Bell, G. K. A., *The Kingship of Christ*. Baltimore: Penguin Books, 1954.

Brown, Robert McAfee, *The Significance of the Church*. Philadelphia: The Westminster Press, 1956, chap. 4.

DeWolf, L. Harold, *A Theology of the Living Church*. New York: Harper & Brothers, 1953, chap. 38.

Filson, Floyd V., *Jesus Christ the Risen Lord*. New York: Abingdon Press, 1956, chap. 9.

Finegan, Jack, *Beginnings in Theology*. New York: Association Press, 1956, chap. 20.

Harkness, Georgia, *Understanding the Christian Faith*. New York: Abingdon-Cokesbury Press, 1947, chap. 11, parts 1, 2.

Houf, Horace T., *What Religion Is and Does*, rev. ed. New York: Harper & Brothers, 1945, chap. 19.

Jenkins, Daniel, *The Strangeness of the Church*. Garden City, N. Y.: Doubleday & Company, Inc., 1955, chaps. 5–7, 12, 15.

Knox, John, *The Early Church and the Coming Great Church*. New York: Abingdon Press, 1955, Introduction, chaps. 1, 3, 4.

Miller, Alexander, *The Renewal of Man*. Garden City, N. Y.: Doubleday & Company, Inc., 1955, chap. 8.

Morton, T. Ralph, *Community of Faith*. New York: Association Press, 1954, chaps. 1–11.

Neil, William, *The Rediscovery of the Bible*. New York: Harper & Brothers, 1954, chap. 27.

Nichols, James Hastings, *Primer for Protestants*. New York: Association Press, 1947, chap. 7.

Rall, Harris Franklin, *Religion as Salvation*. New York: Abingdon-Cokesbury Press, 1953, chap. 15.

Stewart, George, *The Church*. New York: Association Press, 1940, chaps. 2, 3.

25

the life of the church

St. Paul calls the Church "the body of Christ," and this expression may help us to understand it—its own life and its function in the world. It is to the first of these considerations that we now turn. The significance of the term "body of Christ" applied to the life of the Church is three-fold: it must function as a true organism, it must grow to maturity, and it must express its essential inner character established by Christ, its head.

The intimate relation of members to each other was noted when we considered the meaning of the term "member." The New Testament uses the word *koinonia* for this special community brought about through faith. It means "sharing in the company of those who are in Christ." In fact, it is this fellowship that defines the true meaning of friendship (see 1 John 1:1–7). Practically, this means that within the fellowship of the Church personal interests cannot supplant the welfare of the whole body. "The body does not consist of one member but of many" (1 Cor. 12:14). St. Paul drew from this the conclusion that the gift of tongues, for example, dared not be exploited by any individual, but had to be used in ways that contributed to the whole group's welfare. Even more practically, he insisted that each member must make his own contribution to the whole, and to the Thessalonians he wrote that this meant each person had to earn his own living and not be a drag on the community (1 Thes. 4:10–12).

The organic functioning of the body of Christ is dealt with more fully in the Letter to the Ephesians (see Eph. 4:25–5:2). Absolute honesty becomes essential, for no body can function if separate members cannot rely on each other. Nothing—anger, for example—dare be permitted to put members at cross-purposes with each other. Parasites cannot be tolerated. Speech must be governed by a consideration for the welfare of all. In short, if the Church is to be the body of Christ, members must be "imitators of God."

This emphasis on the body as an organism does not mean, however, that there is here an impersonal corporate entity for which individuals can be sacrificed. The Church is not comparable to the modern totalitarian state that ruthlessly exploits its citizens. There can be no health of the body apart from the health of the members, "If one member suffers, all suffer together; if one member is honored, all rejoice together" (1 Cor. 12:26).

But just as the physical body requires nourishment, Christians require nourishing if the body of Christ is to reach maturity. This nourishment can come only from God: it is His grace. Grace refers to God's own nature which He gives to those who will receive it, a gift shown incomparably in the coming of Christ. The question we now ask is how it comes, or what its channel is, or more traditionally, what the *means* of grace are.

1. The study of the scriptures

In Protestantism, certainly, the emphasis is on the "proclamation of the Word." This is a much fuller concept than appears from the superficial meaning of the words. In fact, it has several ramifications. For one thing, it does refer to the preaching of the biblical message. The idea involved is not that God cannot make Himself known by other means, but that the logical place to meet Him is through the book that is a testimony to His dealings with men: the Bible. Other literature is certainly inspiring. But if other literature in any sense is to lead us to Christ, it must be grounded in the written Word.

We have already noted at several points that the words of the Bible become to us God's living Word when they are attested to by the Holy Spirit speaking within us. But this cannot happen unless we give ourselves to a study of those written words. It is as we read them or hear them read that God can make Himself known to us—not in some effusive, immanent feeling, but as He has declared Himself in history. This is one of the reasons Christians generally, and Protestants particularly, have been interested in education for the masses as well as the clergy and the elite. Each person, it is felt, ought to have the opportunity of knowing for Himself that God does speak through the Bible. Most modern literacy movements, as a result, have had their origin in Christian mission programs.

But the Bible was not written by individuals solely for individuals. It belongs to the whole Church, and its message must be heard in the context of Church life. This is the reason for the Protestant emphasis on the preacher and the sermon. There are things we can learn by ourselves. But since our relation to God is not a solitary affair, we learn more completely as a Church where the Word is shared and where, in the context of prayer and worship, we listen in faith to one set apart by the Church for the special task of expounding the scriptures. And again, in this setting, God may confirm through the Holy Spirit what is said by the preacher.

2. Worship

But the process we have been discussing does not take place within a vacuum. That God can speak to men when they least expect it cannot be gainsaid. But the usual atmosphere in which men receive God's grace, in which He imparts to them something of Himself, is that of worship. Worship comes from the Anglo-Saxon *worth-ship* and means "the acknowledgment of God's supreme worth." Quite simply, to worship is to own that God is God.

Since, however, we are human beings with psychological as well as physiological natures, since we function in characteristic ways, the Church worships by enabling its members to worship. And hence any "service of worship," though directed primarily to God, is also patterned to help men direct themselves to God. We must be careful at this point not to think of worship as some technique involving soft lights and mood music aimed little higher than at the creation of a particular feeling in the worshiper. This is a perversion—one which is unfortunately not unknown—resulting from putting man and not

God at the center of concern. Rather, the service of worship enables men to offer themselves to God.

a. Vision. Perhaps the basic pattern of worship can best be traced in the experience of Isaiah in the temple (Isa. 6:1–8). Worship begins with the vision of God: "I saw the Lord sitting upon a throne, high and lifted up." This does not mean that everyone must have a sensual image of God as Isaiah had. But it does mean an awareness of God as God. One reason for having church buildings or places of worship is that through the appeal to the senses, something of the majesty and mystery of God may be conveyed. The soaring arches of Gothic architecture, for example, serve to create this very awareness. Indirectly, the simplicity and even barrenness of the Puritan meeting house worked toward the same end, creating the impression of the utter transcendence of God. In the service proper, the words of scripture often designated the "call to worship," and the hymns of praise not only stimulate our awareness of God but are a response to it, corresponding to the song of the cherubim of Isaiah's vision: "Holy, holy, holy is the Lord of hosts; the whole earth is full of His glory."

b. Confession. For Isaiah, to see God meant not only high spiritual exaltation but an overwhelming sense of his unworthiness: "Woe is me! For I am lost; for I am a man of unclean lips, and I dwell in the midst of a people of unclean lips!" To be aware of God in His purity is a shattering experience, as Christians of all ages have testified. It leads to the awareness of our own sinfulness. And consequently in the service of worship there is opportunity for confession of sin, whether it be the familiar prayer from the Anglican morning service, "Almighty and most merciful Father; we have erred and strayed from thy ways like lost sheep . . ." or some verses of scripture, or a hymn of penitence, or even a period of silence.

c. Renewal. This, however, is not the end of the matter. For true to the whole Christian experience of salvation, confession of sin leads to God's forgiveness and our renewal. So in Isaiah's experience, the seraph cleansed his lips with a coal from the altar. And this experience, too, is reflected in the portions of the service of worship that speak assurance of God's love and forgiveness: "This has touched your lips; your guilt is taken away, and your sin forgiven."

d. Dedication. Some would no doubt want to divide this last step into two: enlightenment and dedication. The point is that, following forgiveness, we are ready to learn God's will for our lives; but we can learn this in its fullness not as a subject of our curiosity, but only as we are willing to obey it. In Isaiah's experience his obedient answer of "Send me" to the question, "Who will go for us?" preceded his instruction about what he was to do and what sort of response he might expect. There is, in other words, an integral relation between willingness to do God's will and the ability to understand it. That is why the reading of the scriptures and the sermon which relates them to our present situation are in the context of worship and are complemented by dedication. The latter is expressed outwardly in the offering of our gifts and praise and inwardly in the offering of ourselves.

Worship has always a two-fold motion: first, God's call to us, and second, our response in offering ourselves. In this sense the entire worship service is an offering to God. This is why the word "service" is used in connection with it. Music is performed not as entertainment, but as an offering. Prayers are offered to God on behalf of the congregation and are not meant primarily as edification for those present. And it is only as everything is directed to God that God can reveal Himself fully to the worshipers, for it is only in this that He is acknowledged as God.

3. Prayer

Usually when we think of personal worship we think more in terms of prayer. Prayer of course has its place in the regular service of worship of the whole congregation, but its essential personal quality was recognized by Jesus when he said that when we pray we ought to enter our room and close the door, praying to God in secret (Matt. 6:6). But the understanding of prayer is often seriously twisted by thinking of it primarily as asking for things. Instead of approaching the matter through asking how God answers prayer, we shall try to see it as fundamentally communion with God.

a. What is prayer? Even when prayer is thought of as asking, what makes it true prayer is that our requests are seen in relation to One Who is over and above them. In other words, if a person can see no more than his problems, he is not praying. He can pray only when he sees them somehow under God's dominion. But what does this mean? Primarily, it means that something more than our needs is involved. It is our whole relation to God. And prayer, in a sense, means exploring that relationship in all its aspects.

As a guide to our thought, we might ask what happens in genuine communion between two persons. Communion indicates that the two are together. But being together in this sense involves a close relationship in which mutual concerns are shared. The depth of the "togetherness" of two people (which is obviously much more than mere physical proximity) is seen in the nature of the concerns they share. In prayer we share our deepest concerns with God—specifically, God's will, our own lives, and the problems involved, those closest to us and all that affects them. Because prayer is a living relationship, these concerns relate to each other and temper and qualify each other. A concern for God's will affects our concern for others, and this in turn affects our understanding of our own lives. In this sense, prayer is truly a conversation dependent upon a dynamic relationship between God and the one who prays.

What can we expect to result from it? First of all, Christian prayer should lead to a finer comprehension of God's will and a firmer trust and commitment to Him. In strictly human terms, we would speak of a growing depth of the friendship; correspondingly, our relation to God deepens. Second, it should lead to our seeing ourselves and others in the objectivity of eternal dimensions. No longer preoccupied with problems, we may see situations as they are. Third, it should lead to a greater willingness to serve, to do God's will in the specific situation that confronts us. And it should strengthen us not only in this particular matter, but through the recognition that all things continue in God's control, even those things which are beyond our doing or understanding. Quite simply, prayer should lead to a discernment of God's will in the specific situation in which we find ourselves and an earnest desire to do His will.

This broader concept of prayer is indicated in the Lord's Prayer itself (Matt. 6:9–13). The initial thought is centered on God, His Kingdom and will. Only then is the petition for daily bread made and immediately woven into the whole matter of human relations seen in the larger context of good and evil. The close of the prayer reaffirms the Kingdom, power, and glory of God.

With this groundwork laid, we are ready for the question of how God answers prayer. Taking the approach we have, we can see that the answer is found in the prayer itself. This does not mean that we ought to hear actual voices giving us some specific program to carry out, but it means that prayer itself changes our view toward our concerns. Part of our problem in seeing this may be that we think of prayer so much in terms of words that we forget it is something we do, which, like everything we do, creates a new situation. Just lifting our concerns to God changes them. And many times as a result, those concerns are resolved in more fundamental issues. Thus a person who prays for personal safety in danger may find that his basic concern lies deeper than mere physical survival. Or the person who prays about some misunderstanding with another may see quite different issues at stake. God answers prayer through prayer, not necessarily by some recountable mystical experience, but through the very nature of prayer as communion rather than soliloquy.

But God also answers prayer through the entire interrelatedness of Himself, persons, and nature. This is not a matter about which we can readily dogmatize. We do not know for certain—particularly since the repudiation of the nineteenth century mechanistic view of nature—where the lines of influence are drawn. But if this is God's world as the Christian affirms (and we have looked critically at that affirmation), then we ought to expect God's will to be carried out in the regular pattern of events and not merely in startling supernatural occurrences.

A starving person, for example, prays for food, and his neighbor, perhaps with absolutely no prompting of voices, no obviously religious overtones, takes him a bowl of soup. The need is met, yet many would dispute the agency of prayer because they cannot appreciate the significance of life's interrelations. Or more specifically, people in other nations are hungry and pray about it. Folk in our country also pray and, as a result, establish relief programs. An individual, not presently associated with a local church but nevertheless affected by the Christian element in all society, sees an advertisement in the bus on his way to work. It points out how a certain quantity of food can be sent to another nation for a small sum. This person, along with hundreds like him, makes that contribution, and the prayers of the hungry are answered, at least partially. Note, however, that the answer to such prayer depends on the willingness of people to abide by God's will, the productivity of the soil, even on conditions of international exchange. These matters are all tied together, but in a universe that is God's.

The concept of natural law often bothers people here. They tend to think of it as some inexorable order that shall never be changed, something absolutely binding on whatever powers may be. But natural law at best is a description of how things happen. If one were to give it a decidedly religious orientation, he might say that natural law describes the normal way God does things in the world. It is descriptive, not legislative. Through this natural order God's will is carried out. Hence, even if our prayers close on a note of asking, we do not necessarily imply interference in the natural order, any more than a friend violates natural law if he asks me to accompany him downtown instead of spending an hour in my study.

Of course we are not to pray for impossible things. Prayer is not magic. Should I lose a leg in an accident, prayer will not make it grow back again. And yet God certainly does not want me to suppress my deepest desires. Prayer becomes a way of distinguishing what cannot be changed from what can, and of getting along creatively with the unchangeable. We need not leave out of our praying fundamental concerns because of some prior concept of what is possible and what is impossible. But those concerns must be held up to God, and in this very act we may find them changing. The Westminster Shorter Catechism states that "prayer is the offering up of our desires unto God for things agreeable to His will," pointing out that the desire itself is offered in a spirit of trust and commitment.

Another question frequently raised is whether, if our prayers for other people are effective, their freedom is not seriously curtailed. If other people are responsible for their own decisions, dare I pray that they make them in a certain way? Some would say that mental telepathy is the mechanism for such intercessory prayer. But when we pray for others, we do not seek to impose our will on them: we hold them in our concern before God. Does this violate their freedom? Actually, anything we may do affects their freedom. My decision to drive my car to town, involving it in particular places at particular times affects the freedom of others. So does my concern for others, or lack of it, for that matter. But when I pray for another person within the context of God's will, this enhances his freedom rather than limits it, for it is in the will of God that his true freedom lies.

b. Providence. We are actually raising here the question of providence, or God's care over the world. Is God's will so absolutely determined that we can only conform to it, or can our prayers influence God's will? On the one hand are those who insist that if God is God His will must be absolute, and therefore nothing can take place which He has not predestined. On the other hand are those who beg for this and plead for that as though God were capricious and their prayers set the course of the whole universe. This question, which has been asked continually for centuries, is not to be answered in a few paragraphs, but we can make some observations which at least will set forth the issues more clearly.

Some things are set by God's will. Sometimes this is spoken of as "general providence." We may think here of the natural order of the universe, or even the moral order of life resting on the righteousness of God. Or again we might think of God's final victory over all evil. The Christian holds that these things are established and inviolable. Evil, in other words, is self-defeating. As some have put it, "A man does not break the moral law: it breaks him."

God's will is related to our particular lives. This is often called "special providence," and it must be relevant to human freedom. God is not a celestial tinkerer, adapting his plans to our latest move, but God's will is relevant to what we do. Part of our difficulty in understanding the will of God is that we are creatures of time, seeing everything in terms of *before and after*. We think of praying and then of God adjusting His will to our prayers, and the idea sounds almost blasphemous. Yet, our prayers may be one of the factors by which God formulates His will.

Since this is God's world, it responds only to Him. But we humans may respond willingly or unwillingly. We do not escape God's jurisdiction by disobeying Him. As the psalmist wrote, "He makes the wrath of men to praise Him" (Ps. 76:10). But men can also respond in faith, making God's will their intention. And in this case God's will can be done through them without circumventing their intention.

Now how does this apply to the question at hand: whether or not our prayers are more than demonstrations of our submission to God's overwhelming authority. Suppose, for example, a community is suffering from severe drought. Will it help matters for the people to pray for rain? Rain comes, we know, only when physical conditions warrant it—that is, when the relative humidity, temperature change, and wind are proper. Under certain conditions, rain cannot be prevented. Without them, rain cannot be produced. Even cloud seeding requires favorable conditions to be successful. Can prayer in any way alter these conditions? Many would say, "Certainly not! This would only make the universe capricious. Think of the confusion conflicting prayers would bring!"

But the real question is not one merely of rainfall. It is a total situation with which we are dealing. God's will cannot be isolated in regard to the matter of rain alone. It involves that, but also people. God's will comprehends all reality so interrelatedly that we cannot isolate "prayer for rain" from "people praying," any more than from "physical conditions necessary for rain." This entire constellation of factors becomes the setting in which God's will is carried out. It seems hardly likely that any one of these is absolute. In this sense our prayers do affect God's will, but not necessarily in getting Him to do something He otherwise would not do.

Someone will ask why pray if God's will is not changed. The answer is several-fold. Prayer's finest benefits may not lie in the realm of changing God's will but in seeing life in relation to it.

Then, as we have been suggesting, our prayers can be one of the factors by which God's will is determined. Finally, prayer is one of the ways through which God's will operates. Some things we simply cannot receive unless we are willing to receive them. Someone might dump a load of bricks on my front lawn as a gift, and the bricks are mine whether I want them or not. But a person cannot share his love of the classics with me unless I am ready to accept it. So also with God's gifts. He may be willing to grant us spiritual insight, but this cannot come unless we are willing to receive it. Our prayer for it makes its coming possible: God could not will it for us otherwise. Yet our prayer does not *change* His will, nor can we say that it changes ours.

In short, the question of providence must be considered in a much wider context than it often is. God is not unresponsive to our need. But we are to an important extent self-determining creatures who must be willing to receive God's choicest gifts if He is to give them to us.

c. Forms of prayer. Prayer in the sense we have been describing it is personal, not because it is nobody's concern but ours, but because it involves all that we are. It goes far beyond mere words. St. Paul suggests that at times we cannot express ourselves in words, but that such prayer is nevertheless real and understood (Rom. 8:26, 27). Simply to recite a set formula is not necessarily to pray. And yet in worship services we frequently join in set prayers and individually use the Lord's Prayer. Of what value are these?

Merely as the repetition of words, they are of no value. One might question, however, whether they are ever *merely* this and nothing more. As guides, they may be invaluable. They may open to us aspects of prayer that we previously had not considered. A book such as John Baillie's *Diary of Private Prayer* can broaden the concerns that we lift up in prayer. Set prayers thus become an example for our own praying.

A less rigid guide may be found in the use of the pattern

appropriate to all worship. Recognition of the need for adoration, confession, and dedication can lead our praying beyond just asking to true communion. Guides for meditation may provide greater variety here than our own imagination might suggest.

But the set prayer may also help us to express more adequately our own concerns and thus deepen them. In this sense it becomes truly our own. People have long thus used the scriptures. We might, for example, pray to be made clean within, with just that simplicity. On the other hand, we may find that the psalmist has put this so succinctly that we can use his words as our own prayer: "Create in me a clean heart, O God, and renew a right spirit within me" (Ps. 51:10, A.V.). Or we may use the collect for purity, again as our own prayer:

Almighty God, unto whom all hearts are open, all desires known, and from whom no secrets are hid; cleanse the thoughts of our hearts by the inspiration of thy Holy Spirit, that we may perfectly love thee, and worthily magnify thy holy Name; through Christ our Lord. Amen.

So the prayers of the person leading worship may be both a stimulus to the individuals of the group and a means of expressing the mutual concerns of the whole body. Sometimes bidding prayers are used—that is, the leader suggests a need for which all pray in silence. Methods and means vary, but the point is that these enable one to develop his own prayer life not merely as technique but in content as well.

In response to Christ's word about praying in his name (John 14:13), most prayers conclude with the formula "in Jesus' name" or "through our Lord Jesus Christ" or something similar, which can mean "in the spirit of Christ." To pray in Jesus' name would mean that we temper and purify our desires so they conform to his character. Selfish prayers cannot be uttered in his name. But the phrase has a deeper significance resting on the whole Christian experience of redemption. We do not come into God's presence because of our merit or efforts. It is through what Christ has done, through what he continually does for us that we can truly approach God at all. When we offer our prayers "through Jesus Christ," we acknowledge this. This simple phrase indicates the uniquely Christian understanding of prayer: it is a way to God opened for us by Christ and therefore a means of His grace.

4. The sacraments

When we think of Bible study, worship, and prayer, we are very likely to think of them in terms of things that we do, so that God, in turn, will bestow His grace on us. But even though the Christian life requires not only our assent but our effort, the testimony of Christians is that it is God's initiative which calls forth this response, that it is because of Who He is and what He has done that we are moved to turn to Him in faith. This is why some have spoken of faith not as something we offer at all, but a trust that God produces within us. Just as my confidence in another person must be generated by that person's trustworthiness, so my trust in God must be generated by God's faithfulness. The means of grace, then, are not things we have instituted, but rather ways which God has provided us through which He can deepen our faith. And particularly when we turn to consider the sacraments, we are much more likely to understand them if we can see them as ways by which God generates and increases our faith.

A sacrament is traditionally defined by the Church as an "outward and visible sign of an inward and spiritual grace." There are thus two parts to a sacrament: the outward act and the inner spiritual reality. Both are necessary. Throughout history, however, people have often distorted their meaning in either of two ways: by teaching that the mere performance of the act conveyed God's grace in an almost mechanical fashion, or by contending that the spiritual reality was independent of the outward act, which truly spiritual people could dispense with entirely.

The need for sacraments arises from the fact that we are not pure spirits. We do not understand everything purely intellectually. We cannot reduce a piece of music to words, because the music conveys a meaning not reducible to words. All great art works have this characteristic. Even literary masterpieces cannot be displaced by short condensations or synopses of plots. In the sacrament we have something that appeals to us not just through intellectual concepts but through sight and action and feeling, as well. The appeal is to our whole selves. For a religion of incarnation where God makes Himself known in history, some form of the sacramental concept is essential. That is, if God can reveal Himself in His fullness only in a human life, then it follows that spiritual truth comes to us through physical means. The sacrament becomes a sign that in a sense certifies to us God's promises. It reminds us of the covenant that God has established with us in Christ.

A good many things in life have a sacramental nature: a period of testing in which genuine courage is born or a rich experience in family living where love is real. The Roman Catholic Church accepts seven sacraments: baptism, confirmation, penance, the Lord's Supper (mass), marriage, extreme unction, and ordination. In each of these God's grace is conveyed in a specific way. But Protestants hold that true sacraments must derive from a specific command of Christ; and whereas many things may be sacramental, only baptism and the Lord's Supper or holy communion are actually sacraments, because only these can be traced to a specific word of Christ. The references are: "Go therefore and make disciples of all nations, baptizing them in the name of the Father, and of the Son, and of the Holy Spirit" (Matt. 28:19); and "This is my body which is broken for you. Do this in remembrance of me" (1 Cor. 11:24).

a. Baptism. Baptism is a ritual washing or cleansing of a person. It was practiced in Judaism before Christ and was required of Gentile converts to signify their purification before becoming members of the community of Israel. John the Baptist gave it a specific reference to sin and held that Jews as well as Gentiles required cleansing to be acceptable to God. Christians accepted baptism as a seal of repentance (Acts 2:38), and St. Paul used the symbolism of immersion to indicate a dying to sin and being raised to new life with Christ (see Rom. 6:1–11). The focus of this renewal was participation in the Christian fellowship. Hence baptism signified one's being ingrafted into Christ (Gal. 3:27). Because this meant a new quality of life, people were often given a new name as a part of the rite, from which act our term "Christian name" is derived. The ingrafting into Christ became "christening."

Two principal concepts of the meaning of baptism have influenced its practice in the churches. In one, its meaning is seen as the confirmation of personal repentance and faith. In this sense baptism cannot be separated from such faith, and hence it must be confined to those who can have it: namely, young people and adults. Churches taking this position deny the validity of infant baptism. Although baptism is regarded as a seal to repentance, it is not repeated because it indicates that a new relationship has been established with God. The faith necessary to baptism is not concerned merely with the act involving water, but with one's whole relation to God. So Martin Luther, when he became discouraged, would say to himself, "I was baptized," not to salve his conscience but to remind himself of his continuing relationship with God.

There are those who hold that the administration of the sacrament in itself conveys the grace of God and that therefore infants benefit from it as much as adults. But a still different position is taken by those who regard the principal meaning of baptism as a sign of belonging to the fellowship of Christ. In view of Jesus' teaching and action towards children (Mark

10:13–16), they feel that children as well as adults belong in the Church, and that since there can be such a thing as a Christian child, the sacrament belongs to children. They regard the Christian community as the society in which God's grace is active, in which the child's faith is stimulated and nourished.

Sometimes the issue is clouded by the question of whether or not a person should be committed to a way of life without his consent. Were Christianity a matter of mere intellectual opinion involving nothing more than a clear choice between obvious alternatives, one might say that children should be allowed to decide for themselves. But Christianity is a life, not an opinion, and one learns of it only through living it. Just as other important matters of life are not left solely to the child's choice—eating, wearing clothes, education—neither is this. Nor do we leave it to the child's choice whether or not he becomes a citizen of his nation or a member of a particular household. Christianity is more a society than an opinion, and hence children are raised in it. Even churches that do not practice infant baptism include children in their circle of concern and fellowship.

Baptism, like all the sacraments, is not a purely personal matter between an individual and God. It is a sacrament of the Church. This means that the baptized child or adult belongs to a fellowship. Although this recognition may appear more important to those groups which practice infant baptism—that is, when the vows are made by the parents in behalf of the child, and they and the whole group commit themselves to bring him up "in the nurture and admonition of the Lord"—it is just as important for adults to recognize that only within the fellowship can the Christian life be real. It was human isolation that Christ sought to overcome (1 John 1:3).

b. The Lord's Supper. Physically, the Lord's Supper is a ceremonial meal of bread and wine commemorating Jesus' last meal with his disciples. Through the centuries it has been central to Christian worship. In this sacrament Christians have known Christ to be especially near to them; in fact, they have spoken of his "real presence." But interpretation of his presence varies. Some insist that the bread and wine actually become the body and blood of Christ. Others feel that their use is a memorial that brings Jesus to mind. But probably all would agree that more is involved than imagining Christ to be present: he actually is.

We should add, however, "present to faith." We do not mean that faith creates his presence, but rather recognizes it. And the purpose of the sacrament is partly to stimulate that faith through which its benefits can be received. Christians believe that God is always present but that our awareness of His presence may be more or less acute. We find Christ near in holy communion not because he is otherwise absent, but because our faith is stimulated to know him. Here as with baptism, the benefits, to some degree, depend on our faith, but the sacrament is given to generate that faith.

Although we speak of Christ's real presence, we recognize that he is not present in the same sense that he was to the disciples in first century Galilee. Some have spoken of this as his "presence in absence." In the ritual of the Lord's Supper we look back to Christ's life, particularly to the moment when he broke bread with his disciples in their last meal together. This is why an integral part of the service is the use of the scripture recalling this moment: "The Lord Jesus on the night when he was betrayed . . ." (1 Cor. 11:23), and why other portions of the gospels are read.

We also look ahead to the completion of Christ's work, to the fulfillment of what we shall later consider under the title "the Christian hope." This simply means that we also remember that Christ shall be victorious over all evil, that he shall be the judge of the living and the dead. St. Paul's words remind us of this dimension of Christ's presence: "As often as you eat this bread and drink the cup, you proclaim the Lord's death until he comes" (1 Cor. 11:26).

The Roman Catholic Church regards this sacrament as a re-enactment of Christ's sacrifice on Calvary, a repetition before the worshipers, for their benefit, although the repetition is dependent on what Christ has accomplished once for all time. Protestants have generally regarded any thought of repetition of Christ's sacrifice as something akin to blasphemy, holding that nothing could be added to what Christ has done. Yet Protestants do hold that something is sacrificed in gratitude for what Christ has done, only it is ourselves as a living offering (see Rom. 12:1). The table from which the bread and wine are served to the congregation is called both a "holy table," referring to the board around which Christ's people are fed, and an "altar," referring to the sacrifice of "praise and thanksgiving" there offered. It is from the Greek word for thanksgiving that the term *eucharist,* which some use for the Lord's Supper, comes.

The Lord's Supper, again, belongs to the whole Church. This is the source of the term *holy communion* which means not only the relation between Christ and the individual believer, but that among believers as well. St. Paul warned that to eat and drink without discerning the body—that is, without recognition of our interrelatedness in Christ—is to bring judgment upon ourselves (1 Cor. 11:29). Churches of the Presbyterian tradition distribute the bread and wine to the whole congregation seated in the pews as symbolic of their participation as a corporate body.

The warning to which we have just referred is sometimes taken to mean that we ought not observe the sacrament if we feel unworthy of it. Repentance is necessary—the earnest desire to obey Christ. But the sacrament is not given as a seal to our worthiness, but rather to God's claiming us though we are unworthy. This is clearly indicated in the words of the Anglican (and by derivation the Methodist) service: "We are not worthy so much as to gather up the crumbs from under thy table." And we participate not because we are already sufficient, but because we need Christ. Actually, St. Paul's warning was not directed toward those who in all humility are painfully aware of their shortcomings, but rather toward those who profaned the service itself by unseemly conduct. It may be hard for us to imagine, but it is nevertheless true that in the early church the Lord's Supper was observed at the end of a large common meal at which some people had gorged themselves while others had become drunk! It was against this sort of thing that these strictures were directed (see 1 Cor. 11:17–34).

c. Marriage. Protestants do not regard marriage as a full sacrament, but because this is often interpreted to mean that they do not take it as seriously as those who do, some word of explanation is in order. We have noted that the Reformers regarded a specific command of Christ as necessary to a full sacrament, and this is missing in the case of marriage. In fact, in the New Testament period, the general counsel was against marriage, in large measure, no doubt, because of the difficulty of the times (see Matt. 19:10–12; 1 Cor. 7:1–9, 25–40).

But it was also recognized that in the complete self-giving of husband and wife, and in the love necessary to maintain wholesome home life, something of the essence of the Kingdom of God is revealed. Therefore the traditional relationship between husband and wife, in which the husband was regarded as superior, is reinterpreted in Christian terms. Authority no longer rests upon accepted social practice, but upon love. The husband's authority is to be exercised like Christ's over the Church: the pattern is not domination but self-giving. In the same way the obedience of the wife is patterned on the self-giving of love based on gratitude and not law or fear. In the unique relation of marriage where the welfare of each partner is identified with that of the other, where self-giving becomes most complete, one can experience something of the intimate relation between Christ and the Church (see Eph. 5:21–33). It is in this sense that marriage is sacramental, though it is not regarded as a full sacrament.

Some groups such as the Quakers have dispensed with outward sacraments entirely, believing that God's spiritual blessings are given in entirely spiritual ways and that perhaps some persons' attitudes toward the sacraments have approached superstition. Yet even Quakers have practices that nourish their faith. So long as we have physical bodies we will probably find that the outward physical signs help us to understand, even to receive, the inward and spiritual grace, just as our knowledge of God depends on God making Himself known in the man Jesus Christ.

5. The ministry

The responsibility for the life of the Church rests on all members. To be a layman is not to be an outsider, as is often thought, but to be one of the people of God. But for practical purposes, some must be delegated certain responsibilities for the smooth and effectual functioning of the whole group. All Christians are ministers of the Gospel, for all are called into the on-going work of God; some people are set aside for special duties, and it is to these that we generally refer when we speak of "the ministry." We have already noted that traditionally there have been three principal offices: deacons, presbyters, and bishops.

There are two principal concepts of the ministry. One sees it as derived from God. Ministers are those who exercise God's authority in the congregation. The administration of the sacraments, teaching, and especially pronouncing God's forgiveness to repentant sinners—all are seen as God's work among His people. There can be no Church, according to this concept, without a duly authorized ministry, and usually this means one derived in an unbroken succession from Christ and the Apostles. These tasks cannot be done at all by a layman because he lacks the authority of God to do them.

The other concept sees the ministry as a delegated function of the life of the congregation as a whole. To accomplish its purpose the church must function smoothly; and so that things can be done decently and in order, the congregation sets apart chosen individuals for special tasks. There is nothing about leading a worship service that a layman could not do it, but one who is trained to do this and does it regularly is more likely to do it better. Since all members cannot have the necessary training and time off from regular employment to do these things, ministers are appointed by the whole church. In the first concept, the authority of the minister is thought to be derived from God directly; in the second, it is thought to come from the congregation or Church.

As might be expected, elements of both views are frequently combined. One's entering the ministry depends on the call of God to him personally and on the action of church authorities confirming that call. The minister is responsible to both God and the congregation: he is not chosen merely to reflect the sentiments of men. Even where the minister is elected, he is expected to exercise God's care over His people, being a true pastor to the members of the congregation.

Some churches (usually those organized on the episcopal pattern) depend on a semi-independent clerical government to supply their ministers; others are radically democratic in allowing each congregation to choose its own; most combine the two, permitting congregational selection within over-all standards and through processes set by a higher authority. Types of church government therefore vary from the episcopal—with authority vested in the highest office—to the independent, in which each congregation governs itself, and the presbyterian in between with its pattern of local authority combined with a higher governing body.

Qualifications for the minister are wide. Not only must he have a solid grounding in the Christian faith and his own tradition—in the forms and usages of his church—but he must be able to relate them to contemporary life. He must understand business management as well as psychology. And he must be able to evidence in his own life his personal religious faith.

Summary

In this chapter we have considered the Church as an end in itself, as the new community that Christ brought into existence, the community of faith. We have looked briefly at what this means in the relation of members to each other. Specifically, we have examined the ways this new life is nourished—the means of grace. But the Church exists not just for its own sake, but to do God's will in the world. To this concern we now turn.

QUESTIONS FOR DISCUSSION

1. Taking a specific order of service, explain how it is a means of grace for the worshipers using it.
2. Why would Christianity more naturally have sacraments than, say, Hinduism?
3. How can prayer be reconciled with God's absolute dominion over the earth?

OTHER SOURCES

General

Brown, Robert McAfee, *The Significance of the Church*. Philadelphia: The Westminster Press, 1956, chap. 6.

Harkness, Georgia, *Religious Living*. New York: Association Press, 1940.

Knox, John, *The Early Church and the Coming Great Church*. New York: Abingdon Press, 1955, chap. 2.

Stewart, George, *The Church*. New York: Association Press, 1940, chap. 4.

Bible

Jenkins, Daniel, *The Strangeness of the Church*. Garden City, N. Y.: Doubleday & Company, Inc., 1955, chap. 8.

Nichols, James Hastings, *Primer for Protestants*. New York: Association Press, 1947, chap. 8.

Worship

Burrows, Millar, *An Outline of Biblical Theology*. Philadelphia: The Westminster Press, 1946, chap. 15.

Pike, James A., *Doing the Truth*. Garden City, N. Y.: Doubleday & Company, Inc., 1955, chap. 9.

Pratt, James Bissett, *Eternal Values in Religion*. New York: The Macmillan Company, 1950, chaps. 1, 2.

Rall, Harris Franklin, *Religion as Salvation*. New York: Abingdon-Cokesbury Press, 1953, chap. 11.

Steere, Douglas V., *Prayer and Worship*. New York: Association Press, 1938, chap. 4.

Underhill, Evelyn, *Worship*. New York: Harper & Brothers, 1937, chaps. 4–6, 12–15.

Prayer

Buttrick, George Arthur, *Prayer*. New York: Abingdon-Cokesbury Press, 1942.

DeWolf, L. Harold, *A Theology of the Living Church*. New York: Harper & Brothers, 1953, chaps. 16, 42.

Gilkey, James Gordon, *A Faith to Affirm*. New York: The Macmillan Company, 1940, chap. 6.

Harkness, Georgia, *Prayer and the Common Life*. New York: Abingdon-Cokesbury Press, 1948.

——, *Understanding the Christian Faith*. New York: Abingdon-Cokesbury Press, 1947, chap. 9.

Houf, Horace T., *What Religion Is and Does*, rev. ed. New York: Harper & Brothers, 1945, chap. 12.

Rall, Harris Franklin, *A Faith for Today*. New York: Abingdon Press, 1936, chap. 15.

Steere, Douglas V., *On Beginning from Within*. New York: Harper & Brothers, 1943.

―――, *Prayer and Worship*. New York: Association Press, 1938, chaps. 1, 2.

Whale, J. S., *The Right to Believe*. New York: Charles Scribner's Sons, 1938, chap. 8.

Wickenden, Arthur C., *Youth Looks at Religion*. New York: Harper & Brothers, 1939, chap. 10.

Sacraments

DeWolf, L. Harold, *A Theology of the Living Church*. New York: Harper & Brothers, 1953, chaps. 39–41.

Finegan, Jack, *Beginnings in Theology*. New York: Association Press, 1956, chaps. 21, 22.

Jenkins, Daniel, *The Strangeness of the Church*. Garden City, N. Y.: Doubleday & Company, Inc., 1955, chaps. 9–11.

Rall, Harris Franklin, *Religion as Salvation*. New York: Abingdon-Cokesbury Press, 1953, chap. 13.

Underhill, Evelyn, *Worship*. New York: Harper & Brothers, 1937, chaps. 7, 8.

Ministry

Burrows, Millar, *An Outline of Biblical Theology*. Philadelphia: The Westminster Press, 1946, chap. 14.

Niebuhr, H. Richard, *The Purpose of the Church and Its Ministry*. New York: Harper & Brothers, 1956.

Niebuhr, H. Richard and Daniel D. Williams, eds., *The Ministry in Historical Perspectives*. New York: Harper & Brothers, 1956, chap. 11.

Spann, J. Richard, ed., *The Ministry*. New York: Abingdon-Cokesbury Press, 1949.

26

the task of the church

We have used the New Testament term the "body of Christ" for the new community that God has called into existence and have looked at its inner life—its interrelatedness and its growth toward maturity. But the body of Christ is the means through which he can continue to express himself.

325

Hence we now turn to look at the Church as that people through whom God carries out His purposes in this world. Simply put, the task of the Church is to bring the world to an acknowledgment of the Lordship of Christ, meaning not merely an outward profession of Christianity, but an inner acceptance of Christ as true Lord in all areas of life.

1.   The proclamation of the Gospel

According to St. Mark, when John the Baptist was arrested, Jesus came into Galilee preaching the Gospel: "The time is fulfilled, and the Kingdom of God is at hand; repent, and believe in the Gospel" (Mark 1:15). The Gospel, we have seen, is not a theory or a religious opinion. It is news that concerns every person, the news of what God has done in Jesus Christ, and therefore is meant to be shared. News is shared when it is made public, either in passing from one person to another or in being proclaimed to a crowd. It was because the disciples were commissioned to share the good news that they gave themselves to preaching, for in the New Testament preaching does not mean haranguing as we so often are likely to think, but proclaiming news.

But preaching, to be effective, must be communication. People must hear and understand. Therefore the news must be expressed in such a way that people can comprehend and act on it. This expression, if it is in words, must be phrased in the thought forms and terminology of the hearers. But the expression may be in an even more universal language—action. The task of the Church is to proclaim the Gospel to the world by communicating it to people in the wholeness of human life.

a. Education. Should someone come to us all excited about the fact that $E = mc^2$, unless we knew the significance of these symbols and the relationship they imply, the proclamation that this was indeed so would have no meaning for us. Even were we to know that E stands for energy and m for mass, but had no further knowledge of the problems of modern physics, we still would not be able to understand. Should this same person speak to us in terms of there being the possibility of an interchange between energy and mass, we might be able to see the significance, at least, of what he was saying, although full understanding would depend on highly technical training. The Gospel is proclaimed to men as men rather than as experts in one field or another—even religion—but response to the proclamation depends on an understanding of it.

The people to whom Jesus spoke were not uneducated to his message. Their heritage gave them the concept of God active in human history. They knew the story of the Exodus and their long history interpreted by the prophets. When Jesus announced that God's action had been consummated, they at least knew what he was talking about whether they agreed with him or not. But people in the wider Greco-Roman world did not have this heritage. To most of them the idea of God taking a direct hand in human affairs was incomprehensible. Words could be translated from Aramaic to Greek—*messiah* becoming *christos*—but the meaning of these words would not automatically be attached to the translation. *Messiah*, meaning "anointed one," had a definite implication to the Jew. *Christos* meaning "anointed one" did not have that same implication to a Greek. The Christian message, therefore, merely translated into Greek words did not make sense to the Epicureans and Stoics of the Hellenistic world, as St. Paul learned (Acts 17:16–34). Most early Christian converts were from the lower classes where the appeal was not primarily intellectual (1 Cor. 1:26–31).

But it was shortly recognized that the Gospel was meant for all men, including intellectuals, and to proclaim it to them meant being able to speak their language not just in word translation but in thought pattern as well. It was not long before men were proclaiming the Gospel in terms that at least would be comprehensible to those educated in the various philosophical schools. This desire to communicate was one of the factors influencing the writing of the Fourth Gospel with its concept of the *logos* or Divine Word. The logos or the rational principle in all things was a Greek philosophical concept. It was at least a familiar term to which Christians gave a unique meaning in relation to Christ. In the years immediately following the New Testament period, this work of putting the Gospel into new modes of expression went forward apace. St. Augustine, for example, reworked the Gospel in terms largely those of Neo-platonic philosophy. But one of the most famous attempts to relate the Christian message with current thought was that of St. Thomas Aquinas. When the teaching of Aristotle was reintroduced into Europe, it was transmitted through Arabian scholars who gave it a decided agnostic interpretation. For this reason the works of Aristotle were banned from the University of Paris. But St. Thomas showed how Christian teaching was compatible with Aristotelian principles, and as a result that philosopher was taught officially by church schools.

These attempts at restatement of the Gospel in other terminology must always be examined for fidelity to the central Christian message. There have been restatements throughout the years of church history when the Gospel was falsified. The attempts of the gnostics to fit Christianity into their scheme of cosmic speculation are examples. More recently, the attempt to fit the biblical revelation into an evolutionary framework borrowed from biology has been questioned on this very issue. But the motive behind restatement is not to add something to or to take something from the Gospel but to express it in terms that are readily understood by the generation in question.

It is also true that some thought patterns must be changed before the Gospel can be communicated. In our day there are those who feel that men must first be delivered from a deterministic philosophy before they can even know what Christian preachers are saying.[1] Much of the interest of Christianity in education is to develop and maintain a world view in which Christianity can make sense. St. Thomas did this in the Middle Ages, but it must be done again in each generation. And this work continues on all levels of education. It begins, perhaps, in the high echelons with those who can think through the issues involved. It is carried out from the grammar school to the university.

Most Protestant churches are committed to public school education, which increasingly has come to mean the elimination of specifically religious elements from the curriculum. How far this process can go without betraying the churches' purpose is being debated today. In higher education there is a dual pattern of state and church colleges. Some church schools probably do conceive their role in narrow terms of indoctrination. But the Church's interest in education is wider than simply finding a congenial reception for its message. The Gospel is not exhausted with the news of the historical events associated with the Incarnation, for the implications of these events in all of life's concerns must be worked out. If the meaning of all life is bound up in the Incarnation, then no human problem can be understood apart from it. Most church schools are supported by the conviction that Christianity must be relevant to all of life's concerns. That is, they are maintained not merely to give students additional classes in religion which they otherwise would not have, but to deal with a more serious problem: the implication of the Gospel for science, art, social studies, philosophy, for all the disciplines of human learning. The reason for the church school is that these studies might proceed unprejudiced by prior commitments (which sometimes can be found in state colleges because of their nonsectarian nature) that deliberately exclude Christian thought.

[1] See F. R. Barry, *Recovery of Man* (New York: Charles Scribner's Sons, 1949; London: James Nisbet & Co., Ltd.).

b. Social witness. The proclamation of the Gospel must relate it to the social context in which men live. It necessarily follows from the Christian affirmation that Christ is Lord that this Lordship must be made evident wherever people live. The Church's concern with social problems therefore rests on its faith in one God Who is supreme over all. Social injustice is fundamentally a religious problem because it is a denial that a righteous God rules over men.

This recognition is one of Israel's finest contributions to Christianity. As early as the reign of David there were prophets who championed the cause of social justice against even royal might (see 2 Sam. 11:1–12:15 and 1 Kings 21:1–24). And the famous prophets of the eighth century—Isaiah, Micah, Amos, and Hosea—are remembered for their insistence that ceremonial worship apart from right human relations could not possibly please God. In particular, God was the protector of the poor and helpless just because He was righteous. Old Testament laws are outstanding for their provisions for the powerless. Slaves are to be granted their freedom after six years of service (Deut. 15:12–18). Fields are not to be gleaned by the owner at harvest, but the fallen grain and that in the fence rows is to be saved for the needy and sojourner (Lev. 23:22). Provisions of the Sabbath rest are to be extended to Israelites and non-Israelites alike (Deut. 5:12–15).

This emphasis on social righteousness was taken over by Christians in the concept of the Kingdom of God. The obligation laid on Christians was to live so that God's reign would be evident in their lives. Dr. Jenkins defines the Church as "the community of those who live here and now, in this sinful present age, in the light and by the power of the final consummation of all things in Christ." [2] This means by implication that the fellowship of Christians is not merely a religious society, but

[2] Jenkins, *The Strangeness of the Church,* p. 38.

an agent for the transformation of secular society as well, not so much as a political movement but as a leaven.

Two factors limited the scope of this concept, however. One was the expectation of Christ's imminent return to earth (see Matt. 16:28 and 1 Thes. 4:16, 17). For many, this meant that the world was beyond being improved and one could only be obedient to God in his personal life, enduring evil until the end of the present order (see Rev. 22:10, 11). Slaves were to remain slaves even though they now served willingly rather than under duress (Col. 3:22, 1 Cor. 7:20–24). Masters were to deal gently with those under them (Col. 4:1), although it was recognized that "in Christ" the distinctions of slave and master did not apply (Gal. 3:28). Certain Christian groups today hold this attitude toward the world.

The second factor was the low social status of Christians. By and large, they did not hold positions of leadership and power. St. Paul's legal status as a mere Roman citizen gave him an advantage over most of his companions who lacked even that right (see Acts 16:35–40; 22:22–29). Christians were a minority, with little opportunity for taking the lead in social reform, recognizing, too, that sin is a perennial problem despite a change of social conditions. So they waited for a better day. But as they waited, they established a pattern of behavior that often led to irresponsibility when power did come to rest in their hands.

The dawning recognition of its social responsibility forms an interesting chapter in the history of the church, but one of which we can give only the briefest sketch. The New Testament counsels concerning the expression of love appear to be so perfectionistic that many have thought of them as an interim ethic, appropriate to a short period, but not able to be maintained throughout society over any length of time. When wholesale conversions to Christianity began following the shift of the Roman government's position from persecution to support, two standards evolved: the older and stricter for those who took their faith more seriously—clergy, monks, or nuns—and one less strict, by way of compromise with the bulk of the population. The latter was a type of minimum requirement, and the former a goal toward which the more devout could aspire. Even nominally Christian rulers were sadly deficient in Christian virtues; but eventually the church was able, largely through the rise of papal power, to force even emperors into the outward semblances of morality.

In the Middle Ages the church had achieved something of its dream of governing all of life. The secular aspects of life were under control of the civil rulers, while the sacred were directly under the church, but the two were alike directed toward Christian ends. Unfortunately, however, the Christian position came to be identified with the feudal ordering of society, and when conditions forced a change in the organization of society, the church often became identified with the cause of reaction. Secular often came to mean "anti-clerical."

This trend continued through the Reformation. While the Reformers insisted that New Testament counsels were meant for all men, that there could be no dual standard of Christian behavior, they leaned heavily on the civil rulers for support in their work. As a result, governments were at times given an uncritical support and obedience. All of life was regarded as the context in which one fulfilled his Christian calling; however, the world came to be regarded as not so much God's realm but more of a battlefield in which one had to fight for his own soul's salvation.

The industrial revolution heightened the tension. With the breakdown of the parish system through large population movements and the rise of a power class untrained in social responsibility, there was no effective critique of social conditions, which steadily grew worse. Much Christian teaching emphasized the virtues of obedience and long suffering rather than social justice, so that Karl Marx had some justification for his charge that religion was the opiate of the people. Yet at the same time the church was able, through individual leaders who often expressed themselves in other than traditional ways, to give men a sense of dignity that led to movements of reform and reclamation.

The Roman Catholic Church had always its principle of natural law by which it could make its social teaching relevant to prevailing conditions, and it never gave up its claim to speak with authority in all areas of life. Practically, however, its witness was often extremely conservative. But the beginning of the twentieth century saw a new movement called the "social gospel" within Protestant ranks. It was not novel, for it had roots in the earlier anti-slavery and temperance movements. But it was a recognition of the fact that power structures change, that earlier appeals to individual consciences may have been an effective method of influencing society, but when the power structure is impersonal—as it is in an industrial civilization—other methods of appeal must be found. The logical approach was through the process of government—legislation and the ballot.

The advocates of the social gospel saw that there is little point in admonishing individuals to be Christian if the social context in which they live and work makes this impossible. The name "social gospel" given to the movement was unfortunate because it implied that such social emphasis was not integral to the Gospel itself, whereas the social gospel was the attempt to give wider application to Jesus' teaching about the Kingdom of God. Sometimes, too, the movement was associated with a questionable theology that made progress almost inevitable by overlooking the reality of human sin. But because of it, Christians gave their support to such social legislation as the regulation of working hours, abolition of child labor, establishment of safety regulations, elimination of oppressive monopolistic practices, and the reform of government.

It hardly need be mentioned that Christians do not always
agree on action to be taken on specific problems. The dispute
over pacifism within the churches or over problems of racial
integration is indication enough of this. But the proclamation of
the Gospel does mean that these social problems be brought
under the judgment of God and action taken not merely on
the demands of expediency but on the basis of principle and
purpose. There is also difference of opinion as to whether the
churches themselves should become involved in political or
social action or whether they ought only to lift up and examine
issues in the light of biblical teaching, allowing individuals to
work out their own witness.

It has been in response to this obligation to proclaim the
Gospel in social relations that churches have insisted on their
separation from the state. We have spoken of the practical reason for eliminating sectarian influences from the government:
it leads to an impossible situation in a land where religious
groups are many. But throughout the history of the church
there have been those who protested a state-church link on
religious grounds. It tended to silence the social witness of the
church because of vested interests. The church is to be kept
separate from the state not merely to avoid sectarian disputes
but in order to keep the way clear for criticism of the policies
of the state in the light of the Gospel.

The Gospel proclamation is that Jesus is Lord, not only in
the heavenly regions, but everywhere (Eph. 1:15–23; 4:1–10).
The reality of this conviction can be proclaimed not in words
only, but in action. This means a critical appraisal of all contemporary life in the light of the Gospel, and a use of power
that is available for Christian ends. To deny this means to hold
either that Jesus' Kingdom has no relation to this world or that
it has already been realized in present society.

c. Concern for the individual. A concern for social justice cannot really be divorced from concern for the welfare of individuals, although at times it is made impersonal. But because concern for the individual is so vital to the Gospel—some would say that the most significant contribution of Christianity is belief in the supreme worth of the individual—we shall treat it separately though briefly.

The news that God has entered human history for men means that God counts them in some sense of eternal value. This is the only genuine foundation for individual concern. Only where men believe in the *eternal* worth of the individual do they remain concerned about his temporal condition. Sometimes confused with Christian belief is the idea that man in himself has certain rights. When everything is peaceful, the difference is hard to detect, but when the assumptions of the latter concept are plainly challenged by human perversity, it is left without support and its effect on human affairs quickly disappears. Christian concern rests not on what men in their own character may or may not be, but on the action of God in Christ: "Beloved, if God so loved us, we also ought to love one another" (1 John 4:11). This regard is not confined to those of the "household of faith." That is, this concern extends beyond mutuality. For if Christ is Lord, then all men belong to him whether they recognize this or not. Whenever a Christian sees another person, no matter how high or how low in the social scale, he sees one for whom Christ has given his life. When he so treats that person, he proclaims the Gospel.

Historically, one of the most important implications of this was the change in social status of women and children. Family life takes on a new dimension when human beings are no longer regarded as property, when the foundation of family life is not just the prevailing pattern of social organization but the relation of persons mutually bound to Christ. Roles are no

longer defined by law, but by the will of God (Matt. 19:3–9).
Authority rests on the claims of love (Eph. 5:21–33).

It is on this basis that welfare programs are conducted, and
if they have matured from the older "charity" to methods of
self-help that maintain self-respect, it is because more knowledge and greater wisdom have channeled this basic respect
more constructively. On this same basis medical benefits are
extended to all who need them, education is made available for
all who will receive it, and the responsibility and privilege of
government are shared democratically.

2. Christian vocation

So far we have looked at what it means for the Church to
accept its task of proclaiming the Gospel to the world. But we
are very apt to think of the Church as some impersonal entity
in this regard and speak of what "it" ought to do in much the
same way that we speak of what the government ought to do.
The Church, however, is a society, and a society is made up of
its members. When we focus specifically on what one Christian
does in response to the Gospel and within the community of
faith, we raise the issue of Christian vocation.

a. The meaning of vocation. Essentially a religious word,
vocation means "calling." In the New Testament, to "call" a
person means to summon him to a task of responsibility. It is
used of the whole Christian life, for God first calls men who
may then respond. All Christians are called (Rom. 1:7). This
role is not merely of their own choosing. And the call is specifically to the way of life in which the sole Lordship of Christ is
evident. It is by the call of God that Christians are brought into
the fellowship of the Church (1 Cor. 1:9), and it is by the call
of God that they are set to work in His purpose.

In the Middle Ages the meaning of *vocation* was largely
confined to the life of the religious person—the priest, monk,
or nun. If an individual were to have received a call, he would

likely have left secular concerns and employment to enter some religious order. But at the Reformation, the more universal New Testament teaching was again emphasized: every Christian is called and thus has a vocation. That vocation is to acknowledge in all of daily life the Lordship of Christ.

Difficulty is usually encountered in trying to understand this concept because God is so often limited to a so-called religious realm, and thereby the concern of the Church as well. Thus when we speak of the maid being called as well as the clergyman, many people think that what is meant is that the maid can somehow, through her work, influence people to live Christlike lives as much as a clergyman could, or reach people the clergyman could not. This, of course, would be fine. But this is not the essential meaning of *vocation*. It does not refer to what a person might do of a religious nature while he is employed at some other task. It means that the work itself is a response to God's call: the dusting, or machine tending, or plowing, or study.

All goes back to the recognition that this is God's world, and His dominion is seen in His providing for His creatures. Yet that providence is expressed through man's work. God feeds men, but through the agency of other men who till the soil—and in our day we could expand that simple picture to include the agricultural economist, the scientist, and the merchant. This work is all a response to God. Today we recognize the interrelatedness of all society. Industry, agriculture, commerce, education—all are intricately tied together. And seen from the Christian viewpoint, all in some way relate to God's care over the world.

This does not mean that every human occupation fits into the Christian scheme of vocation. Some simply are irrelevant to God's purpose or may even be contrary to it by being useless or unnecessary or harmful. But it does mean that work which is necessary to human need is within the concept of vocation. It means further that work is to be judged on the basis of results rather than prestige. We need not conceive of necessary work in too narrow terms. Human life is more than physical existence, and the musician or artist who can express man's aesthetic sense may be just as important as the farmer or the carpenter. It is a false simplification to think of necessities in purely physical terms. Yet, although man does not live by bread alone, he does require bread to live. There is nothing inherently more Christian in being a minister, therefore, than in being a manufacturer. There is no scale of vocations shading from less Christian to more Christian, though in any job an ideal may be more or less compromised.

b. Determining one's vocation. How, then, is a person to decide what his calling is—how he, personally, should respond to Christ's Lordship in this world? Two factors are foremost: need and ability, and they cannot really be separated. Each person has some understanding of his abilities, and he may correct or substantiate his self-appraisal by taking into consideration the opinions of wise counselors and friends, in addition to data obtained from aptitude and guidance tests. Even then, however, ability must be relevant to need. Thus, a young person contemplating his future career may take stock of his abilities— skill in getting along with people, a penchant toward science, or musical talents—and he decides whether to become a personnel manager, a clergyman, a research chemist, or a school music director. Here he can make a rather free choice among many possibilities.

But there are times when needs are almost compulsive. Were a town threatened with flood, and all able hands required to sandbag a river levee, one could scarcely plead special abilities as exemption from this primary necessity. A young wife may find her talents lying in some measure unused as she undertakes the routines of housework and child care, without which home life cannot exist. But with the choice relatively open, one finds his vocation where need and ability coincide. Thus the experienced teacher may help sandbag levees when flood waters threaten; but when this danger is not imminent, he is more valuable in the classroom than on the levee. It is not that manual work is a "lower" employment, but that his abilities qualify him for other work. A deep sea diver, when the need presents itself, may have to give first aid to a fellow worker; but normally he leaves the practice of medicine to the qualified physician.

To speak of the "call" of God is to use words that imply the thought that there is one single thing a person ought to do with his life, something that he might expect to discover through some mystical experience. There are people who say that their vocation was made explicit to them in this way. But for most, the call of God is mediated through normal experiences of life. Some possibilities are open; others are not. Some young people have the opportunity for a university education; others do not. Some have a great deal of inner resoluteness which others lack. Most grow up in an environment that definitely conditions their conceptions of possible life work: a person with professional parents rarely becomes an unskilled laborer. We pick up the matter of vocation where we find ourselves and begin with the possibilities open before us.

Lest this sound too matter-of-fact, we must note that the understanding of need and ability as well as one's attitude toward his background is definitely affected by his faith. A Christian and an agnostic regard needs in different lights. The Christian thinks not only in terms of momentary expediency but in terms of the on-going purpose of God. And this affects not only his choice of life work, but his attitude in carrying it out as well.

c. *Fulfilling one's vocation.* One's vocation involves his own response to the call of God, a response set within the Christian fellowship, making it a good deal more than just his own business. And the matter is not solved with the choice of life work. The work is part of it, but it must be seen within the context of God's will and purpose expressed through an historically continuous community of people. This view demands evaluation of one's role both as a worker and as a member of the community. And this can be undertaken only as a cooperative venture.

Only the worker, for example, really knows the situation involved in his job. Criticisms of outsiders are not necessarily irrelevant, but they are often detached and therefore lose their effectiveness. On the other hand, the theologically trained person, or the one skilled in biblical interpretation is able to point out implications of the Gospel on crucial issues which the untrained person might overlook. Within the Christian community, however, these separate contributions can be related, because in this community the interdependence is recognized and appreciated. The pastor makes a contribution to daily work not merely in taking care of the routine of the parish, but in helping parishioners understand their own work in the light of their Christian faith. This help is more than encouragement to give full service for wages. It involves a wide understanding of God's will for life.

At the present time, most churches face a serious shortage of ministers. Moreover, as the conception of the role of a congregation in the total life of a community broadens, additional professional workers such as counselors, educational directors, social workers, and business managers become necessary. The range of abilities needed by the modern church is surprising to most people, particularly when we itemize the needs for teachers in all disciplines, agriculturalists, doctors, economists, and medical technicians for the various mission programs. Denominational headquarters make available lists of specific needs which any person ought seriously to consider in defining the meaning of Christian vocation for his own life.

At the same time it must be remembered that Christ's Lordship extends to all of life. Often a person with an unusually meaningful religious experience interprets it as a call from regular work into the professionally Christian ranks. Thus some of the best leadership is lost to the task of claiming the daily life for God. The Christian, as we have said, lives in two worlds: in the present order and in the Kingdom of God. But he lives to assert the claim of the Kingdom on the present order. The possibility of this lies in the fact that the world does belong to God. The necessity of it lies in the fact that God's purpose is worked out in the context of history in human affairs. The tension between the two worlds is the setting for one's vocation. Vocation, in short, is one's own role in the task of the Church.

QUESTIONS FOR DISCUSSION

1. What effect does the relation of the church to the government have on its proclamation of the Gospel?
2. Does Christian pacifism have any basis other than the commandment against killing? On what basis can participation in wars be defended?
3. What makes a vocation Christian?

OTHER SOURCES

Proclaiming the Gospel

Barry, F. R., *Recovery of Man.* New York: Charles Scribner's Sons, 1949, chaps. 4–6.

Bennett, John C., *Christianity and Our World.* New York: Association Press, 1936.

Brown, Robert McAfee, *The Significance of the Church.* Philadelphia: The Westminster Press, 1956, chaps. 7, 8.

Burrows, Millar, *An Outline of Biblical Theology.* Philadelphia: The Westminster Press, 1946, chap. 17.

Ferre, Nels F. S., *Christian Faith and Higher Education.* New York: Harper & Brothers, 1954.

Gilkey, James Gordon, *A Faith to Affirm.* New York: The Macmillan Company, 1940, chap. 11.

Harkness, Georgia, *Understanding the Christian Faith*. New York: Abingdon-Cokesbury Press, 1947, chap. 11, part 3, chap. 12.

Houf, Horace T., *What Religion Is and Does*, rev. ed. New York: Harper & Brothers, 1945, chap. 20.

Jenkins, Daniel, *The Strangeness of the Church*. Garden City, N. Y.: Doubleday & Company, Inc., 1955, chaps. 13, 14.

Miller, Alexander, *The Renewal of Man*. Garden City, N. Y.: Doubleday & Company, Inc., 1955, chap. 6.

Miller, Randolph Crump, *Education for Christian Living*. Englewood Cliffs, N. J.: Prentice-Hall, Inc., 1956, chaps. 1–5.

Moore, R. W., "The Furtherance of the Gospel," *A Primer of Christianity*, London: Oxford University Press, 1950, Part II, chap. 10.

Morton, T. Ralph, *Community of Faith*. New York: Association Press, 1954, chaps. 12–17.

Niebuhr, H. Richard, *Christ and Culture*. New York: Harper & Brothers, 1951, chap. 1.

Pike, James A., *Doing the Truth*. Garden City, N. Y.: Doubleday & Company, Inc., 1955, chaps. 10–15.

Rall, Harris Franklin, *A Faith for Today*. New York: Abingdon Press, 1936, chap. 19.

——, *Religion as Salvation*. New York: Abingdon-Cokesbury Press, 1953, chap. 17.

Rauschenbusch, Walter, *Christianizing the Social Order*. New York: The Macmillan Company, 1912.

Stewart, George, *The Church*. New York: Association Press, 1940, chap. 4.

Tittle, Ernest Fremont, *Christians in an Unchristian Society*. New York: Association Press, 1939, chaps. 3, 4.

Trueblood, Elton, *Alternative to Futility*. New York: Harper & Brothers, 1948.

Walker, Alan, *The Whole Gospel for the Whole World*. New York: Abingdon Press, 1957.

Wickenden, Arthur C., *Youth Looks at Religion*. New York: Harper & Brothers, 1939, chap. 13.

Williams, Daniel Day, *God's Grace and Man's Hope*. New York: Harper & Brothers, 1949, chap. 7.

Christian vocation

Calhoun, Robert Lowry, *God and the Day's Work*. New York: Association Press, 1943.

Coleman, A. J., *The Task of the Christian in the University*. New York: Association Press, 1947, chaps. 6, 7.

Miller, Alexander, *Christian Faith and My Job*. New York: Association Press, 1946.

———, *The Renewal of Man*. Garden City, N. Y.: Doubleday & Company, Inc., 1955, chap. 7.

Nichols, James Hastings, *Primer for Protestants*. New York: Association Press, 1947, chap. 9.

the church and
the non-christian

Whenever the task of the Church in the world is discussed, someone is sure to ask the emotionally charged question, "Do Christians believe that everyone disagreeing with them is going to hell?" And this leads to other questions about why one religious group should seek to impose its opinions on others, or whether all religions are not basically the same. It is difficult to clarify the real issues in the heat of such discussion, and often the problem is to define the initial assumptions. How can we best approach the matter?

1. The world mission of the Church

To state it quite bluntly, the Church is missionary by its very nature. To deny the missionary activity of the Church is to deny the fundamental reason for its existence. A brief review of the ground we have covered should make this apparent. The Christian understands God—and for good reasons which we have examined—as the One Who is transcendent but Who makes Himself known to men through His action in history. He has called into being a people through whom He can work to accomplish His purpose of redemption. If those who are called defect from their call, His work continues through a faithful remnant. In this sense, the Church exists not for its own sake but for the world. It is God's agent in history, through whom He works by historical processes. Men learn of God and respond to Him in the context of their whole lives as personal, social beings because of the activity of the Christian community.

From the earliest days, Christians have so understood their role. Jesus' understanding of his role was that of a missionary. When the disciples wanted him to settle for a while in one village, he insisted that he go on to preach in other places, "for that is why I came out" (Mark 1:38). His mission carried him not only to his own people but among Gentiles as well. He sent out his disciples, two by two, in the same sort of activity (Mark 6:7). After his resurrection the commission was broadened to include not just the local region but the whole world (Acts 1:8), and early converts such as St. Stephen and his friends accepted this wider mission (Acts 6:1–8; 8:1–4). The Church since the time of Jesus himself has been essentially missionary.

There are those who have mistakenly thought that Christianity was constituted a missionary religion by the command of Christ to preach the Gospel to every creature. . . . We may say that Christianity is missionary, not because it received orders to carry its message to all men, but because it was constructed for that purpose. Missions are not an afterthought, but entered into the plan back in the purposes of God far before Christianity or any other religion came into existence. But it was only "when the time had fully come" that "God sent forth His Son" (Gal. 4:4 R.S.V.).[1]

And this is how the Church came to be established throughout the world. Acts 16:9, 10 recounts a vision that prompted St. Paul to carry his mission into Europe. The history of Christian missions is heroic reading from the days of the Apostles through those of Patrick in Ireland and Boniface who cut down the Teuton's sacred oak, to the present day. By the fourth century the Church was established in India, and in the ninth century there was a flourishing Christian community in China. But the real expansion of Christian missions came in the nineteenth and twentieth centuries. The point we make now is that this was no unusual development but the fulfillment of the purpose of God in Christ in creating the Church. It could not have been otherwise if the Christian community were to be true to its Lord.

2. Cultural imperialism?

The charge is frequently made in our day that this missionary program is a vicious form of cultural aggression, for it reflects an attitude of superiority toward the cultures of other people. There is much misinformation behind the charge, for we often have idealized views of other cultures that gloss over the blighting effects of superstition and fear in human life. But there is also some substance to it, for it is easy to confuse Christianity with a particular culture in which it is expressed. Thus in the early days of the church there were those who insisted that

[1] Edmund Davison Soper, *The Inevitable Choice* (New York: Abingdon Press, 1957), p. 175. Reprinted by permission.

the practices of Judaism were an integral part of the Christian faith. The separation of Christianity from Judaism was a long and agonizing process. In our day it is usually Western culture that is identified with Christianity, largely because Christianity has been one of the formative elements of Western civilization. The prestige of scientific accomplishments and industrialization has often created the impression that Western civilization is superior, at least in meeting man's physical needs. Then, too, in countries with established cultures, mission work has often meant the importation of European languages as well as Western dress, social patterns, music, and literature. The fact that commercial and industrial operations have followed or accompanied the missionary has added to the confusion—so has Western control of the Christian mission program and frequently of the churches developing from it.

But the identification of the mission of the Church with extension of a particular civilization is false. True, while some aspects of culture are matters of indifference—the style of dress, for example—some are quite vital to the Gospel. A Christian could hardly be indifferent about the practice of burning a widow alive along with the body of her deceased husband. Nevertheless, Christianity can be expressed in a variety of cultures, each making its own significant contribution.

In our day the younger mission churches are taking on their own characteristics, adapting their practices to the customs of their own lands, using their own traditional art forms in worship, developing a leadership among local people themselves. Whereas in the past the contribution was from the West, the tide is now turning, and a world Christianity is being enriched by contributions from many sources. Too seldom we hear of the mission activity of the churches of the Philippine Islands, for example, or of Japan. Particularly in the World Council of Churches the voice of Christians the world over, with their unique approaches in thought and practice, is being heard. The result may be a faith deepened not only by Greek thought—as New Testament Christianity certainly was—but by Oriental, Indian, and African patterns, too.

3.   Is Christianity superior?

Like it or not, we live in a world where there is a growing interchange of ideas, and Christian missions have historically been one of the most important factors in opening this commerce. The resulting comparison of ideas and ways of life will always be a challenge for all parties entering into the discussion. But in response to what prompting do Christians deliberately try to convert others to their faith?

Here is the same confusion that exists in all human motivation. At times the drive has been unworthy of Christianity because it has been a drive to increase the ranks of the earthly church, which is not always the same thing as bringing men to acknowledge the Lordship of Christ. We have already learned to be wary of separating the Church as God's people from its earthly manifestation in particular churches. But the two are not identical, and the authentic motivation to Christian missions is not to make more Methodists or Presbyterians or Baptists, but to make Christ's Lordship evident. The fact that denominationalism has been more readily overcome in the missionary field than in America or Europe would indicate that the missionary motive is purer than is often thought.

One of the most important traditional motivations, and still effective with more conservative groups, is the desire to "save souls." Beginning with the conviction that God sent His Son in order that men could find salvation, they reason that if men could have been saved some other way, Christ's birth and death would not have been necessary. Therefore, if men are to be saved, Christ must be preached to them. Hence it is our Christian duty, out of sheer human compassion, to convert men in order to keep them from the eternal torments of hell. Regardless of what we may think of such reasoning, there can be no question of the love, courage, and devotion of missionaries who held, and still hold, this view.

The reaction to this line of thought has been a questioning whether God as revealed in Christ is One Who would commit millions of souls to hell through no fault of their own because of the unfortunate fact that the Gospel was never preached to them. There has been a weakening of the conviction that all who have not heard of Christ are damned. Sometimes the agent of this weakening has been the glib assurance that sincerity alone saves a person, glib because in no other area of life is sincerity enough. Sincerity cannot make up for ignorance or lack of skill or confusion of purpose.

Popularly this emphasis on the sufficiency of sincerity is expressed in the statement that "all religions are the same." This becomes a dogma just as much as any creedal statement of Christianity. It is not verified but rather contradicted by the evidence. There is a crucial and undeniable difference between a religion that insists God declares Himself in history and one that says history is a totally meaningless delusion in which God has no part at all. The types of activity derived from two such contrary premises should make it obvious that all religions are not the same.

Sometimes this older conviction that men must be saved from hell has been weakened by the recognition that the question of the soul's salvation of any person is ultimately God's to decide. And this recognition is essentially biblical: "I will have mercy on whom I will have mercy" (Exo. 33:19; Rom. 9:15). We shall turn shortly to consider this matter of God's choosing a people. But here we can note that this recognition does not mean the end of mission motivation, for it may be that the Christian mission is the avenue by which God shows mercy.

Many liberal Christians justify missions not on the basis of any desire to keep the "heathen" from hell, but on the basis of certain areas of superiority of Christianity over other religions. Dr. James B. Pratt lists some of these: Christianity's creedal clarity, the identification of God's righteousness with love, the winsomeness of Jesus as a person, the expression of religious devotion in social service, and finally the greater interest in education and higher skill and energy in propagating the faith.[2] These mean a fuller life for non-Christian people, and this fuller life becomes the real drive behind missions rather than the attempt to change the symbols of religious expression from those which are characteristically Indian, say, to those traditionally Hebrew.

Christians simply do not agree at this point on the reason behind missions, though instinctively they recognize their importance. Perhaps the emphasis on God's revelation in history that we have carried throughout this book can shed other light on the situation. This emphasis reminds us that basically the Gospel is not an idea, but good news, and that Christianity is the whole response of people called forth by the proclamation of that news. This means that to consider merely the beliefs of a religion is to miss the important aspects of that religion. Dr. Soper writes:

If it were true that religion is basically the acceptance of a body of beliefs or the practice of a set of laws or regulations, it would not be unreasonable to aim at a synthesis of some kind, but such is not the case in Christianity. Our religion is at bottom a loyalty or a commitment to a person, an allegiance to Jesus Christ not only as Saviour, but as Lord and Master of our lives.[3]

This of course means that Christianity is definitely exclusive— one cannot serve two masters—but exclusiveness is not narrowness, incapable of recognizing good in other people. Dr. Soper compares the situation to that found in Christian marriage, in

---

[2] James Bissett Pratt, *Can We Keep the Faith?* (New Haven: Yale University Press, 1941; London: Oxford University Press), pp. 167–71. Used by permission.
[3] Soper, *The Inevitable Choice*, p. 143.

which a man and a woman bind themselves to each other exclusively for life; yet it is only in Christian lands, where this concept of marriage prevails, that men and women may associate socially with freedom. The harem or purdah, where women are secluded, is never associated with the exclusiveness attendant to the Christian idea of marriage.[4]

The Christian, in order to remain a Christian, need not deny that other people have important knowledge of God. Since there is but one God, wherever knowledge of Him exists, it is only because to some extent He has there revealed Himself. Most of the world's great religions have a remarkably similar core of ethical teaching, though it is not always equally emphasized, and this could hardly be by chance. There can very well be respect for the transcendence of Allah found in Islam, or the immanence of the Hindu Brahman, and not only respect but a willingness to learn from them as well.

Emphasis on the revelation of God in history affirms the importance of the processes of historical transmission. The spread of Christianity, like news, is from one person to another. Mankind does not conceive an idea simultaneously. Even religions such as the Hindu, which stress God's immediate presence in every man, depend on an historical tradition to transmit the beliefs from one generation to another. The association of holy men around a teacher, the time-honored role of the ascetic, the paths and ways and noble truths memorized and recited—what are these if not unconscious acknowledgments in the face of conscious denials of the importance of history? On what basis then does a person decide to whom he will turn for guidance? Is he to have a choice, or must national tradition be regarded as the final arbiter of truth, or social position, or total numbers of believers? There may have been missionaries who insisted that their position alone was right and all others wrong, but Christianity has made its appeal to men's freedom to decide the God

[4] *Ibid.*, pp. 144f.

Whom they should serve, and it has recognized that one must know alternatives to decide intelligently.

Historical emphasis has a third indication: that one's inclusion in the Christian ranks has nothing to do with superior merit on his part, nor does it give him superiority before other men. St. Paul in discussing the puzzling question of why Judaism should have rejected Christ goes back to the Old Testament insistence that God's call of Israel depended only on His grace and not on Israel's worthiness. And he goes on to say that the inclusion of the Gentiles in God's people has the same foundation. All grounds for boasting are therefore removed. He compares their inclusion among God's people with the grafting of a wild olive branch onto a cultivated olive tree and he warns, "If God did not spare the natural branches, neither will He spare you" (Rom. 11:21).

Our Christianity today rests on what we might call an "historical accident" but which St. Paul and other New Testament writers would call "the mystery of God's grace." (Incidentally, St. Paul thought that Israel's rejection of Christ was providential, that it forced the apostles to go to the Gentiles in order that God's purpose to save all men, including the Jews, might be fulfilled.) However it came about, our being Christian has nothing to do with our own inferiority or superiority. Objection to missions on the basis that "other people are just as good as we are" is not relevant, for Christianity is not the fellowship of the best people, but of those who acknowledge Christ as Lord. Missions are not supported because Christians think they are better than others, but because they have been included in a movement and commissioned to a work that is larger than they —God's work among men. And if people challenge this premise that God's work through the Christian community is different from His work in the rest of the world, we must simply retrace our steps through the concept of an historical revelation.

Finally, so long as the Christian recognizes that he is saved through faith, he cannot dogmatize about God's eternal disposition of the world's people. We are saved through our trust in God and not our adherence to a particular code of laws nor our acceptance of a certain list of religious propositions. Of course faith demands some content for its existence. Faith is more than sincerity. But faith is something of which men cannot be adequate judges. Even St. Paul spoke of people "without the law" doing by nature what the law required (Rom. 2:14, 15). Jesus spoke of other sheep "not of this fold" who would heed his voice (John 10:16). The Christian does not, and cannot, say, "It is only on me and my kind that God has shown, or can show, mercy." At the same time, he must bear witness to God's revelation in history in Israel and the Church.

Summary

The relation of the Church to the non-Christian is of primary concern to the Christian. Because of his understanding of his relation to the Christian community, the Christian is personally involved with the existence of non-Christian fellows. God has laid an obligation on him: "Woe is me if I do not preach the Gospel" (1 Cor. 9:16). And this concern is beyond any recognition of his moral superiority or inferiority to the other person. One simply cannot be a member of the Church which Christ established and think in terms of only himself. To be one of God's people is to be assigned a role in the on-going purpose of God that the Bible says was declared to Abraham and made clear in Christ, a purpose including every generation of men.

QUESTIONS FOR DISCUSSION

1. It is often said, "Only circumstances of birth make us Christian." Analyze the statement in terms of the Christian concept of God's revelation in history.
2. Buddhism, Christianity, and Islam are the three great missionary religions. Compare their motivations for seeking new adherents.

OTHER SOURCES

Braden, Charles S., *Jesus Compared*. Englewood Cliffs, N. J.: Prentice-Hall, Inc., 1957.

Finegan, Jack, *Beginnings in Theology*. New York: Association Press, 1956, chap. 11.

Jenkins, Daniel, *Believing in God*. Philadelphia: The Westminster Press, 1956, chap. 6.

———, *The Strangeness of the Church*. Garden City, N. Y.: Doubleday & Company, Inc., 1955, chap. 16.

Pratt, James Bissett, *Can We Keep the Faith?* New Haven: Yale University Press, 1941, chap. 12.

Soper, Edmund Davison, *The Inevitable Choice*. New York: Abingdon Press, 1957, chaps. 7, 8.

———, *The Philosophy of the Christian World Mission*. New York: Abingdon-Cokesbury Press, 1943, chaps. 11–14.

Wolf, William J., *Man's Knowledge of God*. Garden City, N. Y.: Doubleday & Company, Inc., 1955, chap. 12.

28

the christian hope

The Church is the meeting point of the Gospel and the world because it is the community brought into being by the good news of Jesus Christ, and it, in turn, is commissioned to proclaim that news to the rest of the world. The question that cannot be avoided in all this, however, is whether it can expect success in its work in this world or whether it will meet increasing resistance and be able to claim only a portion of the world's people. The way it conducts its mission vitally depends on how this question is answered. But the answer is not an easy one, for it involves our understanding of the final purpose of all things, the goal toward which everything is seen to move. The study of this particular concern is called *eschatology* (a word derived from the Greek word for "last things"), the doctrine of the consummation of history.

1.   Two contrasting conceptions

While it may seem strange to us to use the technical term *eschatology*, it is not strange for us to think about what we might expect in the future, not necessarily within a few months or even years, but in terms of the general trend events will take. Simply discarding the word does not dismiss the concern, for rational people inevitably think in eschatological terms, whether they are aware of it or would admit it.

If we were to ask an average person what lies ahead, he would probably reply that there might be ups and downs; but, on the whole, progress towards man's perfection is being made, and things are consequently getting better. Upon our further questioning he could no doubt give examples which he feels indicate that such progress is genuine and which give some assurance that the same trend will continue. He might mention the expected span of human life that has about doubled in the past century. He might speak of improved communication that brings people all over the world within a fraction of a second of each other instead of months apart. He might mention the gradual abolition of slavery and the more glaring examples of exploitation, at least in Western lands.

If he has a Christian orientation, he probably will speak in terms of the gradual realization of the Kingdom of God on earth. By this he would mean that an increasing number of men will learn the foolishness and danger of selfish ways and come to obey the law of love in all their relationships. Ultimately, society will be ruled by God. He would probably mention that there might be setbacks from time to time, like the Nazi brutality in World War II, but that in the long run the Kingdom of God will come, and for this reason we ought to do our part to hasten it by making the world a better place to hand on to future generations.

On the other hand, this average person might answer in an entirely different manner by giving examples of how things are going from bad to worse. He might speak of the good old days when people could be trusted and personal initiative prevailed. He may point to world tension with the threat of atomic warfare, or to the increase of juvenile delinquency, or to the growing restlessness of native peoples, or to the increasing dependence of people on their governments, using these as examples of growing decay and disintegration. If he has a Christian orientation, he might speak of the way that evil will gain strength until a titanic struggle develops between the forces of good and those of evil, a struggle with outcome uncertain until God intervenes to subdue evil forever and thus inaugurate His Kingdom.

These two positions may sound poles apart—as in many respects they actually are—but in one important consideration they are agreed: the final victory will be God's. Christ will speak the last word. This, in essence, is the Christian hope in contrast to ideas that history merely repeats itself or has no meaning at all. And it is this faith that distinguishes the Christian hope from wishful thinking or shallow optimism. As an attitude toward life, it is more stable than a mood of the moment. It does not simply reflect the hopefulness of earthly situations. Some people are optimistic when all goes well but morose when they encounter opposition. Christian hope means looking confidently ahead, not because everything is necessarily working out well, but because one's trust is in God. But how can two such diverse ideas arise from the same ultimate conviction?

2. The Kingdom present and yet to come

There are two emphases in the Gospel about the coming of God's Kingdom. The first of these is that it is a present reality now that Christ has come. "Truly," Jesus says to his disciples, "many prophets and righteous men longed to see what you see, and did not see it, and to hear what you hear, and did not hear it" (Matt. 13:17). Or again, "If it is by the Spirit of God that I cast out demons, then the Kingdom of God has come upon you" (Matt. 12:28). And again, "Now is the judgment of this world, now shall the ruler of this world be cast out" (John 12:31). And this emphasis is repeated throughout the New Testament: "This is what was spoken by the prophet Joel" (Acts 2:16); "When the time had fully come, God sent forth His Son" (Gal. 4:4); "He has delivered us from the dominion of darkness and transferred us to the Kingdom of His beloved Son" (Col. 1:13).

This is not interpreted as a purely spiritual coming—that is, in the hearts of men—while the world itself remains unaffected. The new reign of God is evident in history. Things have changed. "The blind receive their sight, the lame walk, lepers are cleansed, and the deaf hear, the dead are raised up, the poor have good news preached to them" (Luke 7:22). The powers of evil have been defeated, and a new era has begun. In this sense, the decisive battle has been fought, and what remains is a clean-up campaign in which the results of that victory are made evident. Hence, what we might expect is the increasing rule of God over human life until the process is completed.

But there is another emphasis in the Gospel. The coming of the Kingdom of God is seen as a future event brought about by the power of God alone, and the prelude to this event is not a gradual "Christianization" of this world but rather a growing tension between good and evil. "Nation will rise against nation, and kingdom against kingdom, and there will be famines and earthquakes in various places. . . . Because wickedness is multiplied, most men's love will grow cold. . . . False Christs and false prophets will arise and show great signs and wonders, so as to lead astray, if possible, even the elect. . . . Then all the tribes of the earth will mourn, and they will see the Son of man coming on the clouds of heaven with power and great glory. . . . But of that day and hour no one knows, not even the angels of heaven, nor the Son, but the Father only. . . . Therefore you also must be ready; for the Son of man is coming at an hour you do not expect." (The whole passage is found in Matt. 24:3-51.) Similar passages are found in 1 Thes. 4:13-5:11 and 2 Thes. 2:1-11, which introduces the figure of the "man of lawlessness" who will precede the return of Christ. The book of the Revelation elaborates this theme with its bizarre pictures of increasing chaos on earth and the appearance of Antichrist before the final victory of God at the battle of Armageddon.

These passages introduce us to a rather strange way of speaking about things, namely the *apocalypse*. The conception of the last stages of history in terms of conflict and tension is characteristic of apocalyptic expression and a further trait is its framework of strange beasts, angels, trumpets, sealed books, and cryptic language. We shall consider the reason for this shortly.

But what are we to make of this theme of the second coming of Christ and the inauguration of the Kingdom? Some people have taken it quite literally and have understood it as a prediction for the future, the date of which is to be arrived at by deciphering the weird allusions to historical events. People are constantly predicting the end of the world on this basis, and dates have been set for it ever since the Christian Church began, for had not Jesus himself said, "This generation will not pass away till all these things take place" (Matt. 24:34)?

Earthly tyrants from Nero to Stalin have been identified with the beast whose number is six hundred and sixty-six (Rev. 13:18).

Others, unable to take this sort of thing seriously, have regarded the apocalyptic details as a carry-over from Judaism but in no sense an integral part of the Christian message. Apocalypse developed from the prophetic movement within Israel, particularly in the years following the exile when earthly fortunes seemed so contrary to the Jewish people that the fulfillment of God's promise was pushed into the future and almost separated from the course of history. Confidence in God's faithfulness could not be shaken; but when events seemed to belie the establishment of righteousness, these disappointing happenings were fitted into a larger picture that saw the increase of wickedness as necessarily preceding the intervention of God in human affairs. In the period between the two Testaments, the apocalyptic hope grew. It was part of the popular mood in Jesus' time. Those who dismiss it feel that it was an attempt to rationalize the Jews' inability to realize their dreams and that we can forget it because we know that the Kingdom must be brought on earth through the remaking of men and society.

3. The significance of apocalyptic thought

In recent years, however, this attitude has become increasingly suspect because the expectation of the return of Christ is so engrained in the New Testament that it would be sheer arbitrariness to strike it out. Some scholars regard it as the only authentic New Testament teaching. Most, however, take a more moderate view; and while the old dispute continues, there is a growing understanding of the apocalyptic emphasis in relation to that of the present reality of the Kingdom. And this new understanding stems largely from an appreciation of the essential historical factor in biblical thought that we have all along been considering.

We began with religion as dealing with the meaning of life. When we consider what our experience means and how it is tied together, we necessarily involve ourselves in religion. But the total meaning of life must come from a source outside ourselves. We looked at the main line of biblical thought that saw this meaning revealed in history, in human events rather than in some so-called spiritual realm divorced from our daily living. We noted how the exodus from Egypt was the key by which the Israelites interpreted their nation's history and their own lives. And we saw that the interpretation raised important questions whose answers were given in the Incarnation of Jesus Christ. Here is where the meaning of history is revealed.

But *revealed* and not *realized*, for the total meaning of history cannot be seen until history is complete. I may interpret events in my childhood and youth in terms of my present experience, but this is only a tentative interpretation. Only when I view my whole life can I interpret it adequately, but I cannot have such a view at any time within my life. The concept of the "whole of life" actually marks the bounds of my rational inquiry. It is beyond my knowledge as we usually think of knowledge, though I may quite well have some intuition of its meaning. In a somewhat similar way, the images associated with the second coming of Christ represent the limits of our thought, but they give an indication of the meaning of the whole by which, alone, the meaning of the parts can be seen. When, in this eschatological sense, we speak of the "end" of history, we are thinking of the consummation of history, the end in the sense of fulfillment of purpose of everything that has gone before.

Professor Reinhold Niebuhr speaks of two different meanings of time in seeking to clarify this.[1] We usually think of the pas-

[1] Reinhold Niebuhr, *The Nature and Destiny of Man*, II, 287.

sage of time as the point dividing the future from the past. In this sense, the present is of only infinitesimal duration. But time in the eschatological sense does not run out to infinity on either side of the present. Time in this sense is cumulative: every past moment is included in the present, and—from our viewpoint within history—every future moment as well. Hence, the fulfillment of history is not an event in history at all, because all is now completed. Nothing lies on the "other side" because everything is caught up in this fulfillment. Or as Professor C. H. Dodd puts it, "To conceive any further event on the plane of history would be like drawing a check on a closed account.[2]

Having said this, we can return to the significance of this line of thought for the present in our lives and the life of the Church. The fulfillment of history or the end of history means far more than the world going up in smoke through excesses of atomic warfare or natural catastrophe. It means rather a picture of the meaning of the whole process by which we can understand that portion of history that falls into our ken. We are much less ready today to think in terms of the world and human life continuing forever than we were a generation ago. Hence, we are not so likely to think that apocalyptic pictures are sheer foolishness. But we dare not relegate eschatology to imaginary pictures of the "end of the world." To think of the end of all things is to understand every moment of the present in terms of God's final purpose, because this does stand over and against every moment.

But when we speak of the "end" even in this sense, we use the future tense, which can easily be misunderstood. The customary use of the future tense is inadequate, but there is no verb tense that refers to something continuously relevant by incorporating all meaning. We might use the progressive present and say, "The end is coming," indicating a process under

[2] C. H. Dodd, *The Apostolic Preaching*, p. 144. Reprinted by permission of Hodder & Stoughton, Ltd., London.

way. But we mean more than just this, because we are referring to something already complete. There is no way out of this ambiguity of verb tenses, but our awareness of the meaning involved can prevent us from misinterpreting the terms.

That these things to which we have been referring have this present reference is borne out in Christian worship. In the Apostles' Creed, for example, the same article speaks of faith in Jesus Christ who was conceived, was born, suffered, died, was buried, descended, rose, and ascended into heaven (all in the past tense), then sits on the right hand of God (in the present), and shall come to judge (in the future). The Christ in whom the Church rests its faith is all these at once. Again it can be seen in the service of holy communion where Christ is present but where he is at the same time remembered and anticipated (see Chapter 25, "b. The Lord's Supper").

4. Images of the end

We have noted that the "fulfillment of history" or "the end" is a limit to our thought because it refers to the total meaning of all human events, which we cannot possibly know. Yet this cannot remain merely a question mark if it is to have any significance for us. Nor can it be expressed in a strictly logical form. If the Christian faith is to be expressed here, it must be in terms of images that convey significant meaning but which cannot be literally interpreted. Three of the most familiar and important of these images are the second coming of Christ, the last judgment, and the resurrection.

a. The second coming of Christ. So extreme at times have been those who expect a literal return of Christ that for many others the very concept is suspect. People who cannot accept the picture of Jesus descending bodily from outer space frequently fail to see that literal interpretation may obscure other important meaning here involved. What the second coming indicates is that the conflict with love in this world that makes the cross necessary for the Christian as well as for Christ cannot be permanent, that beyond the suffering of love is love's victory. As we have said, this victory is not strictly speaking "within" history, and yet it is not foreign to history, either. It goes beyond the meaning of life as we can see it, but in essentially the same direction.

This is what is involved in the picture of Christ's *second* coming. The revelation in Jesus of Nazareth is not supplanted but confirmed. Professor Dodd writes, "Thus the idea of a second coming of Christ appears along with the emphatic assertion that his coming in history satisfies all the conditions of the eschatological event, *except* that of absolute finality." [3] This gives character to the Christian hope, for it is not merely the expectation of better times in general, but the fulfillment of what we already know in Christ. And it is this that sets the tone of Christian life in the present. As Karl Barth puts it, that life "is still wandering and it is still not the goal, but wandering directed by the goal." [4]

b. The last judgment. One of the most persistent problems we face is the relativity of human existence. Our knowledge is partial, and what we think is good at the moment turns out to be evil in the long run. Things we think are ultimate turn out to be merely temporal. Within history, moreover, we have no final criteria by which we can make permanent judgments. To pretend that we have is idolatry (see Chapter 9). But neither can we relax into sheer relativity as though distinctions between good and evil do not matter at all. The Christian belief in the last judgment is the conviction that all our achievements are to be seen in an eternal light where right and wrong are finally seen as they are.

No accomplishment within history itself is final in the sense that everything else must be judged by it. The last judgment

[3] *Ibid.*, p. 161.
[4] Barth, *Dogmatics in Outline*, p. 132.

is beyond human achievements, even beyond the realization of choice ideals. As Bishop Barry puts it, "The Kingdom is ever coming into history, but no future development of earthly history can ever be the Kingdom of God on earth." [5] Here is the clear recognition of the lack of finality in our human life and the refutation of the conviction that at the present moment we can ever have the last word. In Jesus' parable of the last judgment (Matt. 25:31–46) the final separation of the righteous from the wicked upsets men's estimates of themselves. Those who counted themselves righteous are judged, and those who are vindicated are surprised.

Vivid and even threatening pictures have been painted of the last judgment with its separation of the "sheep from the goats" for all eternity; but the Christian belief in the final judgment is essentially hopeful, for the judge is not a foreign figure but Christ himself, who first came to redeem the world. There are those who completely divorce the Christ of Galilee from Christ the judge. They depict the former as humble and loving and the latter as stern and forbidding. Probably this view of the change in personality is drawn from our knowledge of people who become entirely different when great power is given them. Christ is thought of as praying for forgiveness of his persecutors while he hung on the cross, but of exacting vengeance when he came into power. This, however, is not the New Testament teaching. There is something terrifying about the eradication and judgment of all evil, for we are aware of how much we participate in it. Judgment means that there is a final reckoning which is inescapable. But the judge is the same as he who came in love to redeem men. Christ does not change. It is this faith that is expressed in the creed where, consummating Jesus' earthly life, we speak of his coming again "to judge the quick [living] and the dead."

   c. *Resurrection of the dead.* We have discussed the meaning

[5] F. R. Barry, *Recovery of Man*, p. 108.

of resurrection in terms of eternal life for the individual believer, but now we must look at it again in the light of the whole Christian understanding of all life and history. Secular dreams conceive a Utopia in the future for which we may work and strive, but which will be enjoyed only by the generation alive at that time. Sometimes this is baldly admitted, as in the communist willingness to sacrifice millions of lives to achieve the new order. Sometimes it is disguised by the poetic fiction that the dead live on in the memory of the living. Christianity holds that the meaning of human life can be preserved only as each person participates in the fulfillment of its purpose. Individual lives have permanent rather than merely transitory meaning, even though in themselves they are not final. It is because we live in the present but also in the dimension of these "last things" that we can serve God in our earthly life. "Those who have loved and served the Kingdom here are not scrapped in the winning of the victory. Their goal, their inheritance, and their reward is in the communion of the saints in light." [6] It is in this sense that Professor Niebuhr speaks of eternity as fulfilling rather than annulling history.[7] But he also points out again the major emphasis of this section, that the hope lies in God rather than in the trend of human achievements, for resurrection is beyond human achievement. It is not even an inherent power of man, as immortality might suggest. And this is another way of saying what Christianity has always maintained, that the meaning of life is not found in life itself but in God who has made it known through Jesus Christ.

Summary

The content of the Christian hope is that God's will shall prevail, that His rule shall extend over all human relations, that evil shall finally be destroyed. This hope is to be distinguished from

[6] *Ibid.*, p. 109.
[7] Reinhold Niebuhr, *The Nature and Destiny of Man*, II, 295.

mere wishful thinking. Its foundation is the faithfulness of God rather than any transient promise of human conditions. It is more than an expectation for the future: it is a way of understanding the present and the past. Because of the transcendent meaning involved, the Christian hope must be expressed in other than literal terms. Traditional images are the victory and return of Christ, the last judgment, and the resurrection.

IN CONCLUSION . . .

It is because Christianity is a life rather than an intellectual concept that a written explanation of it is so inadequate. We have tried to remember this in our study, noting that doctrine is only a part of Christianity, and that understanding it or even accepting it does not necessarily make one a Christian. More important for our study, we have tried to see that the doctrine is an outgrowth of the life.

We do not first accept certain doctrinal statements as true without any foundation for them in our experience. If we do, our acceptance is superficial. Rather, we respond as whole selves to what we recognize as real. Consequently, Christianity does not introduce us to a new opinion about religious matters, but makes known to us certain facts about reality to which we must respond. It confronts us with the Lord of all.

We present Christian doctrine, therefore, as the most profound understanding of our relation to ourselves, our fellow men, our world, and God. Christianity is a revealed religion because at its center is the self-disclosure of God in Jesus Christ. At the outset of our Christian lives we may not accept the statements of Christian faith as finally true. But as our experience expands and as we reflect upon it, we come to find that what other men of faith have said in the historic creeds bears relevantly on our own experience. Consequently, our affirmation, to be honest, must be foremost in terms of believing in God, not as an opinion which we could readily exchange for another under sufficient pressure, but rather as the foundation of all our living. Probing the depths of that belief, we also discover the truth of the doctrine. At least Jesus was willing to ground doctrine in experience (John 7:17).

We have therefore emphasized the Church as the fellowship in which this faith is lived. Particularly have we stressed the life of the Church as a community within itself and in relation to the rest of the world. For it is in the living that Christianity becomes real. It is as our whole lives are shaped by the conviction that Jesus is Christ and Lord that we are Christian.

We do not comprehend Christianity intellectually. We comprehend it as whole persons, as in one area of life after another we acknowledge that all final meaning of life centers in him, and we respond in trust and obedience.

QUESTIONS FOR DISCUSSION

1. What is the practical importance of the teaching found in Jesus' parables of the wise and foolish maidens and the talents found in Matt. 25:1–30?
2. What current "eschatological" concepts challenge the Christian understanding of the fulfillment of history?

OTHER SOURCES

Anderson, Bernhard W., *Rediscovering the Bible*. New York: Association Press, 1951, chap. 10.

Baillie, John, *The Belief in Progress*. New York: Charles Scribner's Sons, 1951, chap. 5.

Barry, F. R., *Recovery of Man*. New York: Charles Scribner's Sons, 1949, chap. 6.

Barth, Karl, *Dogmatics in Outline*, trans. G. T. Thomas. New York: Philosophical Library, 1949, chaps. 20, 24.

Bright, John, *The Kingdom of God*. New York: Abingdon-Cokesbury Press, 1953, chap. 9.

Burrows, Millar, *An Outline of Biblical Theology*. Philadelphia: The Westminster Press, 1946, chap. 11.

DeWolf, L. Harold, A *Theology of the Living Church*. New York: Harper & Brothers, 1953, chaps. 33, 35, 36.

Dodd, C. H., *The Apostolic Preaching*. Chicago: Willett, Clark & Company, 1937, Appendix: "Eschatology and History."

Filson, Floyd V., *Jesus Christ the Risen Lord*. New York: Abingdon Press, 1956, chap. 11.

Finegan, Jack, *Beginnings in Theology*. New York: Association Press, 1956, chaps. 17, 23.

Jenkins, Daniel, *The Strangeness of the Church*. Garden City, N. Y.: Doubleday & Company, Inc., 1955, chaps. 17, 18.

Niebuhr, H. Richard, *Christ and Culture*. New York: Harper & Brothers, 1951.

Niebuhr, Reinhold, *The Nature and Destiny of Man*. New York: Charles Scribner's Sons, 1943, Vol. II, chap. 10.

Rall, Harris Franklin, *Christianity*. New York: Charles Scribner's Sons, 1940, chap. 17.

———, *Religion as Salvation*. New York: Abingdon-Cokesbury Press, 1953, chaps. 16–18.

Robinson, H. Wheeler, *The Religious Ideas of the Old Testament*. London: Duckworth, 1913, chap. 8.

Shinn, Roger L., *Life, Death, and Destiny*. Philadelphia: The Westminster Press, 1957, chaps. 4–7.

Spurrier, William A., *Guide to the Christian Faith*. New York: Charles Scribner's Sons, 1952, chap. 11.

Whale, J. S., *Christian Doctrine*. New York: The Macmillan Company, 1941, chap. 8.

Williams, Daniel Day, *God's Grace and Man's Hope*. New York: Harper & Brothers, 1949, chaps. 4, 5.

appendix

HISTORIC CREEDS OF THE CHURCH

The Apostles' Creed

I believe in God the Father Almighty, Maker of heaven and earth.

And in Jesus Christ, His only Son, our Lord; who was conceived by the Holy Ghost, born of the Virgin Mary; suffered under Pontius Pilate, was crucified, dead, and buried; He descended into hell; the third day He rose again from the dead; He ascended into heaven, and sitteth on the right hand of God the Father Almighty; from thence He shall come to judge the quick and the dead.

I believe in the Holy Ghost; the holy Catholic Church, the communion of saints; the forgiveness of sins; the resurrection of the body; and the life everlasting. Amen.

The Nicene Creed

I believe in one God, the Father Almighty, Maker of heaven and earth, and of all things visible and invisible.

And in one Lord Jesus Christ, the only-begotten Son of God, begotten of the Father before all worlds, God of God, Light of Light, very God of very God, begotten, not made, being of one substance with the Father; by whom all things were made; who for us men, and for our salvation, came down from heaven, and was incarnate by the Holy Ghost of the Virgin Mary, and was made man, and was crucified also for us under Pontius Pilate; He suffered and was buried; the third day He rose again according to the Scriptures; and ascended into heaven, and sitteth on the right hand of the Father; and He shall come again with glory to judge the quick and the dead; whose kingdom shall have no end.

And I believe in the Holy Ghost, the Lord and Giver of life, who proceedeth from the Father and the Son; who with the Father and the Son together is worshiped and glorified; who spake by the Prophets.

And I believe in one holy Catholic and Apostolic Church.

I acknowledge one Baptism for the remission of sins; and I look for the resurrection of the dead, and the life of the world to come. Amen.

The Christological Formula of the Council of Chalcedon

Following the holy Fathers, we all with one consent teach men to confess one and the same Son, our Lord Jesus Christ, the same perfect in Godhead and also perfect in Manhood; truly God and truly man, of a reasonable soul and body; con-substantial with the Father according to the Godhead, and con-substantial with us according to the Manhood; in all things like unto us, without sin, begotten before all ages of the Father according to the Godhead, and in these latter days, for us and for our salvation, born of the Virgin Mary, the Mother of God, according to the Manhood; one and the same Christ, Son, Lord, Only-begotten, to be acknowledged in two natures, inconfusedly, unchangeably, indivisibly, inseparably; the distinction of natures being by no means taken away by the union, but rather the property of each nature being preserved, and concurring in one Person and one Subsistence, not parted or divided into two Persons, but one and the same Son, and only-begotten, God the Word, the Lord Jesus Christ; as the prophets from the beginning [have declared] concerning him, and the Lord Jesus Christ himself has taught us, and the Creed of the holy Fathers has handed down to us.

CURRENT SOURCES OF THE PROTESTANT CONFESSIONS

For students who want to relate their study of Christian doctrine to the traditional Protestant confessions, this list of current sources from which they may be readily obtained is attached.

Lutheran

All the doctrinal symbols of the Lutheran Churches are available in the *Concordia Book of Concord* published by the Concordia Publishing House, 3558 South Jefferson Avenue, St. Louis 18, Missouri. An edition of Dr. Martin Luther's Small Catechism containing also the Augsburg Confession is available from the Augustana Press of Rock Island, Illinois.

In addition to these, a copy of the Augsburg Confession may be obtained for a few cents from the Concordia Publishing House, and a similarly inexpensive copy of Luther's Small Catechism from the Augustana Press.

Reformed

The doctrinal statements of the Presbyterian tradition including the Westminster Confession and Catechisms are available in *The Constitution of the Presbyterian Church in the U.S.A.* published by the Westminster Press, Witherspoon Building, Philadelphia 7, Pennsylvania. Inexpensive copies of the Westminister Shorter Catechism are obtainable from the same source.

The Heidelberg Catechism which is standard for many continental Reformed Churches and American denominations derived from them is available in an inexpensive paperbound edition from Wm. B. Eerdmans Publishing Company of Grand Rapids, Michigan.

The Roman Catholic Catechism

At least two inexpensive editions of the Baltimore Catechism, No. 3, are available: the New Confraternity Edition, published by Benziger Bros., Inc., 131 Hudson St., New York 13; and another for schools and colleges published by the St. Anthony Guild Press, 508 Marshall St., Patterson 3, N. J.

ınɒex of bıblıcal references

OLD TESTAMENT

NEW TESTAMENT

375

GENERAL INDEX

C

Date Due

OCT. 2 6 1972			